JUSTIN JORDAN   **ARIELA KRISTANTINA**   **BEN WILSONHAM**

DEEP STATE

VOLUME ONE \ DARKER SIDE OF THE MOON

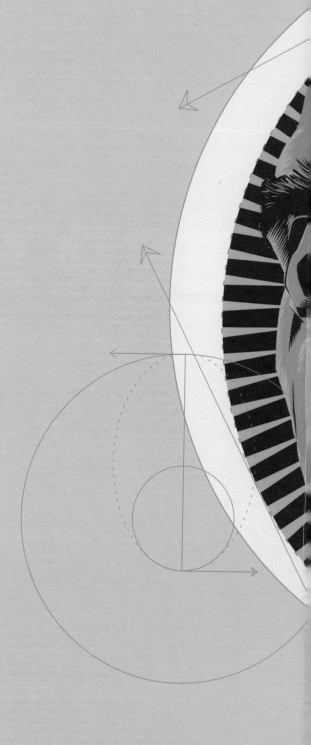

ROSS RICHIE .... CEO & Founder
MARK SMYLIE .... Founder of Archaia
MATT GAGNON .... Editor-in-Chief
FILIP SABLIK .... President of Publishing & Marketing
STEPHEN CHRISTY .... President of Development
LANCE KREITER .... VP of Licensing & Merchandising
PHIL BARBARO .... VP of Finance
BRYCE CARLSON .... Managing Editor
MEL CAYLO .... Marketing Manager
SCOTT NEWMAN .... Production Design Manager
IRENE BRADISH .... Operations Manager
CHRISTINE DINH .... Brand Communications Manager
DAFNA PLEBAN .... Editor
SHANNON WATTERS .... Editor
ERIC HARBURN .... Editor
REBECCA TAYLOR .... Editor
IAN BRILL .... Editor
WHITNEY LEOPARD .... Associate Editor
JASMINE AMIRI .... Associate Editor
CHRIS ROSA .... Assistant Editor
ALEX GALER .... Assistant Editor
CAMERON CHITTOCK .... Assistant Editor
MARY GUMPORT .... Assistant Editor
KELSEY DIETERICH .... Production Designer
JILLIAN CRAB .... Production Designer
KARA LEOPARD .... Production Designer
MICHELLE ANKLEY .... Production Design Assistant
DEVIN FUNCHES .... E-Commerce & Inventory Coordinator
AARON FERRARA .... Operations Coordinator
JOSÉ MEZA .... Sales Assistant
ELIZABETH LOUGHRIDGE .... Accounting Assistant
STEPHANIE HOCUTT .... PR Assistant
HILLARY LEVI .... Executive Assistant
KATE ALBIN .... Administrative Assistant

 DEEP STATE Volume One, March 2015.
Published by BOOM! Studios, a division
of Boom Entertainment, Inc. Deep State
is ™ & © 2015 Justin Jordan. Originally
published in single magazine form as DEEP
STATE No. 1-4. ™ & © 2014, 2015 Justin Jordan. All rights reserved.
BOOM! Studios™ and the BOOM! Studios logo are trademarks of
Boom Entertainment, Inc., registered in various countries and
categories. All characters, events, and institutions depicted herein
are fictional. Any similarity between any of the names, characters,
persons, events, and/or institutions in this publication to actual
names, characters, and persons, whether living or dead, events,
and/or institutions is unintended and purely coincidental. BOOM!
Studios does not read or accept unsolicited submissions of ideas,
stories, or artwork.

A catalog record of this book is available from OCLC and from
the BOOM! Studios website, www.boom-studios.com, on the
Librarians page.

BOOM! Studios, 5670 Wilshire Boulevard, Suite 450, Los Angeles,
CA 90036-5679. Printed in USA. First Printing.

ISBN: 978-1-60886-492-8, eISBN: 978-1-61398-346-1

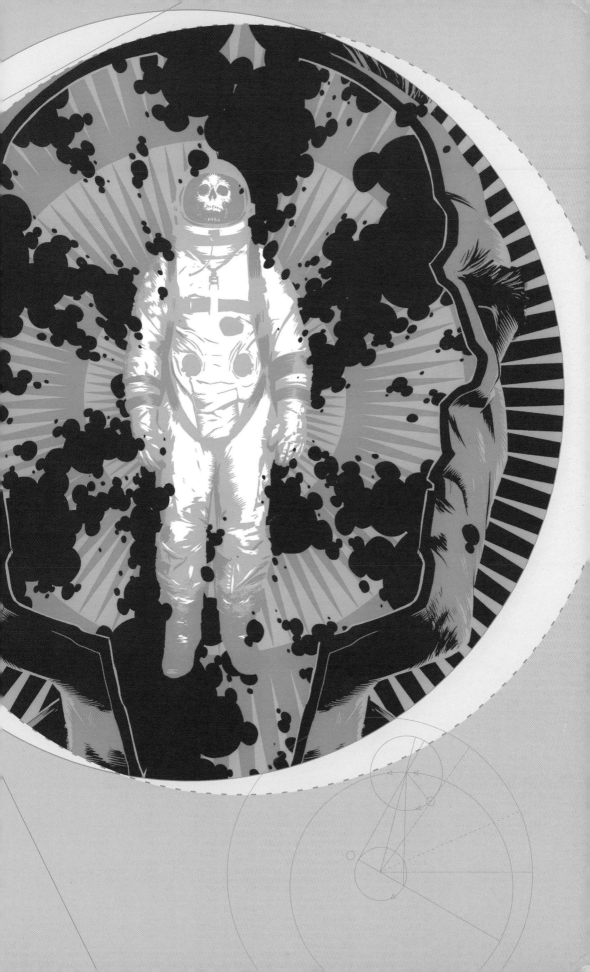

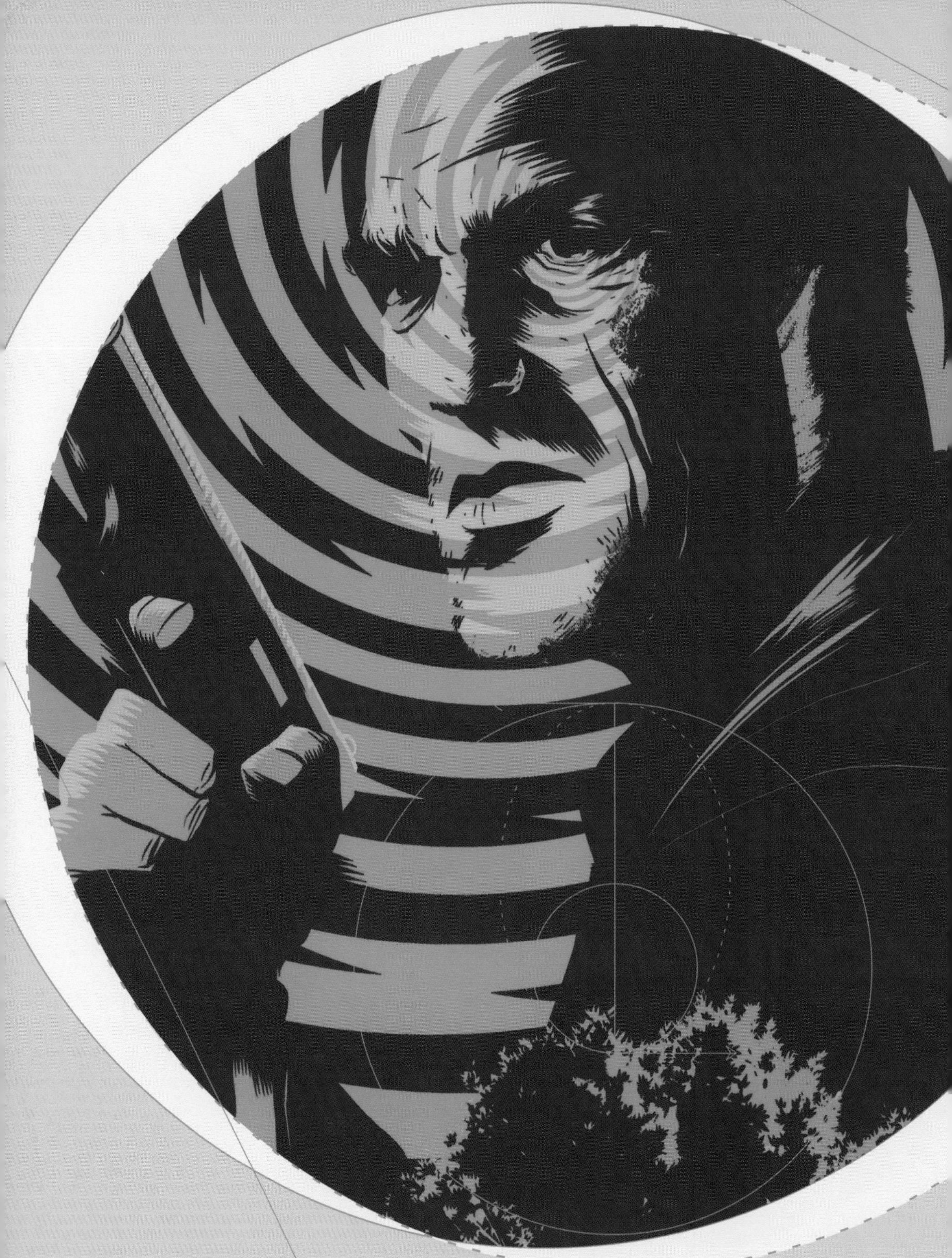

WRITTEN BY
JUSTIN JORDAN

ILLUSTRATED BY
ARIELA KRISTANTINA

COLORS BY
BEN WILSONHAM

LETTERS BY
ED DUKESHIRE

COVER BY
MATT TAYLOR

DESIGNER **KELSEY DIETERICH**

ASSISTANT EDITOR **CAMERON CHITTOCK**

EDITOR **ERIC HARBURN**

DEEP STATE™
CREATED BY
JUSTIN JORDAN

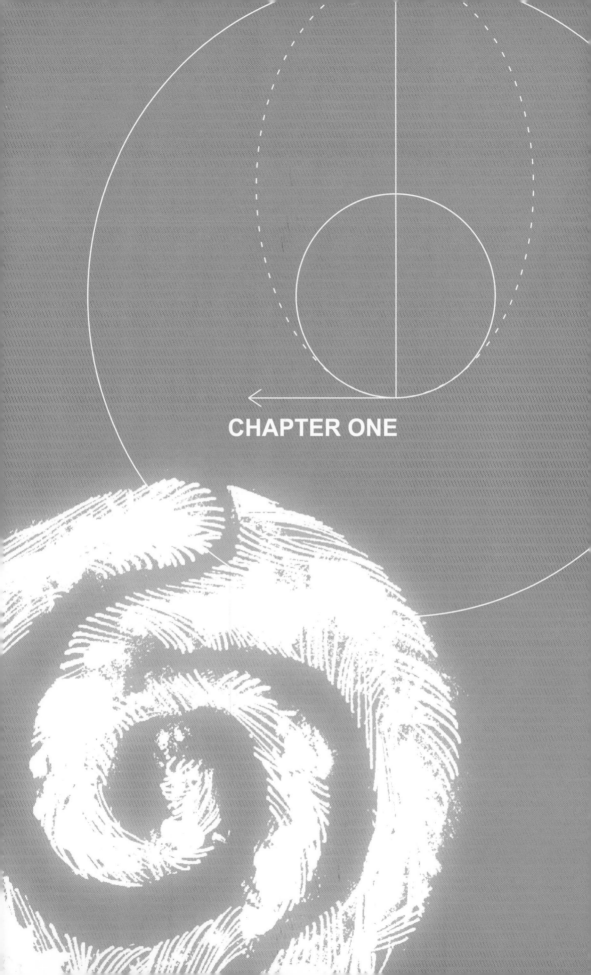

CHAPTER ONE

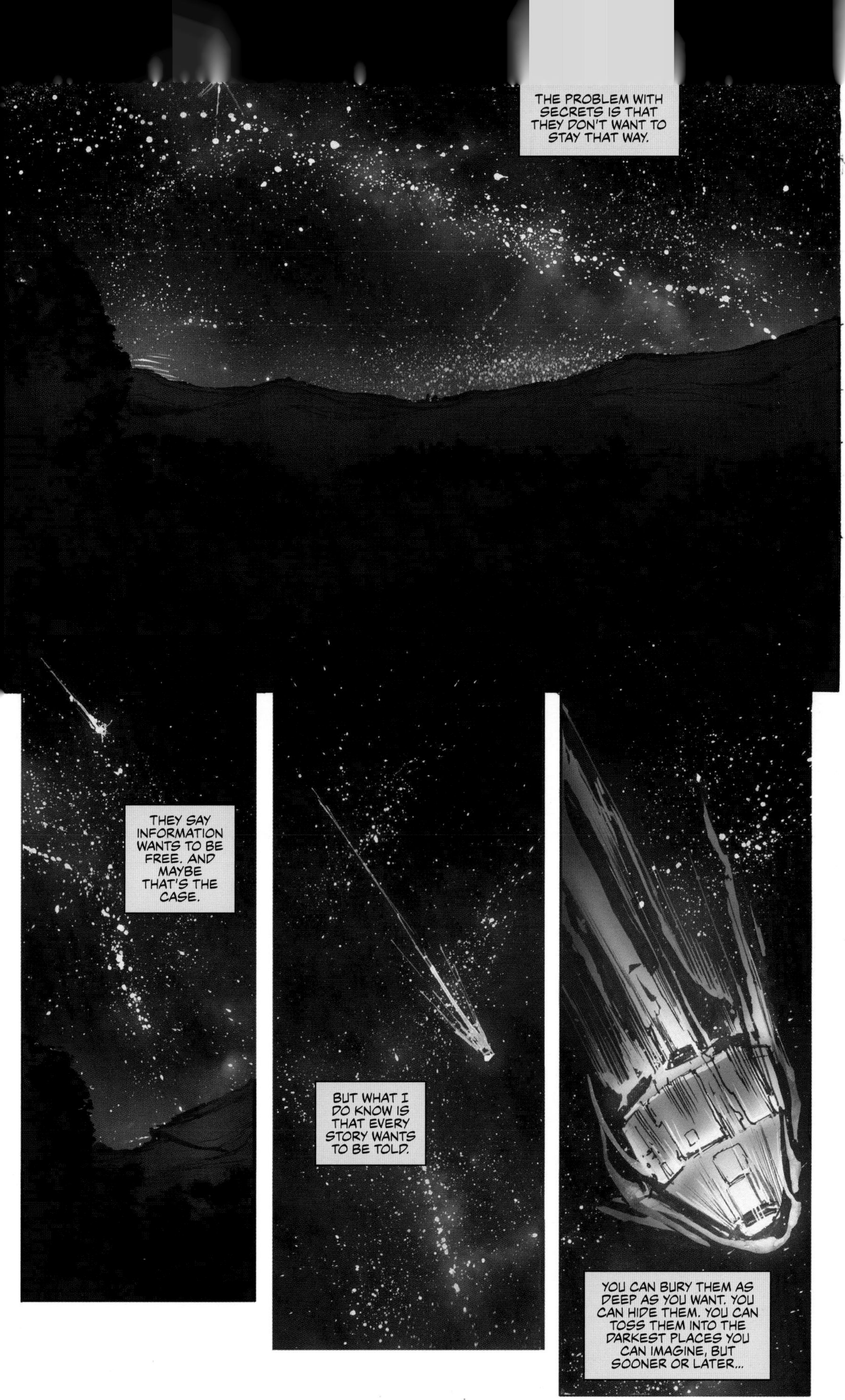
THE PROBLEM WITH SECRETS IS THAT THEY DON'T WANT TO STAY THAT WAY.
THEY SAY INFORMATION WANTS TO BE FREE. AND MAYBE THAT'S THE CASE.
BUT WHAT I DO KNOW IS THAT EVERY STORY WANTS TO BE TOLD.
YOU CAN BURY THEM AS DEEP AS YOU WANT. YOU CAN HIDE THEM. YOU CAN TOSS THEM INTO THE DARKEST PLACES YOU CAN IMAGINE, BUT SOONER OR LATER...

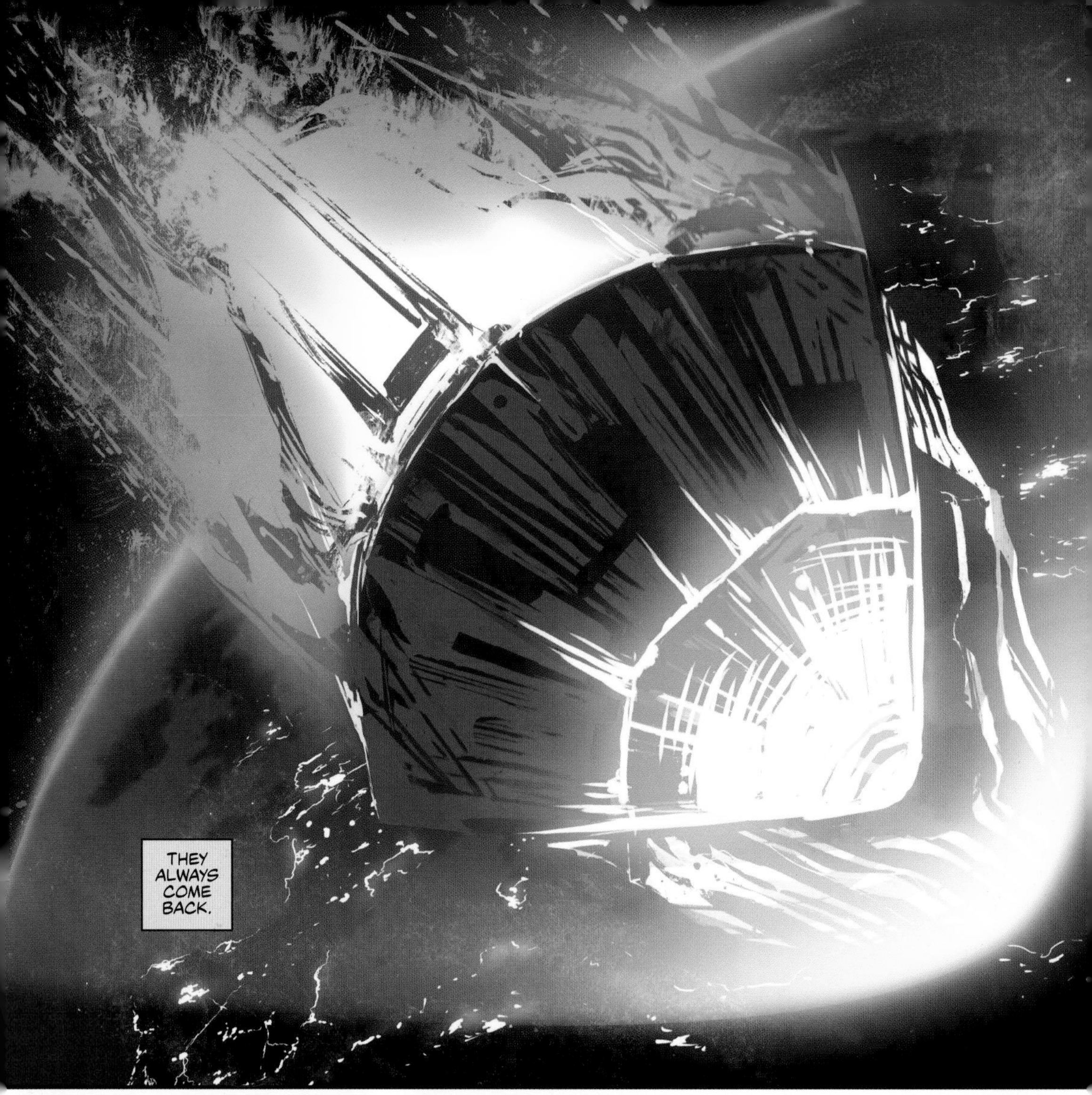
THEY ALWAYS COME BACK.

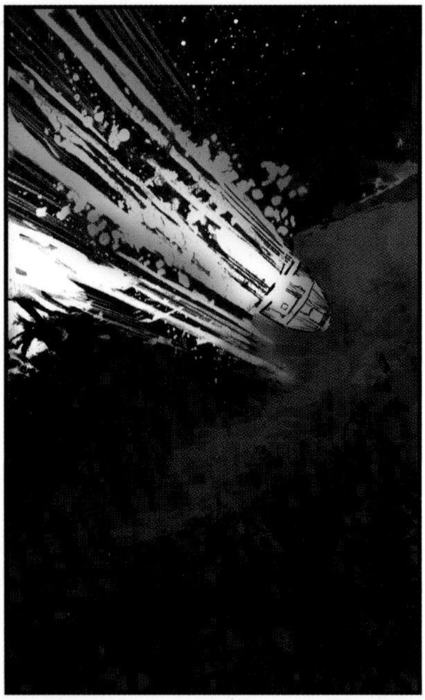

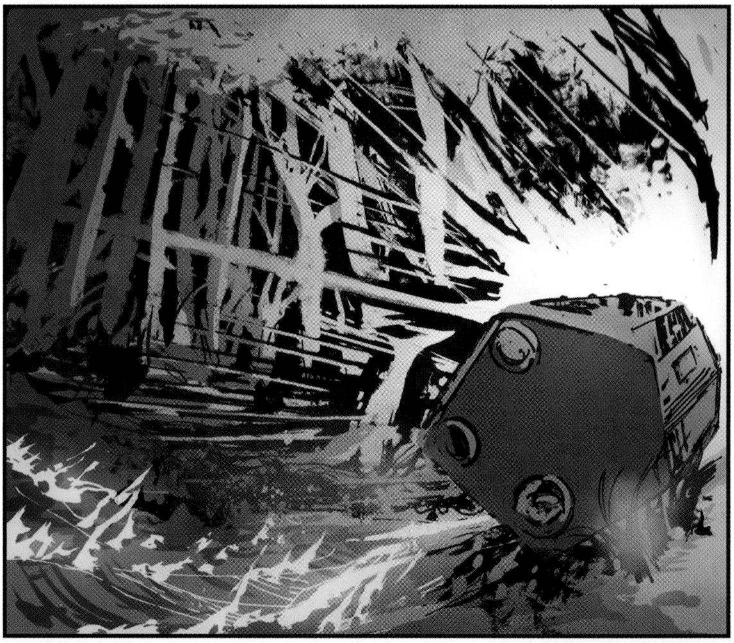

THUNK
CRUNCH

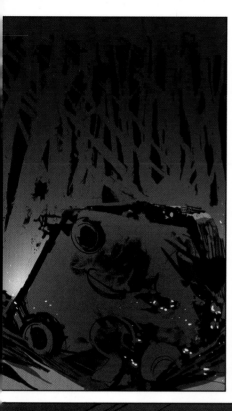

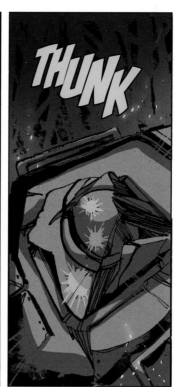

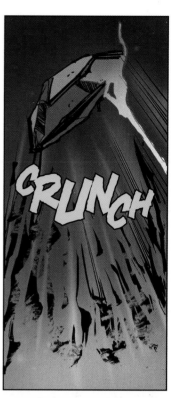

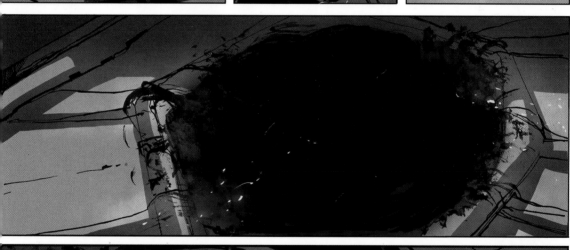

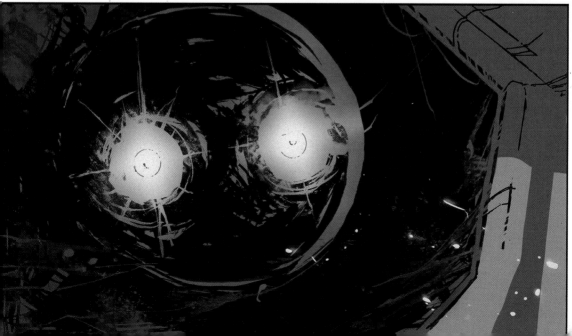

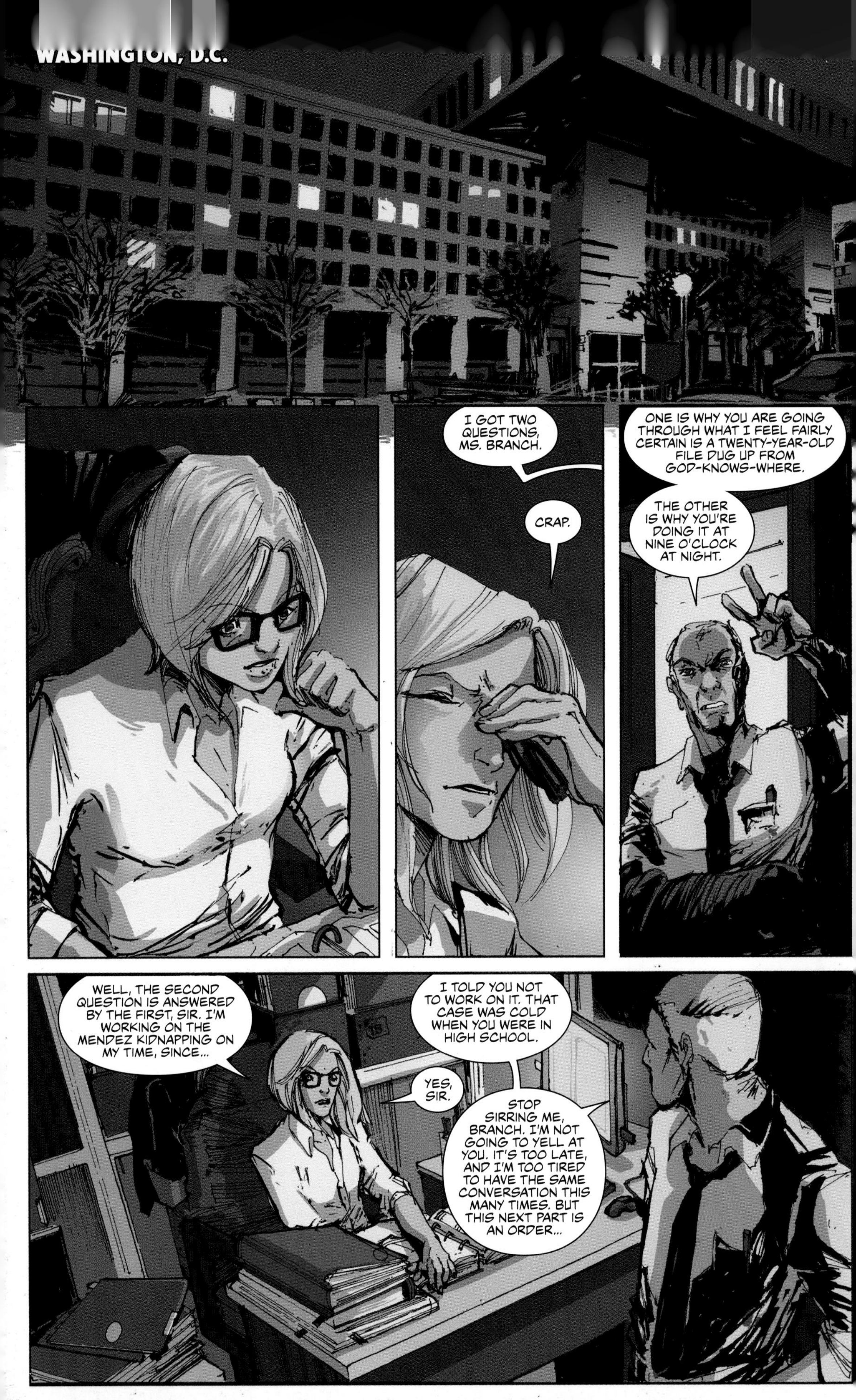
WASHINGTON, D.C.
I GOT TWO QUESTIONS, MS. BRANCH.
CRAP.
ONE IS WHY YOU ARE GOING THROUGH WHAT I FEEL FAIRLY CERTAIN IS A TWENTY-YEAR-OLD FILE DUG UP FROM GOD-KNOWS-WHERE.
THE OTHER IS WHY YOU'RE DOING IT AT NINE O'CLOCK AT NIGHT.
WELL, THE SECOND QUESTION IS ANSWERED BY THE FIRST, SIR. I'M WORKING ON THE MENDEZ KIDNAPPING ON MY TIME, SINCE...
I TOLD YOU NOT TO WORK ON IT. THAT CASE WAS COLD WHEN YOU WERE IN HIGH SCHOOL.
YES, SIR.
STOP SIRRING ME, BRANCH. I'M NOT GOING TO YELL AT YOU. IT'S TOO LATE, AND I'M TOO TIRED TO HAVE THE SAME CONVERSATION THIS MANY TIMES. BUT THIS NEXT PART IS AN ORDER...

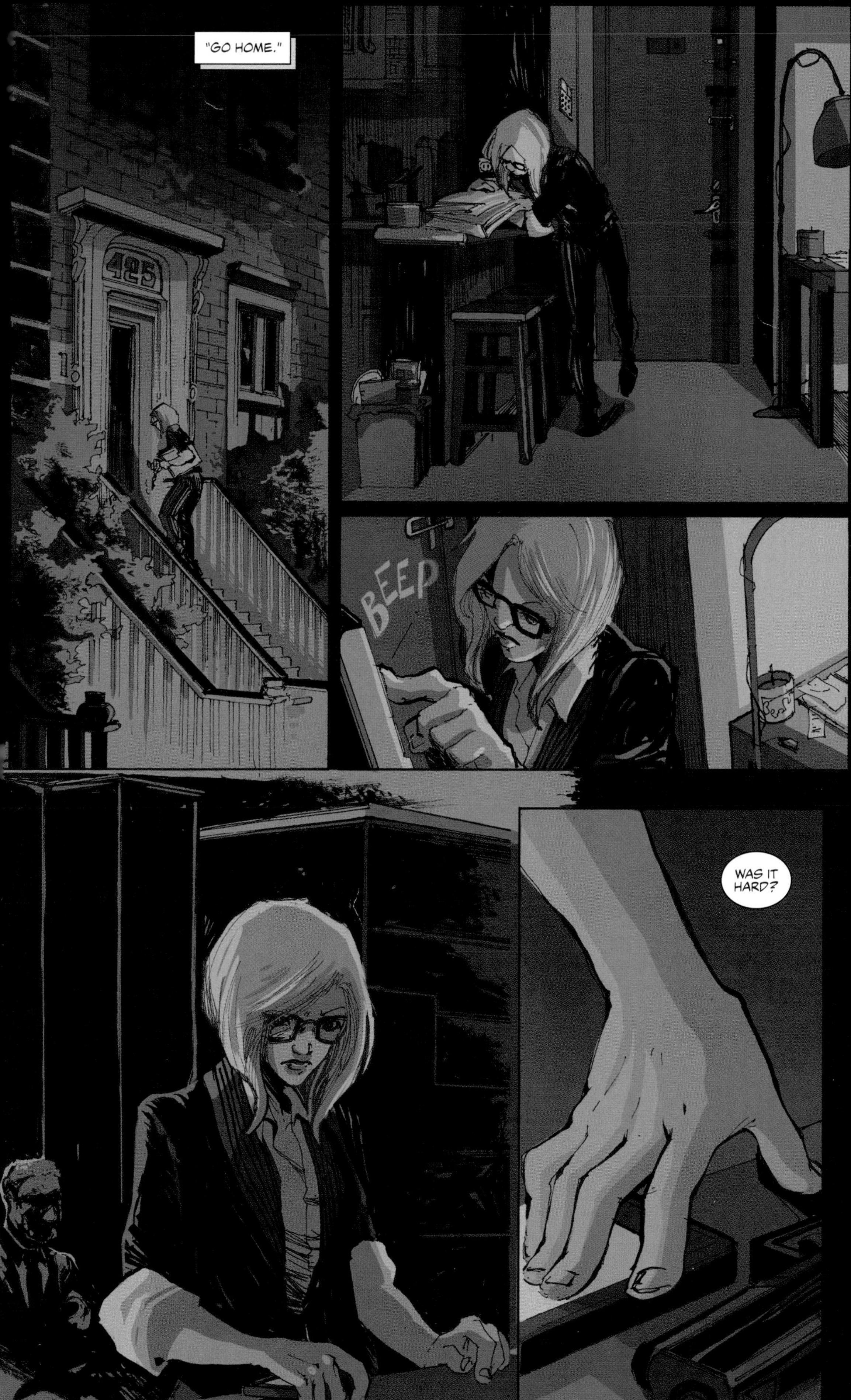
"GO HOME."
BEEP
WAS IT HARD?

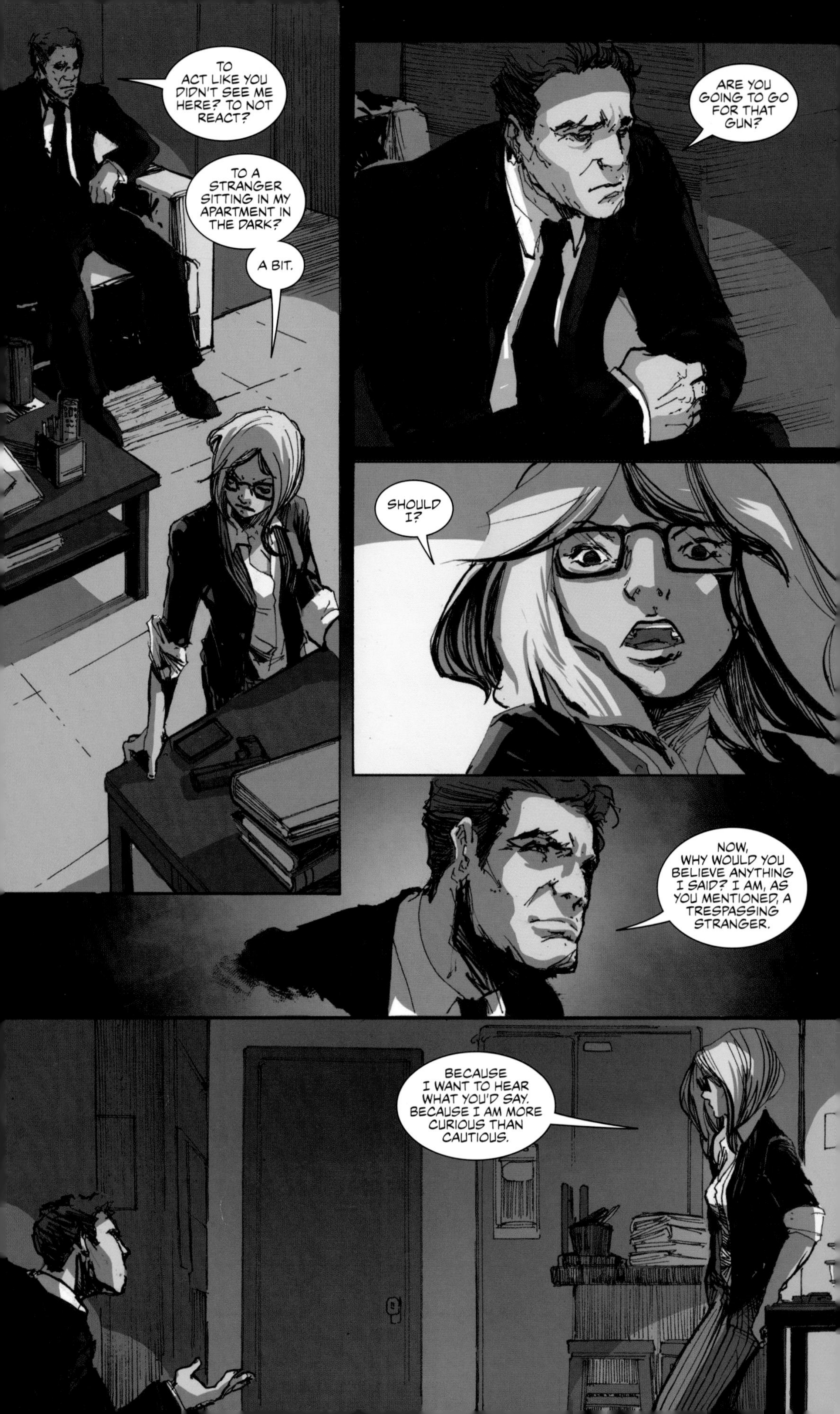
TO ACT LIKE YOU DIDN'T SEE ME HERE? TO NOT REACT?
TO A STRANGER SITTING IN MY APARTMENT IN THE DARK?
A BIT.
ARE YOU GOING TO GO FOR THAT GUN?
SHOULD I?
NOW, WHY WOULD YOU BELIEVE ANYTHING I SAID? I AM, AS YOU MENTIONED, A TRESPASSING STRANGER.
BECAUSE I WANT TO HEAR WHAT YOU'D SAY. BECAUSE I AM MORE CURIOUS THAN CAUTIOUS.

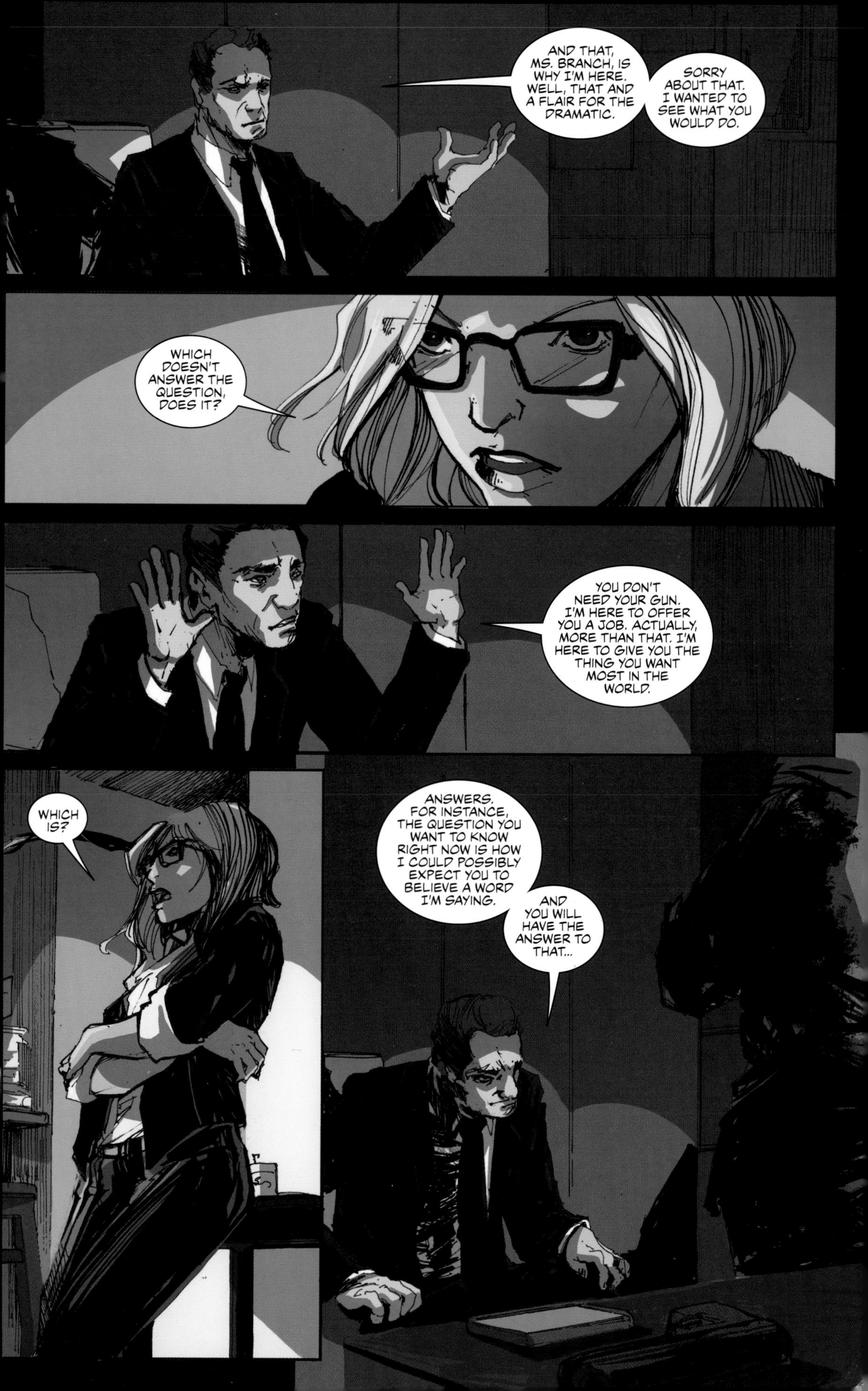
AND THAT, MS. BRANCH, IS WHY I'M HERE. WELL, THAT AND A FLAIR FOR THE DRAMATIC.
SORRY ABOUT THAT. I WANTED TO SEE WHAT YOU WOULD DO.
WHICH DOESN'T ANSWER THE QUESTION, DOES IT?
YOU DON'T NEED YOUR GUN. I'M HERE TO OFFER YOU A JOB. ACTUALLY, MORE THAN THAT. I'M HERE TO GIVE YOU THE THING YOU WANT MOST IN THE WORLD.
WHICH IS?
ANSWERS. FOR INSTANCE, THE QUESTION YOU WANT TO KNOW RIGHT NOW IS HOW I COULD POSSIBLY EXPECT YOU TO BELIEVE A WORD I'M SAYING.
AND YOU WILL HAVE THE ANSWER TO THAT...

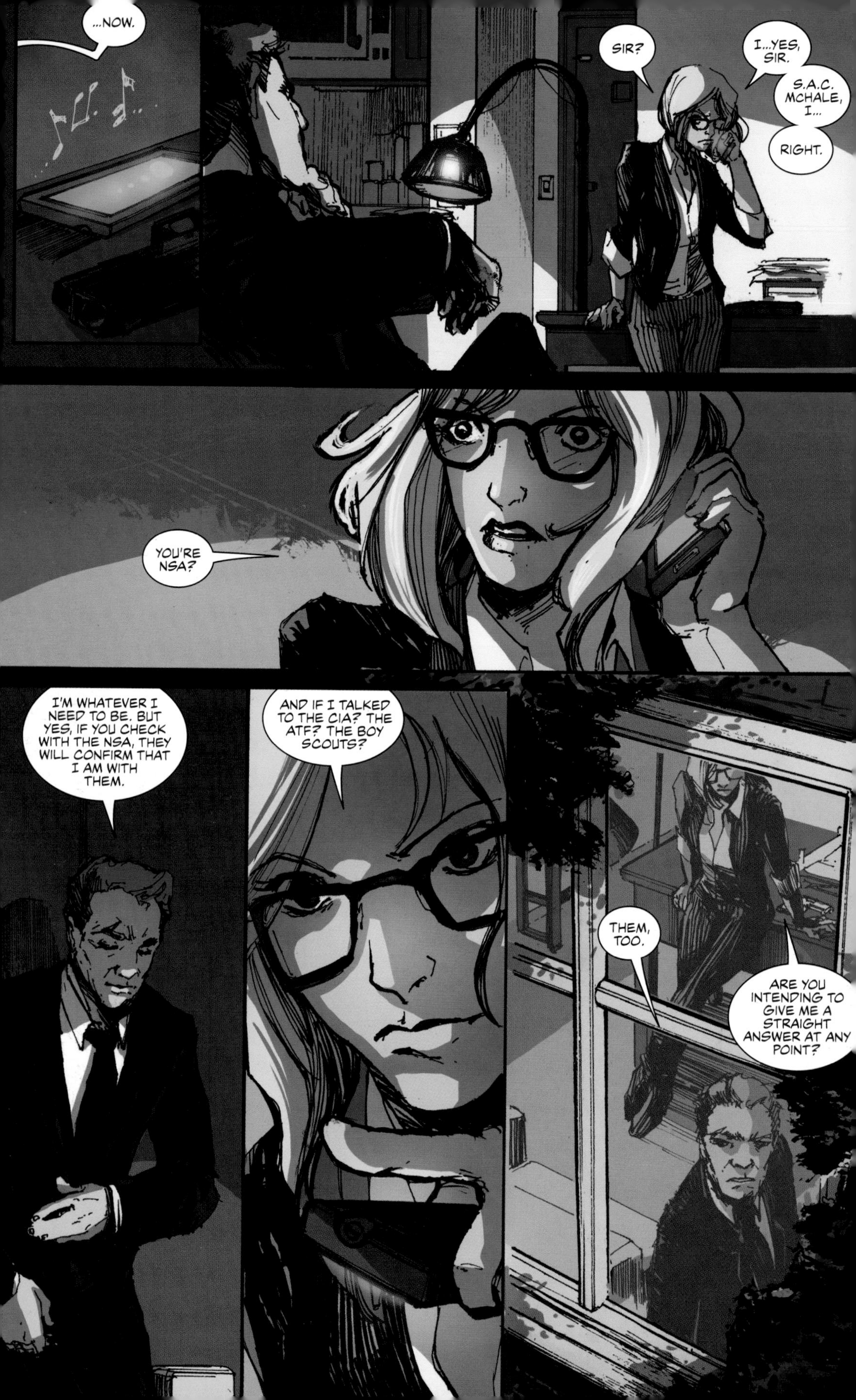
...NOW.
SIR?
I...YES, SIR.
S.A.C. MCHALE, I...
RIGHT.
YOU'RE NSA?
I'M WHATEVER I NEED TO BE. BUT YES, IF YOU CHECK WITH THE NSA, THEY WILL CONFIRM THAT I AM WITH THEM.
AND IF I TALKED TO THE CIA? THE ATF? THE BOY SCOUTS?
THEM, TOO.
ARE YOU INTENDING TO GIVE ME A STRAIGHT ANSWER AT ANY POINT?

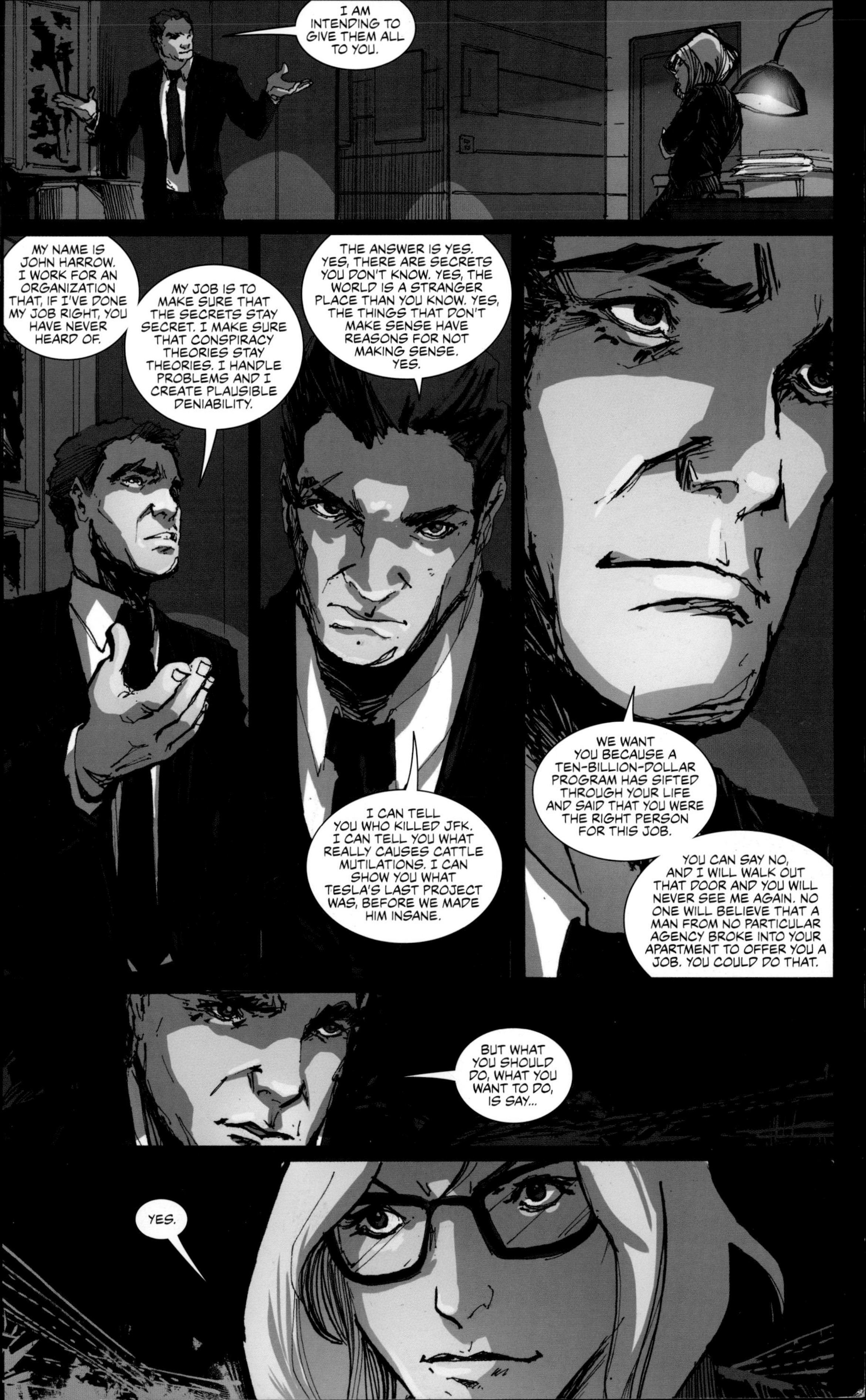
I AM INTENDING TO GIVE THEM ALL TO YOU.
MY NAME IS JOHN HARROW. I WORK FOR AN ORGANIZATION THAT, IF I'VE DONE MY JOB RIGHT, YOU HAVE NEVER HEARD OF.
MY JOB IS TO MAKE SURE THAT THE SECRETS STAY SECRET. I MAKE SURE THAT CONSPIRACY THEORIES STAY THEORIES. I HANDLE PROBLEMS AND I CREATE PLAUSIBLE DENIABILITY.
THE ANSWER IS YES. YES, THERE ARE SECRETS YOU DON'T KNOW. YES, THE WORLD IS A STRANGER PLACE THAN YOU KNOW. YES, THE THINGS THAT DON'T MAKE SENSE HAVE REASONS FOR NOT MAKING SENSE. YES.
I CAN TELL YOU WHO KILLED JFK. I CAN TELL YOU WHAT REALLY CAUSES CATTLE MUTILATIONS. I CAN SHOW YOU WHAT TESLA'S LAST PROJECT WAS, BEFORE WE MADE HIM INSANE.
WE WANT YOU BECAUSE A TEN-BILLION-DOLLAR PROGRAM HAS SIFTED THROUGH YOUR LIFE AND SAID THAT YOU WERE THE RIGHT PERSON FOR THIS JOB.
YOU CAN SAY NO, AND I WILL WALK OUT THAT DOOR AND YOU WILL NEVER SEE ME AGAIN. NO ONE WILL BELIEVE THAT A MAN FROM NO PARTICULAR AGENCY BROKE INTO YOUR APARTMENT TO OFFER YOU A JOB. YOU COULD DO THAT.
BUT WHAT YOU SHOULD DO, WHAT YOU WANT TO DO, IS SAY...
YES.

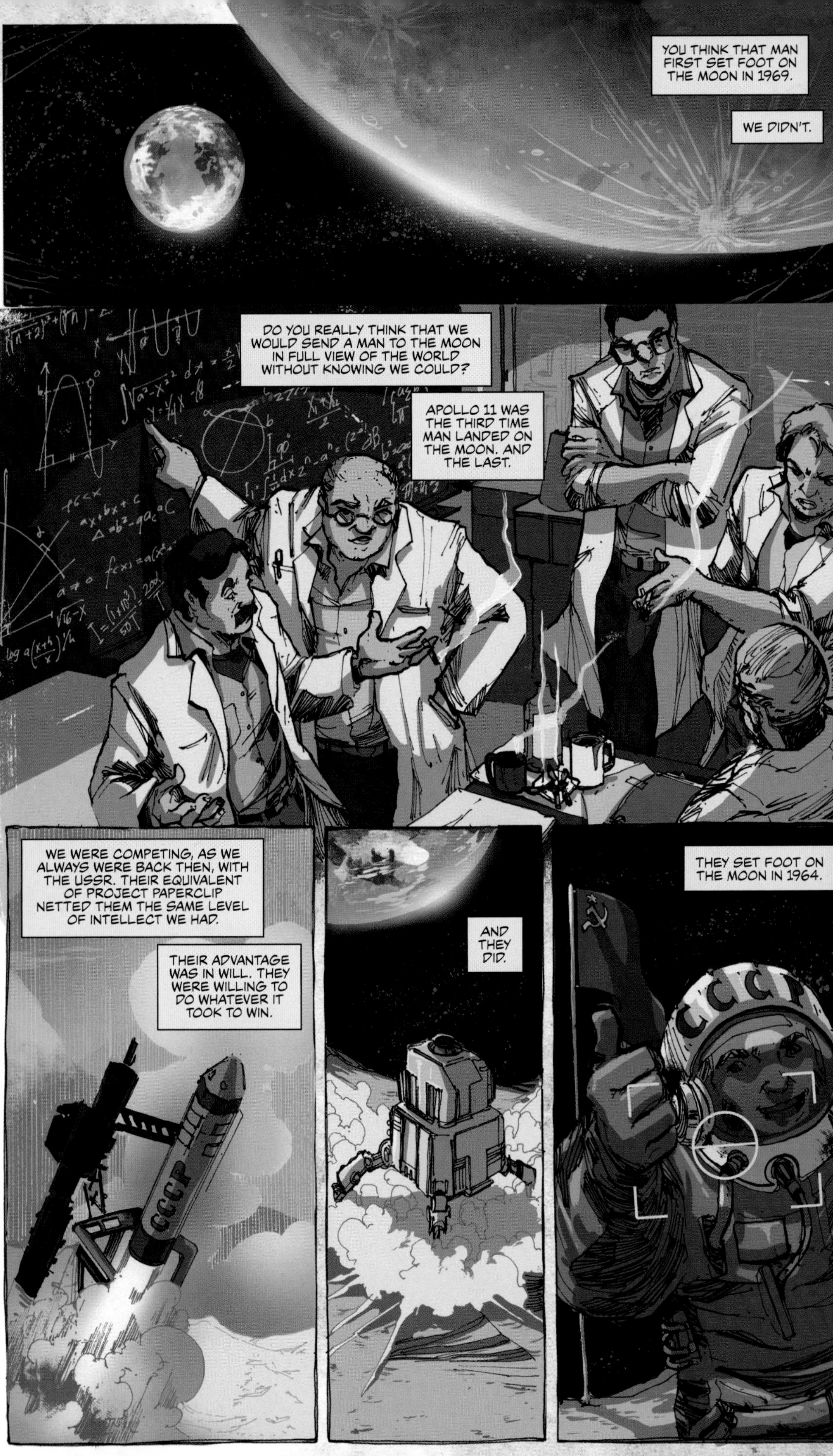
YOU THINK THAT MAN FIRST SET FOOT ON THE MOON IN 1969.
WE DIDN'T.
DO YOU REALLY THINK THAT WE WOULD SEND A MAN TO THE MOON IN FULL VIEW OF THE WORLD WITHOUT KNOWING WE COULD?
APOLLO 11 WAS THE THIRD TIME MAN LANDED ON THE MOON. AND THE LAST.
WE WERE COMPETING, AS WE ALWAYS WERE BACK THEN, WITH THE USSR. THEIR EQUIVALENT OF PROJECT PAPERCLIP NETTED THEM THE SAME LEVEL OF INTELLECT WE HAD.
THEIR ADVANTAGE WAS IN WILL. THEY WERE WILLING TO DO WHATEVER IT TOOK TO WIN.
CCCP
AND THEY DID.
THEY SET FOOT ON THE MOON IN 1964.
CCCP

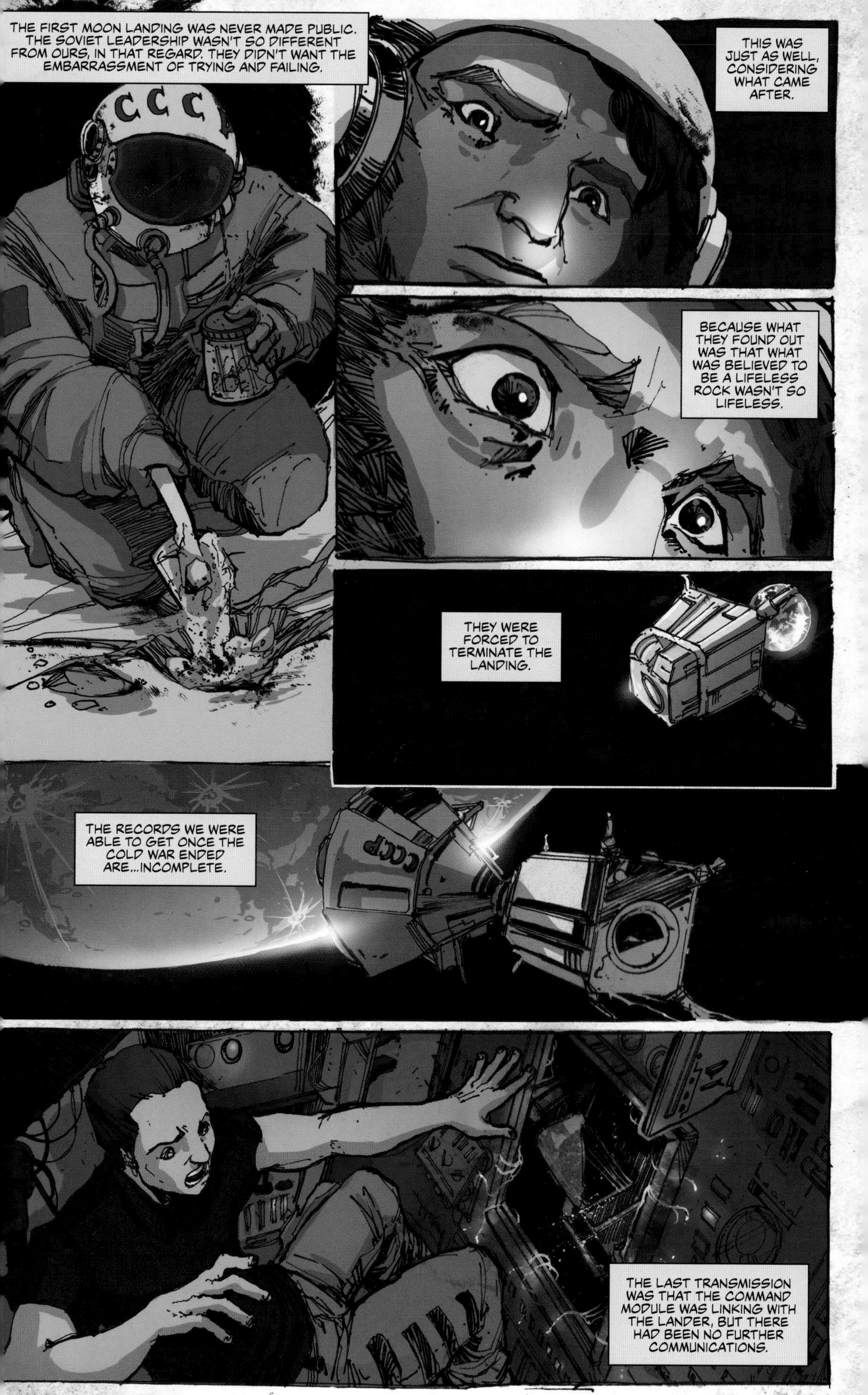
THE FIRST MOON LANDING WAS NEVER MADE PUBLIC. THE SOVIET LEADERSHIP WASN'T SO DIFFERENT FROM OURS, IN THAT REGARD. THEY DIDN'T WANT THE EMBARRASSMENT OF TRYING AND FAILING.
CCCP
THIS WAS JUST AS WELL, CONSIDERING WHAT CAME AFTER.
BECAUSE WHAT THEY FOUND OUT WAS THAT WHAT WAS BELIEVED TO BE A LIFELESS ROCK WASN'T SO LIFELESS.
THEY WERE FORCED TO TERMINATE THE LANDING.
THE RECORDS WE WERE ABLE TO GET ONCE THE COLD WAR ENDED ARE...INCOMPLETE.
CCCP
THE LAST TRANSMISSION WAS THAT THE COMMAND MODULE WAS LINKING WITH THE LANDER, BUT THERE HAD BEEN NO FURTHER COMMUNICATIONS.

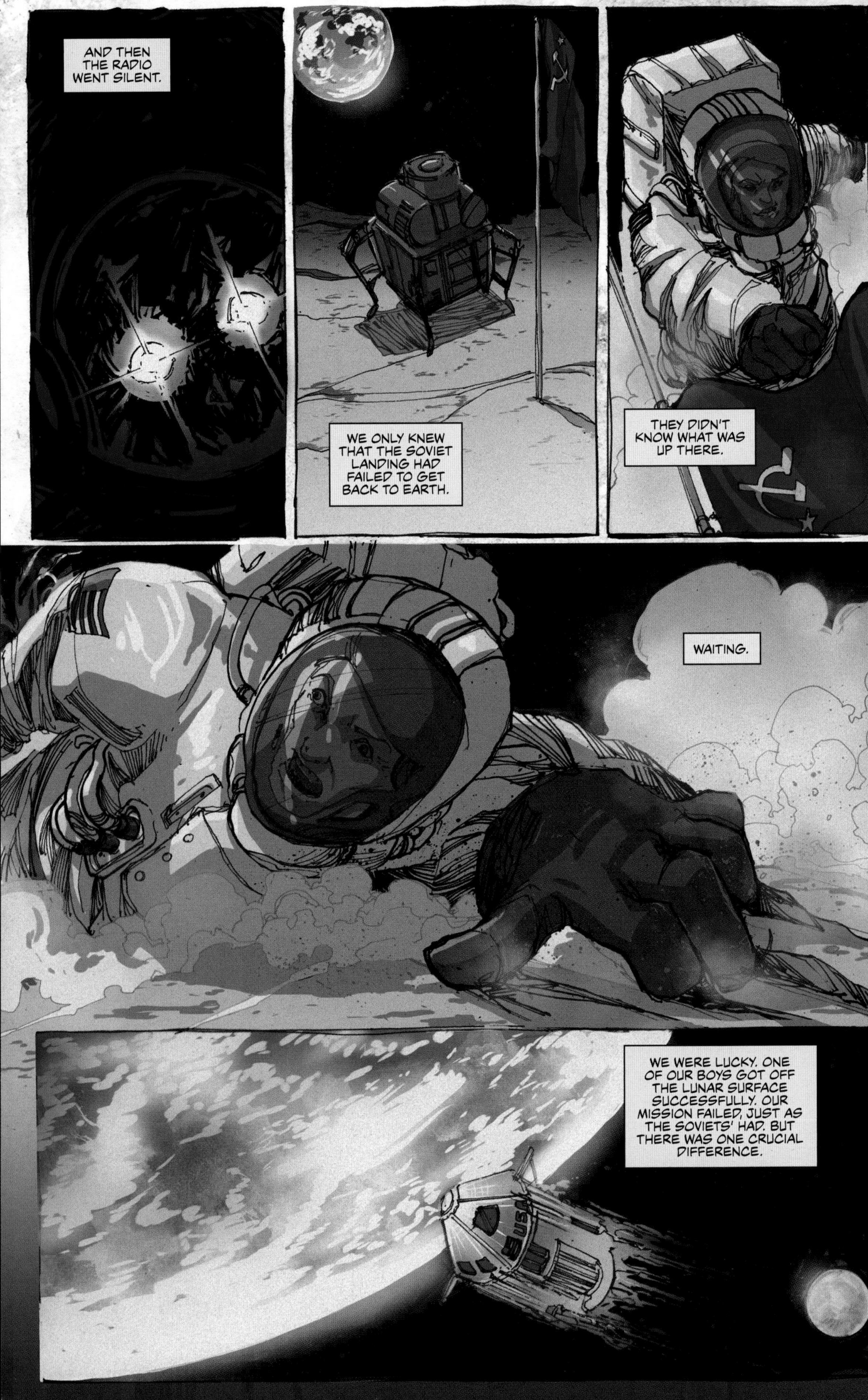
AND THEN THE RADIO WENT SILENT.
WE ONLY KNEW THAT THE SOVIET LANDING HAD FAILED TO GET BACK TO EARTH.
THEY DIDN'T KNOW WHAT WAS UP THERE.
WAITING.
WE WERE LUCKY. ONE OF OUR BOYS GOT OFF THE LUNAR SURFACE SUCCESSFULLY. OUR MISSION FAILED, JUST AS THE SOVIETS' HAD. BUT THERE WAS ONE CRUCIAL DIFFERENCE.
USA

WE CAME BACK.

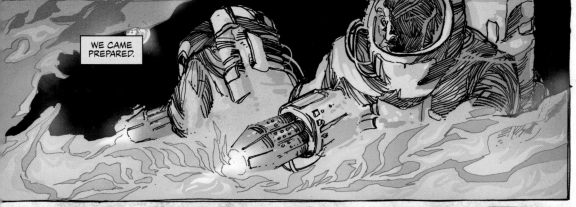

WE CAME PREPARED.

WE BROUGHT OUR BOYS HOME.

EVERYTHING YOU THINK YOU KNOW ABOUT IT? HAPPENED AFTER. WE NEEDED A WIN.

THE RUSSIAN COMMAND MODULE WAS NEVER RETRIEVED.

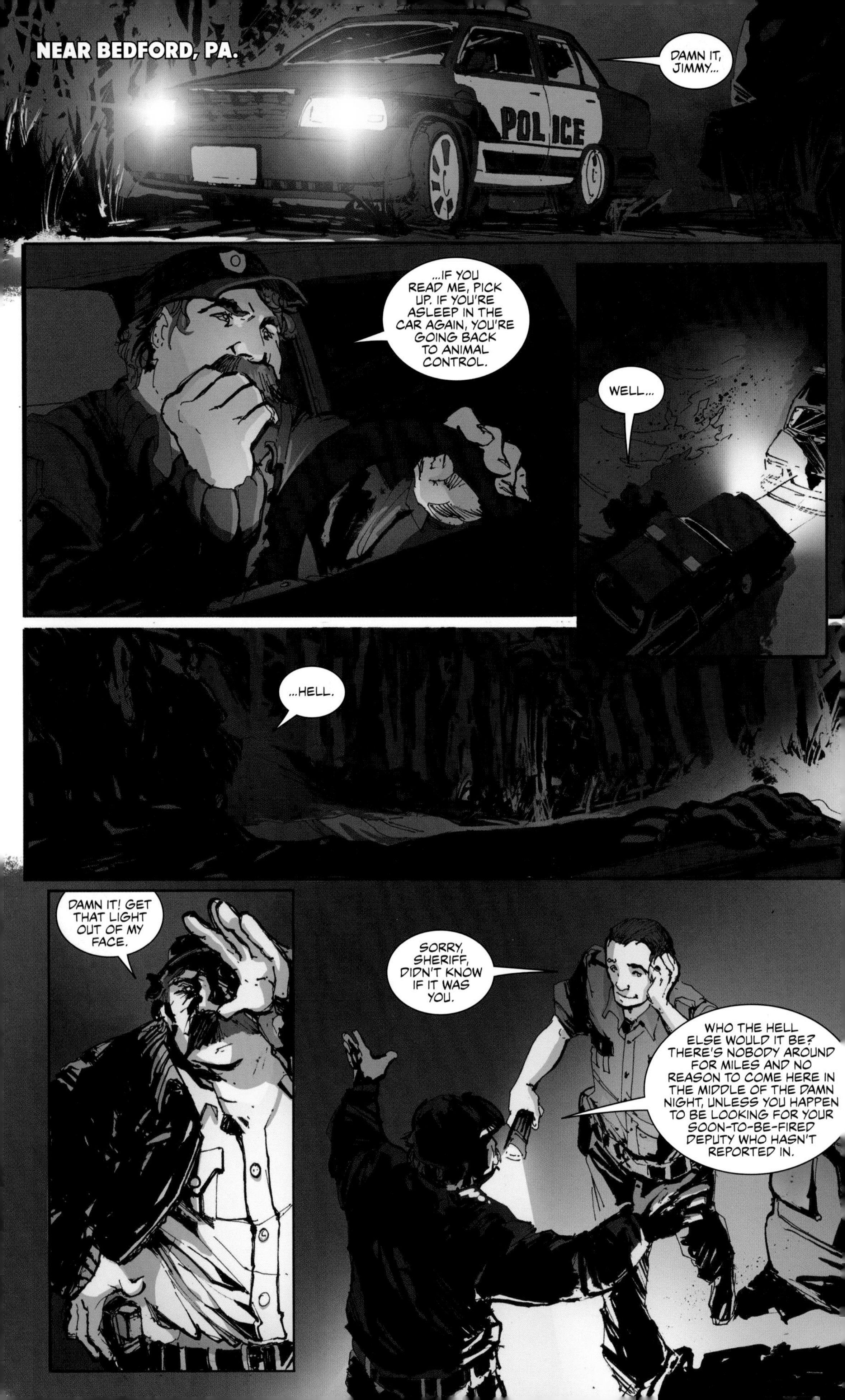
NEAR BEDFORD, PA.
DAMN IT, JIMMY...
...IF YOU READ ME, PICK UP. IF YOU'RE ASLEEP IN THE CAR AGAIN, YOU'RE GOING BACK TO ANIMAL CONTROL.
WELL...
POLICE
...HELL.
DAMN IT! GET THAT LIGHT OUT OF MY FACE.
SORRY, SHERIFF, DIDN'T KNOW IF IT WAS YOU.
WHO THE HELL ELSE WOULD IT BE? THERE'S NOBODY AROUND FOR MILES AND NO REASON TO COME HERE IN THE MIDDLE OF THE DAMN NIGHT, UNLESS YOU HAPPEN TO BE LOOKING FOR YOUR SOON-TO-BE-FIRED DEPUTY WHO HASN'T REPORTED IN.

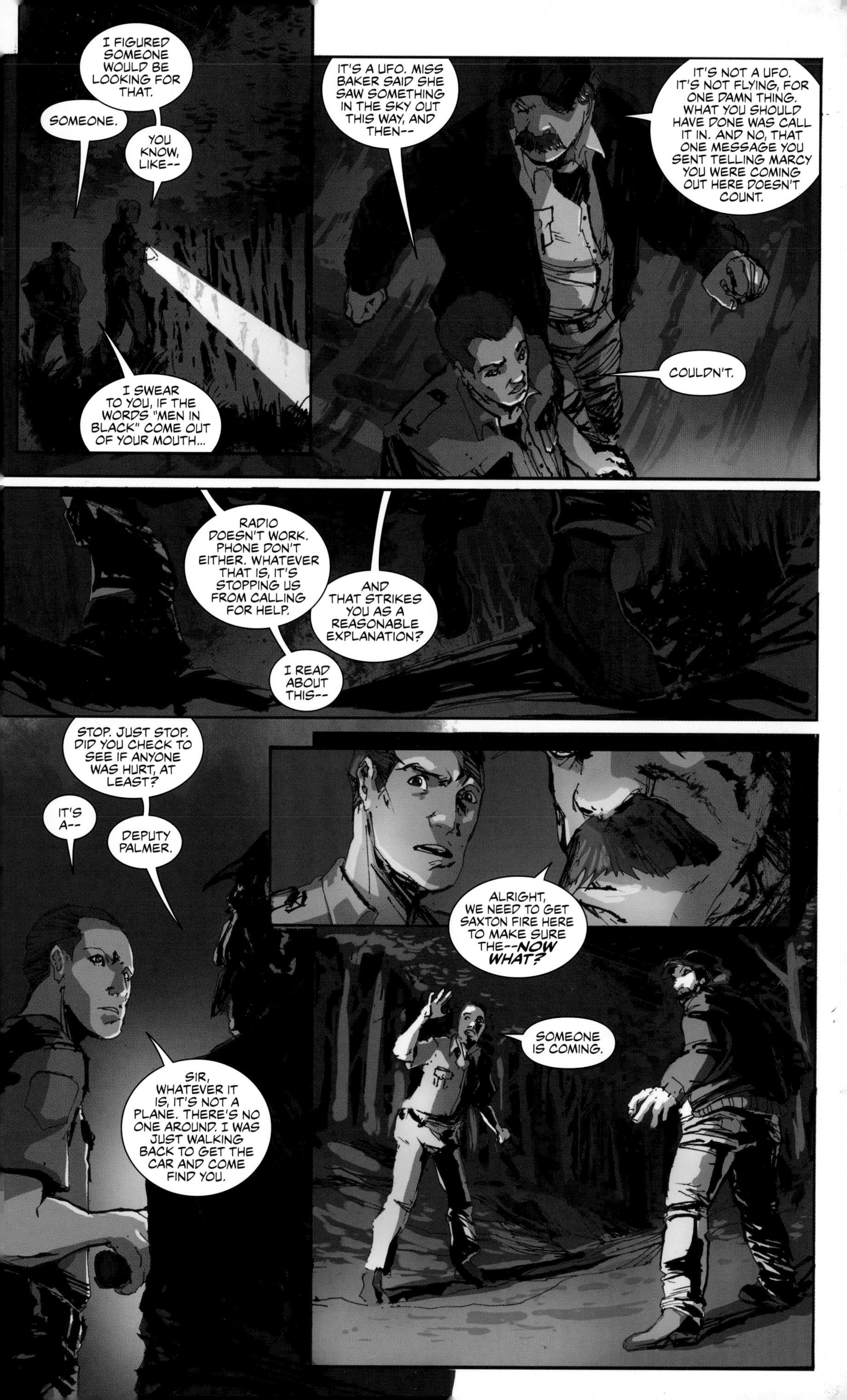

I FIGURED SOMEONE WOULD BE LOOKING FOR THAT.
SOMEONE.
YOU KNOW, LIKE--
I SWEAR TO YOU, IF THE WORDS "MEN IN BLACK" COME OUT OF YOUR MOUTH...
IT'S A UFO. MISS BAKER SAID SHE SAW SOMETHING IN THE SKY OUT THIS WAY, AND THEN--
IT'S NOT A UFO. IT'S NOT FLYING, FOR ONE DAMN THING. WHAT YOU SHOULD HAVE DONE WAS CALL IT IN. AND NO, THAT ONE MESSAGE YOU SENT TELLING MARCY YOU WERE COMING OUT HERE DOESN'T COUNT.
COULDN'T.
RADIO DOESN'T WORK. PHONE DON'T EITHER. WHATEVER THAT IS, IT'S STOPPING US FROM CALLING FOR HELP.
AND THAT STRIKES YOU AS A REASONABLE EXPLANATION?
I READ ABOUT THIS--
STOP. JUST STOP. DID YOU CHECK TO SEE IF ANYONE WAS HURT, AT LEAST?
IT'S A--
DEPUTY PALMER.
SIR, WHATEVER IT IS, IT'S NOT A PLANE. THERE'S NO ONE AROUND. I WAS JUST WALKING BACK TO GET THE CAR AND COME FIND YOU.
ALRIGHT, WE NEED TO GET SAXTON FIRE HERE TO MAKE SURE THE--*NOW WHAT?*
SOMEONE IS COMING.

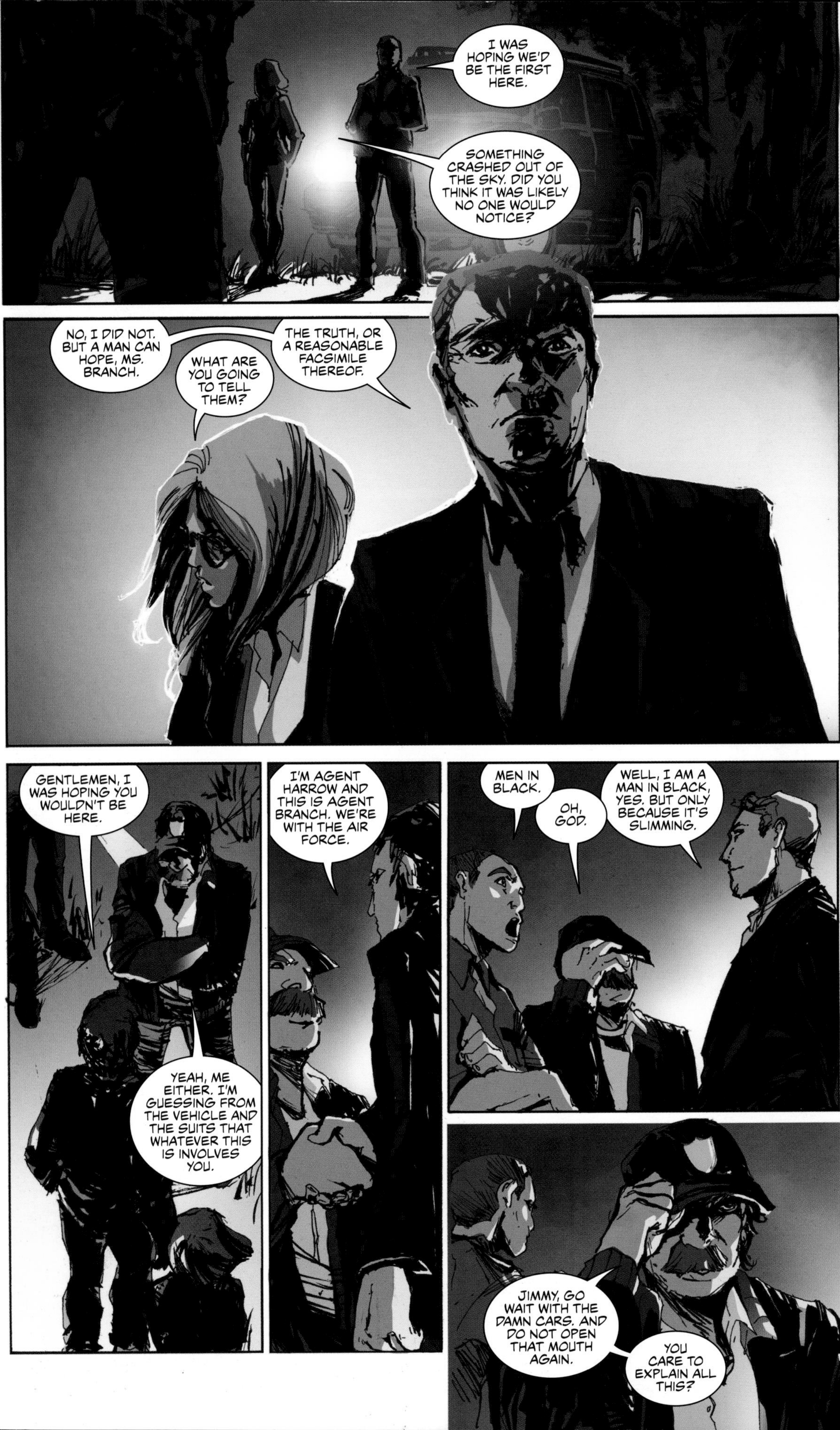
I WAS HOPING WE'D BE THE FIRST HERE.
SOMETHING CRASHED OUT OF THE SKY. DID YOU THINK IT WAS LIKELY NO ONE WOULD NOTICE?
NO, I DID NOT. BUT A MAN CAN HOPE, MS. BRANCH.
WHAT ARE YOU GOING TO TELL THEM?
THE TRUTH, OR A REASONABLE FACSIMILE THEREOF.
GENTLEMEN, I WAS HOPING YOU WOULDN'T BE HERE.
YEAH, ME EITHER. I'M GUESSING FROM THE VEHICLE AND THE SUITS THAT WHATEVER THIS IS INVOLVES YOU.
I'M AGENT HARROW AND THIS IS AGENT BRANCH. WE'RE WITH THE AIR FORCE.
MEN IN BLACK.
OH, GOD.
WELL, I AM A MAN IN BLACK, YES. BUT ONLY BECAUSE IT'S SLIMMING.
JIMMY, GO WAIT WITH THE DAMN CARS. AND DO NOT OPEN THAT MOUTH AGAIN.
YOU CARE TO EXPLAIN ALL THIS?

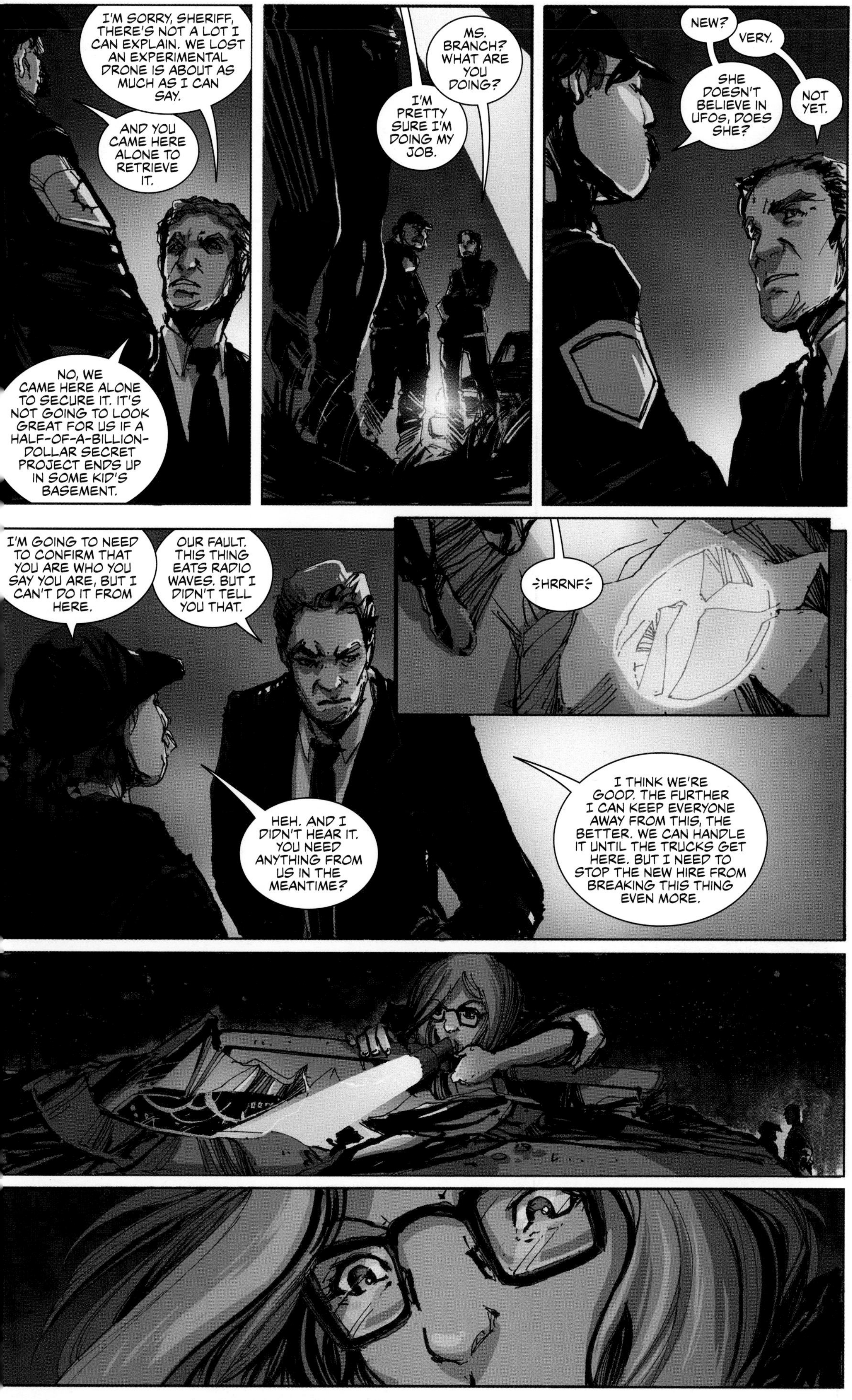
I'M SORRY, SHERIFF, THERE'S NOT A LOT I CAN EXPLAIN. WE LOST AN EXPERIMENTAL DRONE IS ABOUT AS MUCH AS I CAN SAY.
AND YOU CAME HERE ALONE TO RETRIEVE IT.
NO, WE CAME HERE ALONE TO SECURE IT. IT'S NOT GOING TO LOOK GREAT FOR US IF A HALF-OF-A-BILLION-DOLLAR SECRET PROJECT ENDS UP IN SOME KID'S BASEMENT.
MS. BRANCH? WHAT ARE YOU DOING?
I'M PRETTY SURE I'M DOING MY JOB.
NEW?
VERY.
SHE DOESN'T BELIEVE IN UFOS, DOES SHE?
NOT YET.
I'M GOING TO NEED TO CONFIRM THAT YOU ARE WHO YOU SAY YOU ARE, BUT I CAN'T DO IT FROM HERE.
OUR FAULT. THIS THING EATS RADIO WAVES. BUT I DIDN'T TELL YOU THAT.
HRRNF
HEH. AND I DIDN'T HEAR IT. YOU NEED ANYTHING FROM US IN THE MEANTIME?
I THINK WE'RE GOOD. THE FURTHER I CAN KEEP EVERYONE AWAY FROM THIS, THE BETTER. WE CAN HANDLE IT UNTIL THE TRUCKS GET HERE. BUT I NEED TO STOP THE NEW HIRE FROM BREAKING THIS THING EVEN MORE.

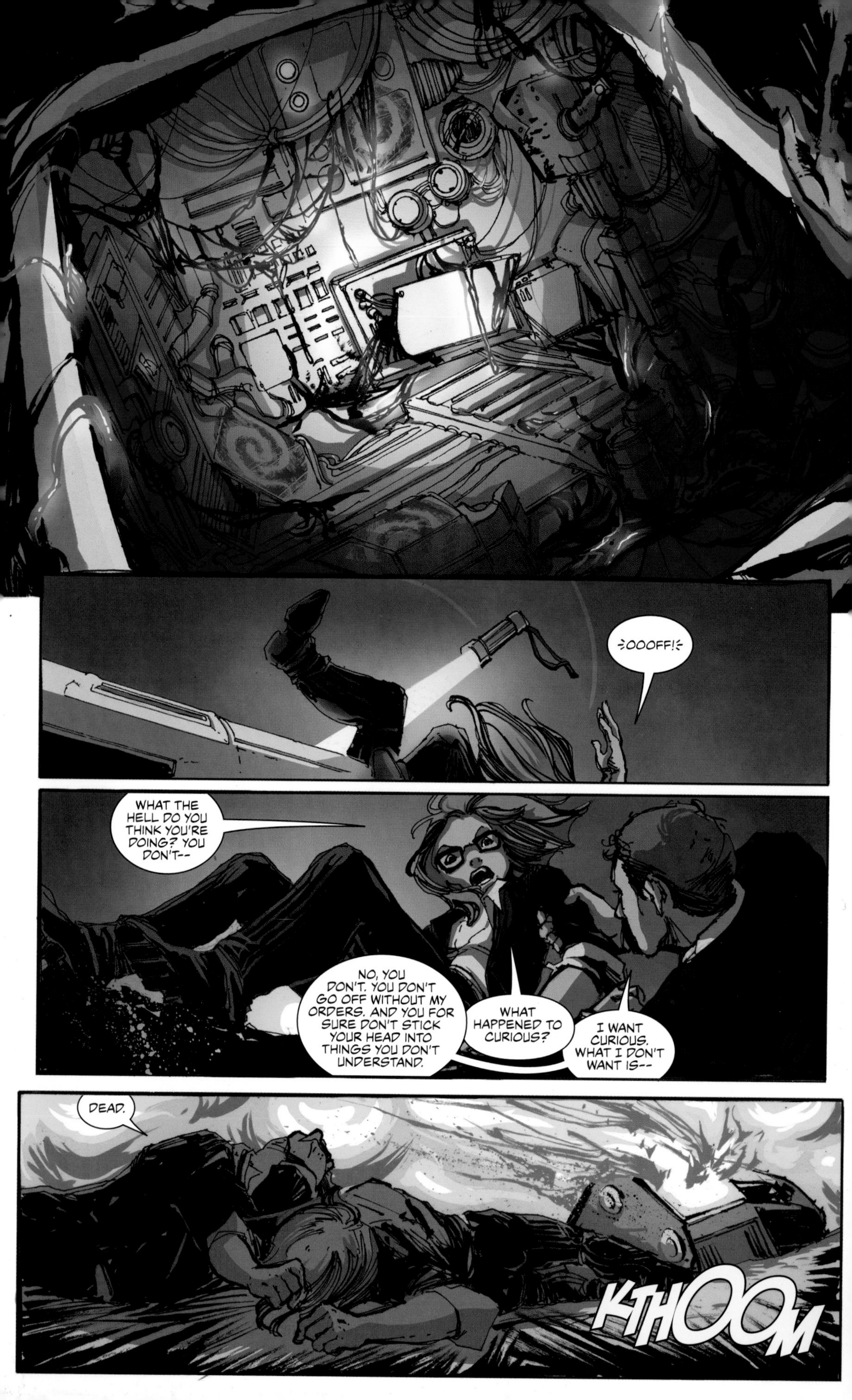
OOOFF!
WHAT THE HELL DO YOU THINK YOU'RE DOING? YOU DON'T--
NO, YOU DON'T. YOU DON'T GO OFF WITHOUT MY ORDERS. AND YOU FOR SURE DON'T STICK YOUR HEAD INTO THINGS YOU DON'T UNDERSTAND.
WHAT HAPPENED TO CURIOUS?
I WANT CURIOUS. WHAT I DON'T WANT IS--
DEAD.
KTHOOM

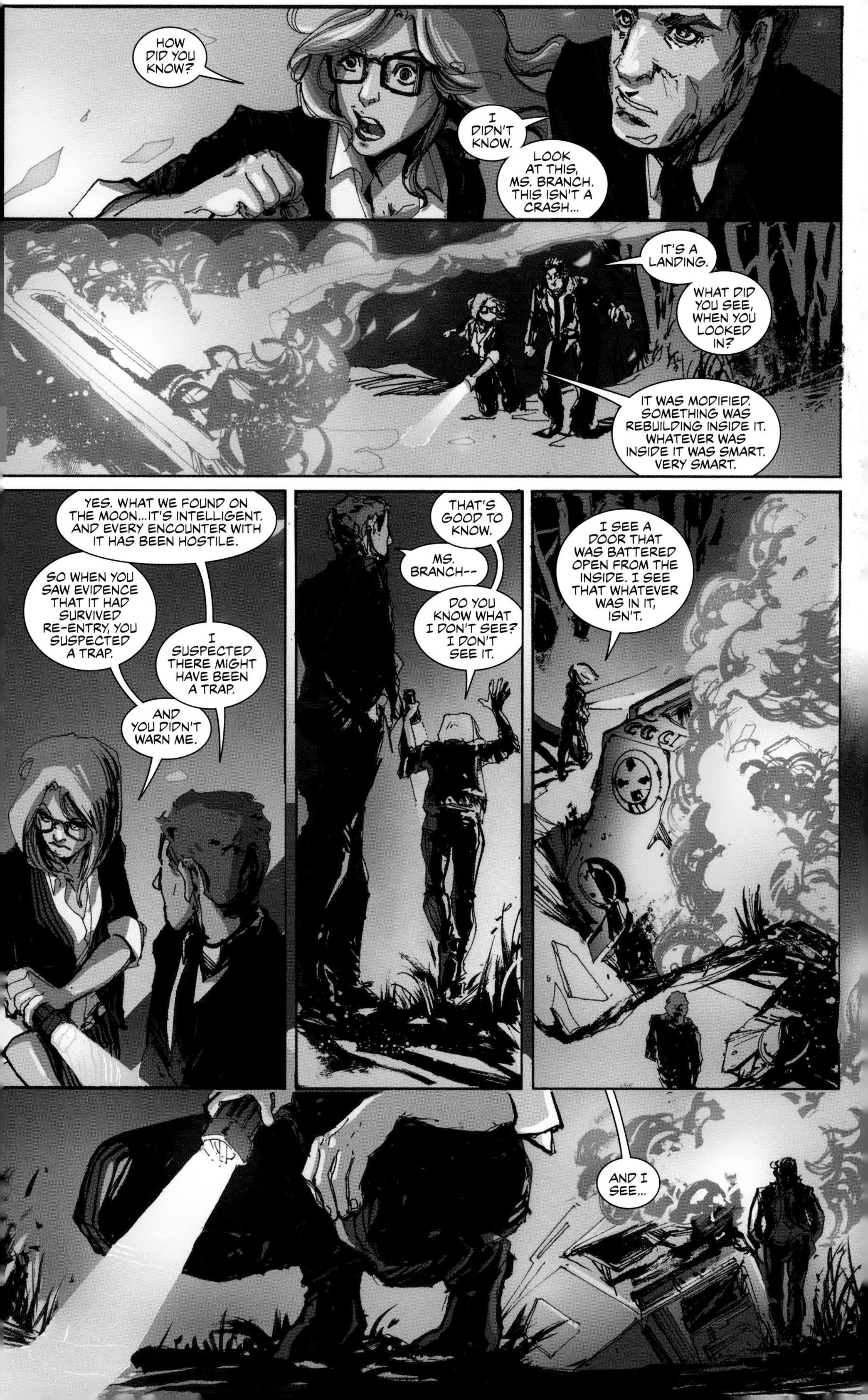

HOW DID YOU KNOW?
I DIDN'T KNOW.
LOOK AT THIS, MS. BRANCH. THIS ISN'T A CRASH...
IT'S A LANDING.
WHAT DID YOU SEE, WHEN YOU LOOKED IN?
IT WAS MODIFIED. SOMETHING WAS REBUILDING INSIDE IT. WHATEVER WAS INSIDE IT WAS SMART. VERY SMART.
YES. WHAT WE FOUND ON THE MOON...IT'S INTELLIGENT. AND EVERY ENCOUNTER WITH IT HAS BEEN HOSTILE.
SO WHEN YOU SAW EVIDENCE THAT IT HAD SURVIVED RE-ENTRY, YOU SUSPECTED A TRAP.
I SUSPECTED THERE MIGHT HAVE BEEN A TRAP.
AND YOU DIDN'T WARN ME.
THAT'S GOOD TO KNOW.
MS. BRANCH--
DO YOU KNOW WHAT I DON'T SEE? I DON'T SEE IT.
I SEE A DOOR THAT WAS BATTERED OPEN FROM THE INSIDE. I SEE THAT WHATEVER WAS IN IT, ISN'T.
AND I SEE...

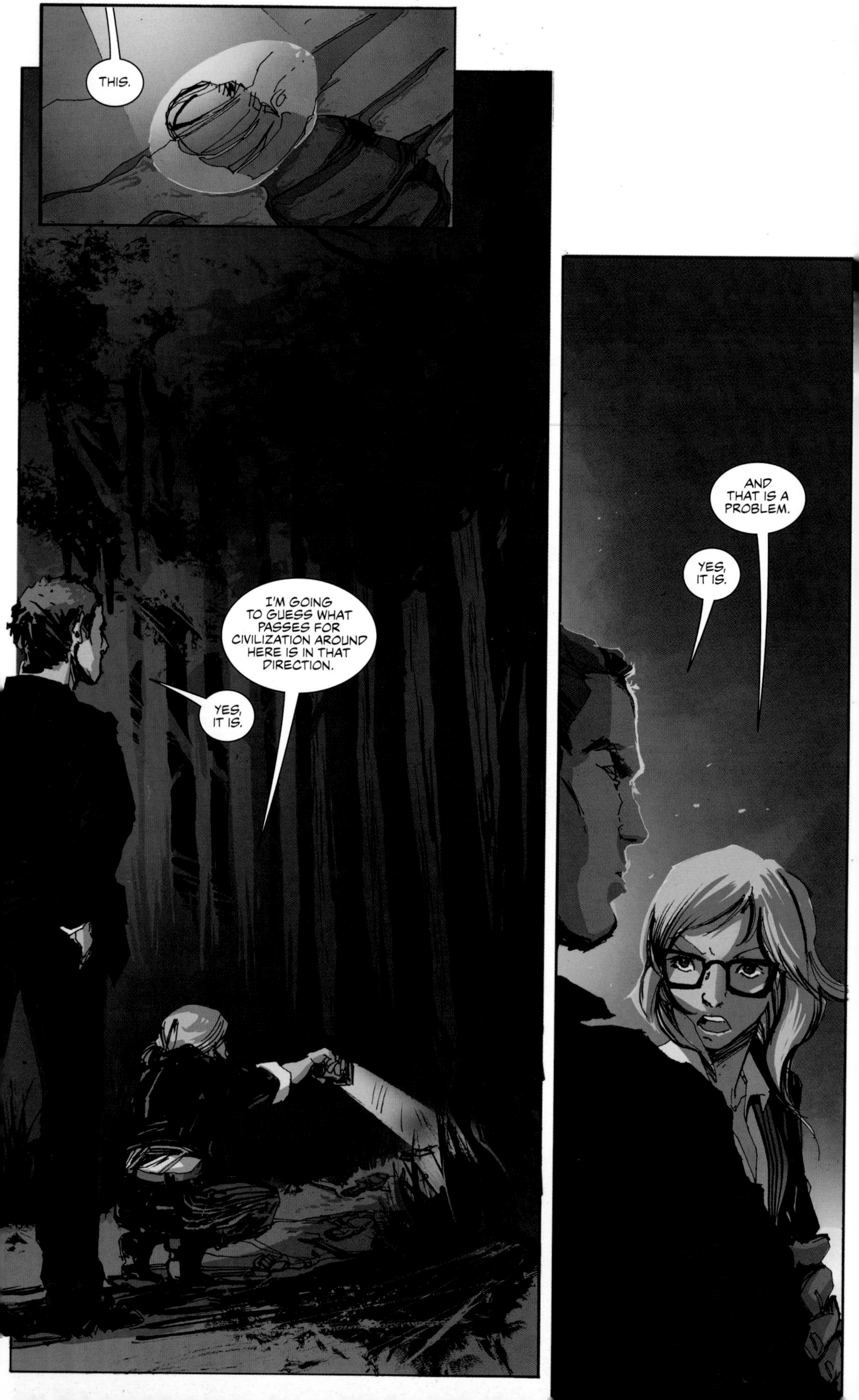
THIS.
I'M GOING TO GUESS WHAT PASSES FOR CIVILIZATION AROUND HERE IS IN THAT DIRECTION.
YES, IT IS.
YES, IT IS.
AND THAT IS A PROBLEM.

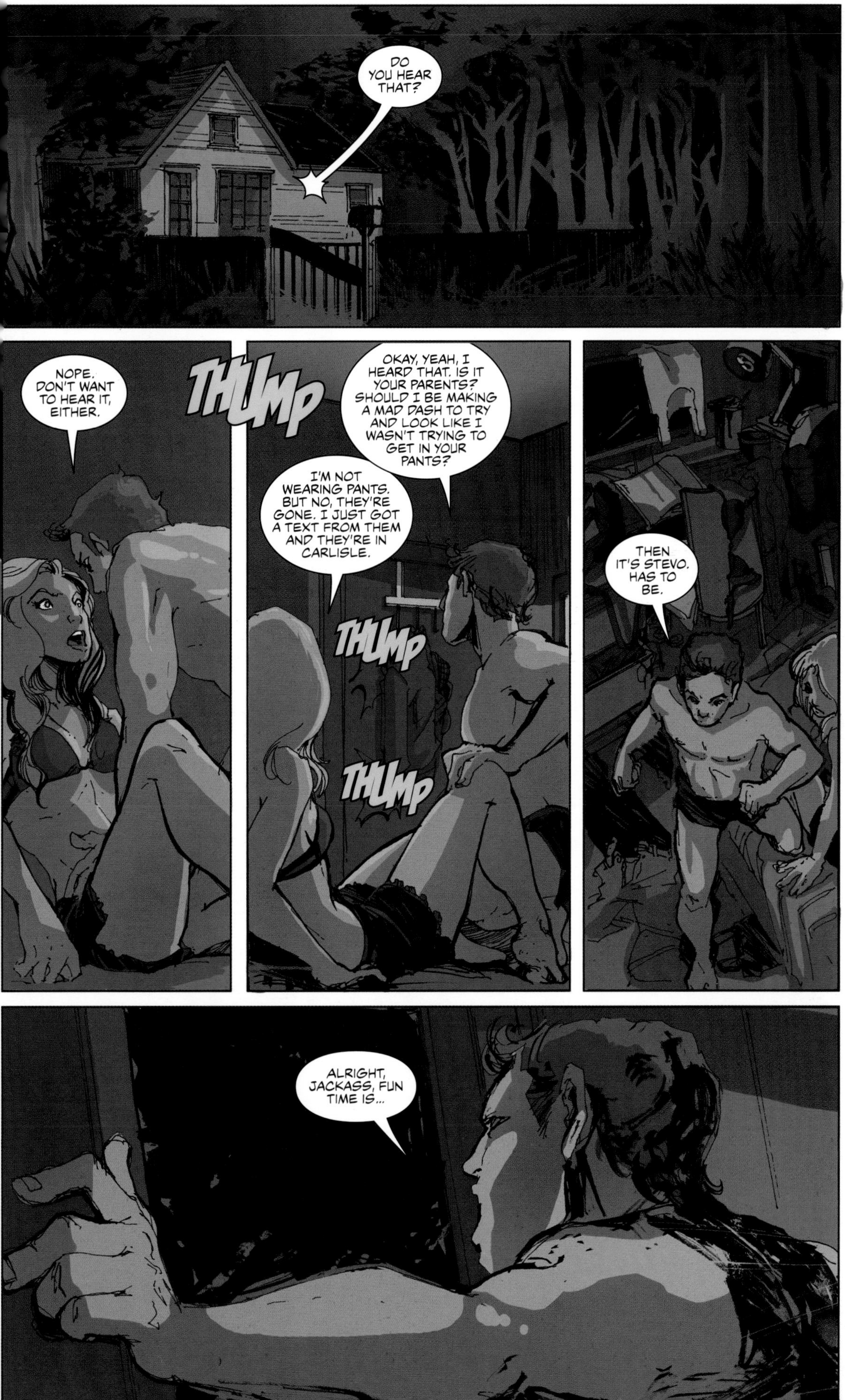
DO YOU HEAR THAT?
NOPE. DON'T WANT TO HEAR IT, EITHER.
THUMP
OKAY, YEAH, I HEARD THAT. IS IT YOUR PARENTS? SHOULD I BE MAKING A MAD DASH TO TRY AND LOOK LIKE I WASN'T TRYING TO GET IN YOUR PANTS?
I'M NOT WEARING PANTS. BUT NO, THEY'RE GONE. I JUST GOT A TEXT FROM THEM AND THEY'RE IN CARLISLE.
THUMP
THUMP
THEN IT'S STEVO. HAS TO BE.
ALRIGHT, JACKASS, FUN TIME IS...

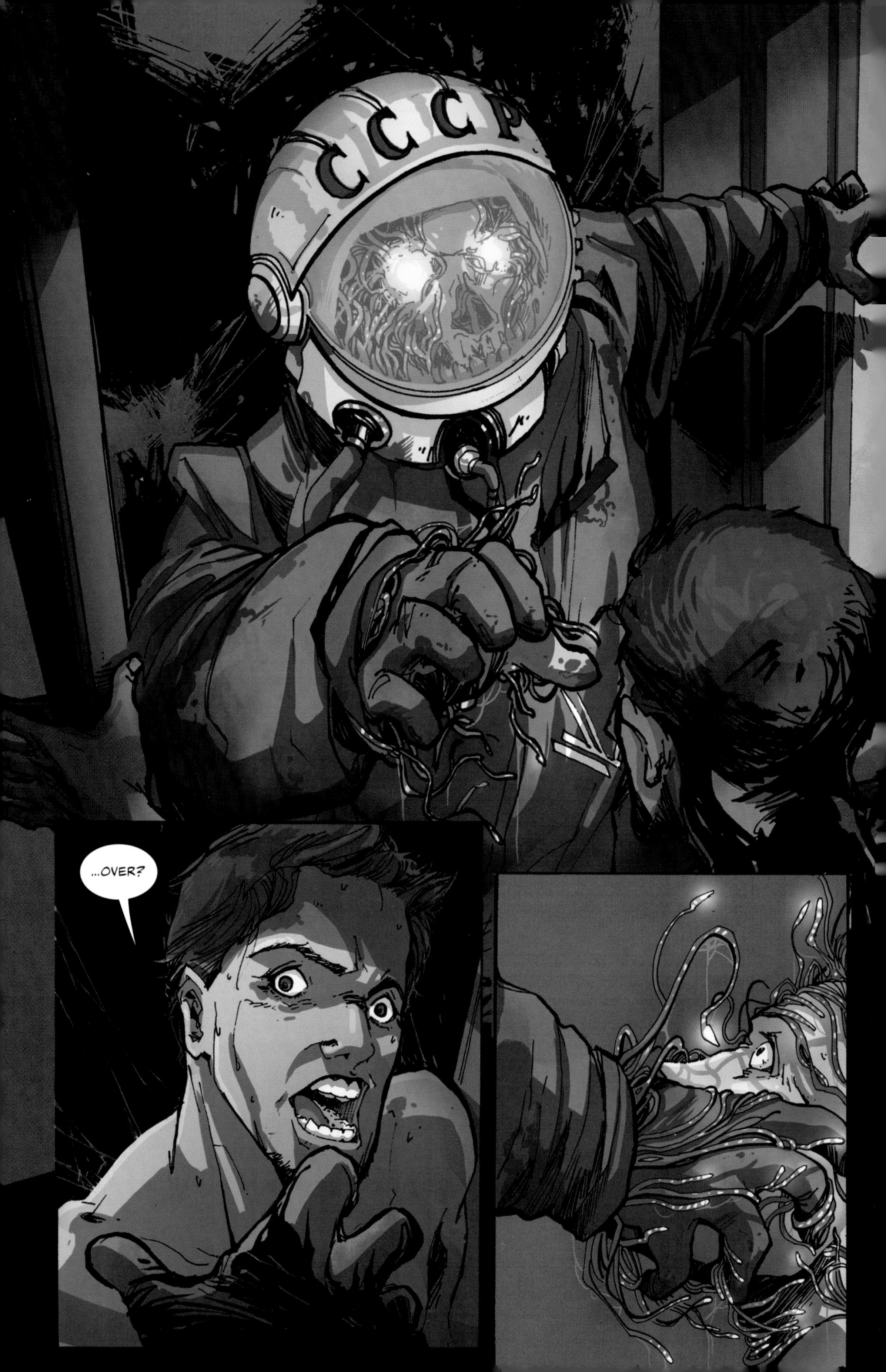
CCCP
...OVER?

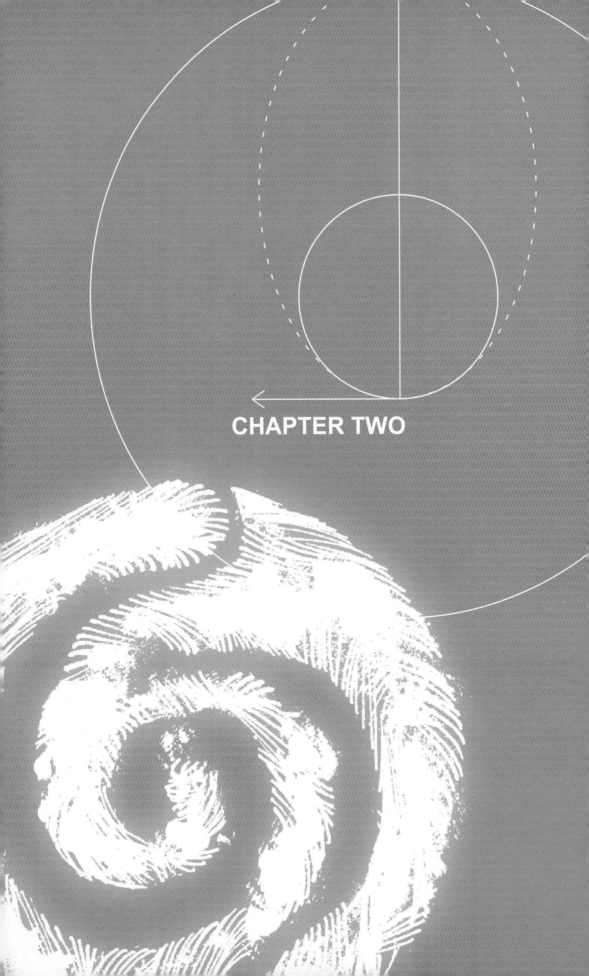

CHAPTER TWO

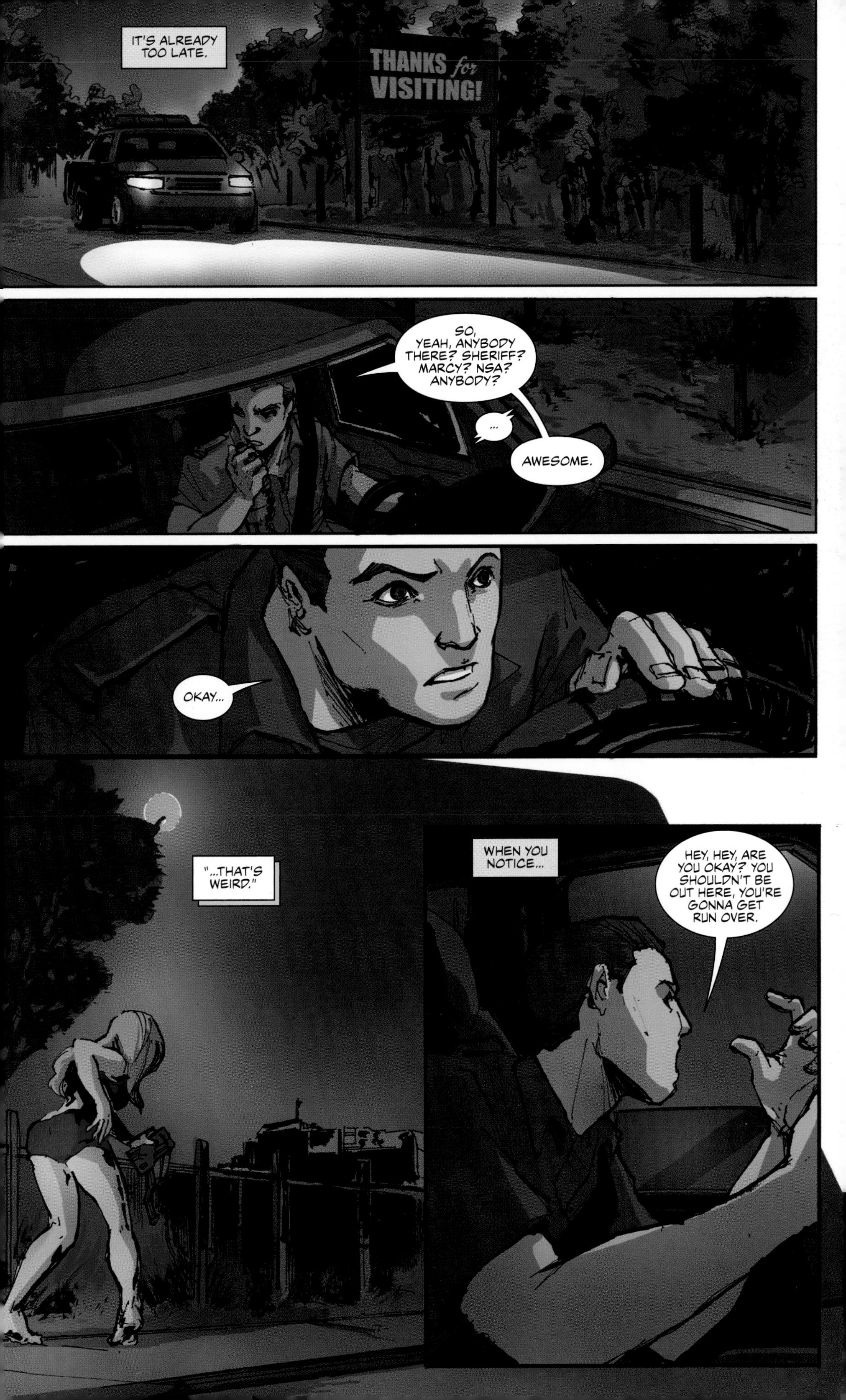
IT'S ALREADY TOO LATE.
THANKS for VISITING!
SO, YEAH, ANYBODY THERE? SHERIFF? MARCY? NSA? ANYBODY?
...
AWESOME.
OKAY...
"...THAT'S WEIRD."
WHEN YOU NOTICE...
HEY, HEY, ARE YOU OKAY? YOU SHOULDN'T BE OUT HERE, YOU'RE GONNA GET RUN OVER.

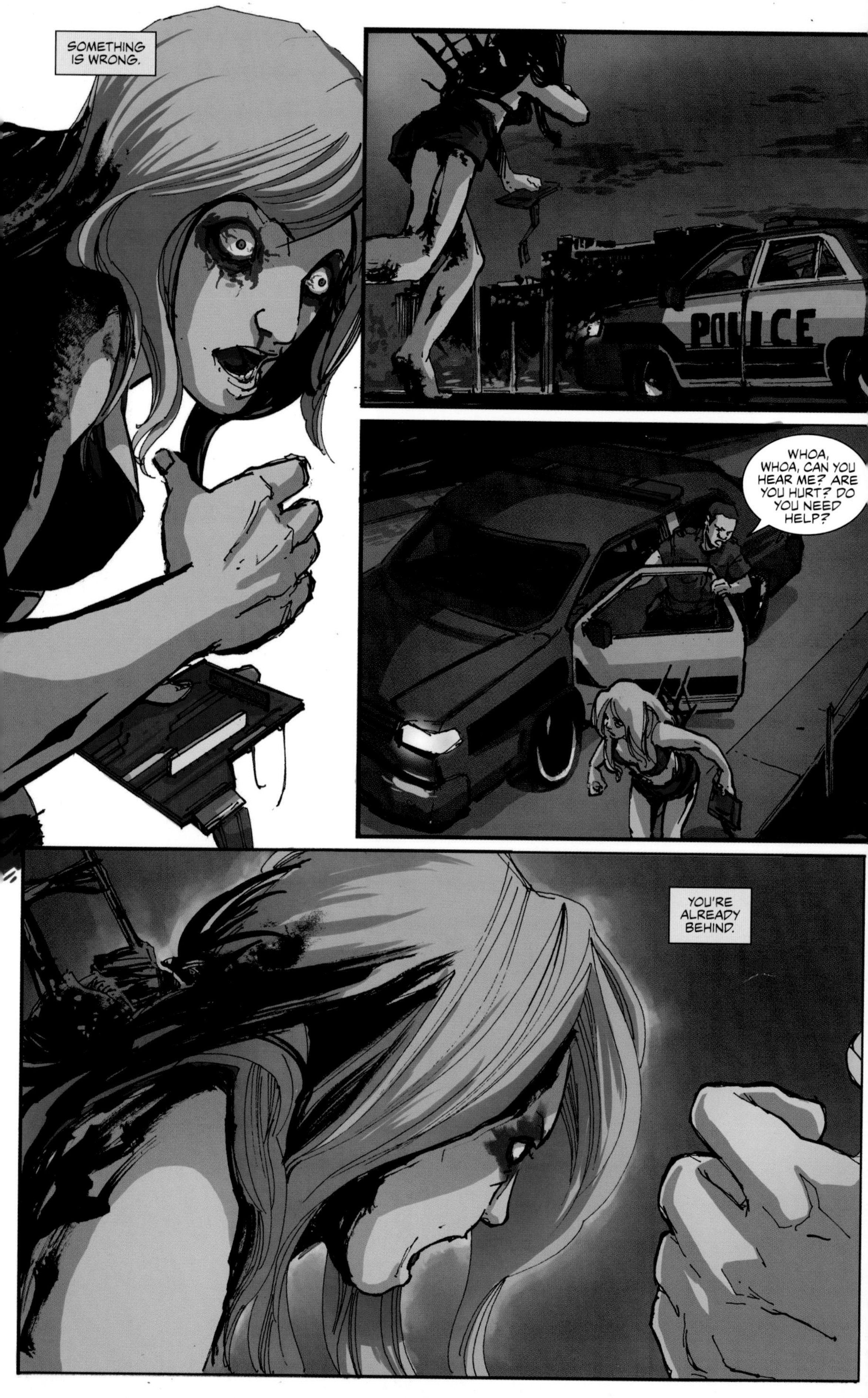
SOMETHING IS WRONG.
POLICE
WHOA, WHOA, CAN YOU HEAR ME? ARE YOU HURT? DO YOU NEED HELP?
YOU'RE ALREADY BEHIND.

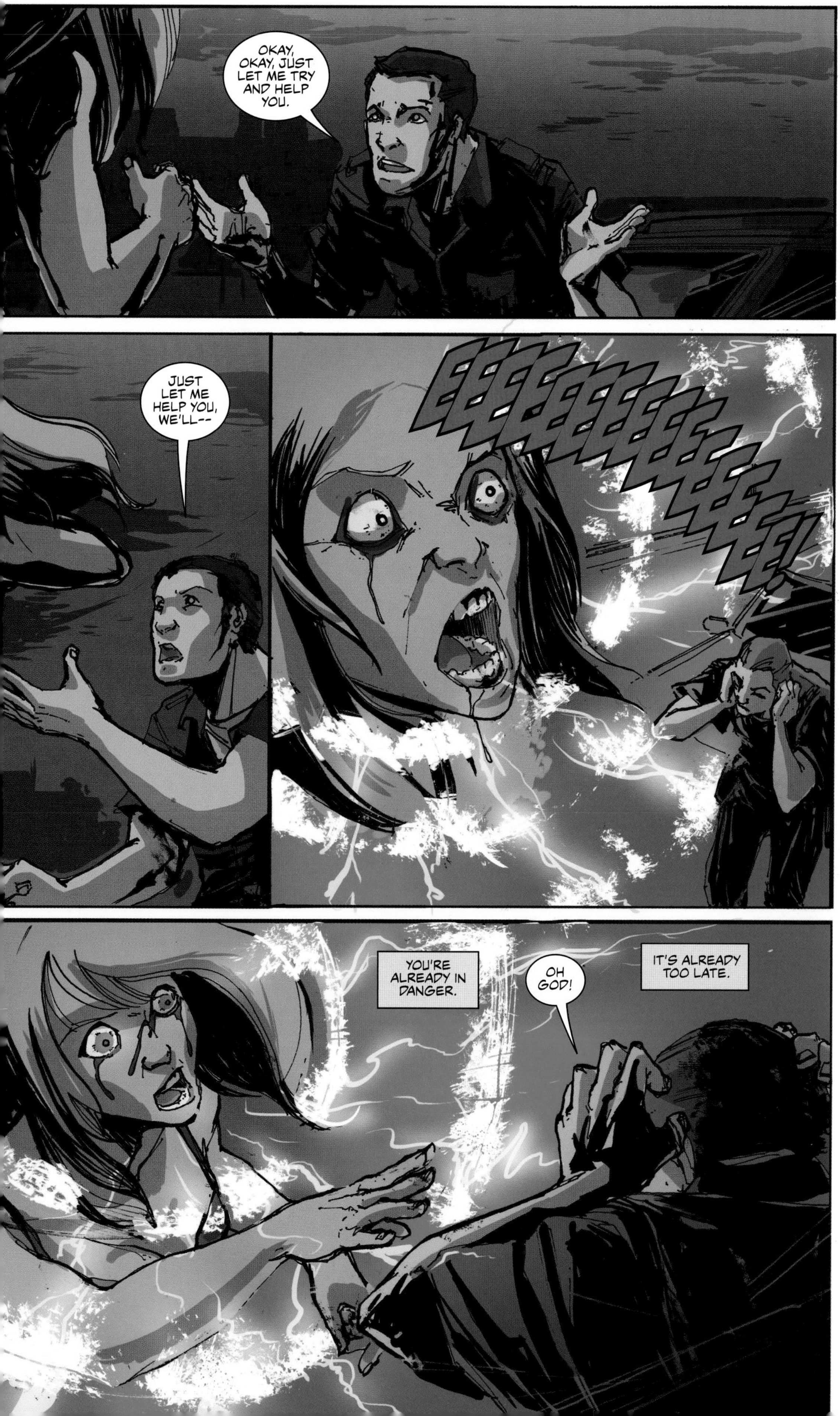
OKAY, OKAY, JUST LET ME TRY AND HELP YOU.
JUST LET ME HELP YOU, WE'LL--
EEEEEEEEEEEEEEEEEEEEEEEEE!
YOU'RE ALREADY IN DANGER.
OH GOD!
IT'S ALREADY TOO LATE.

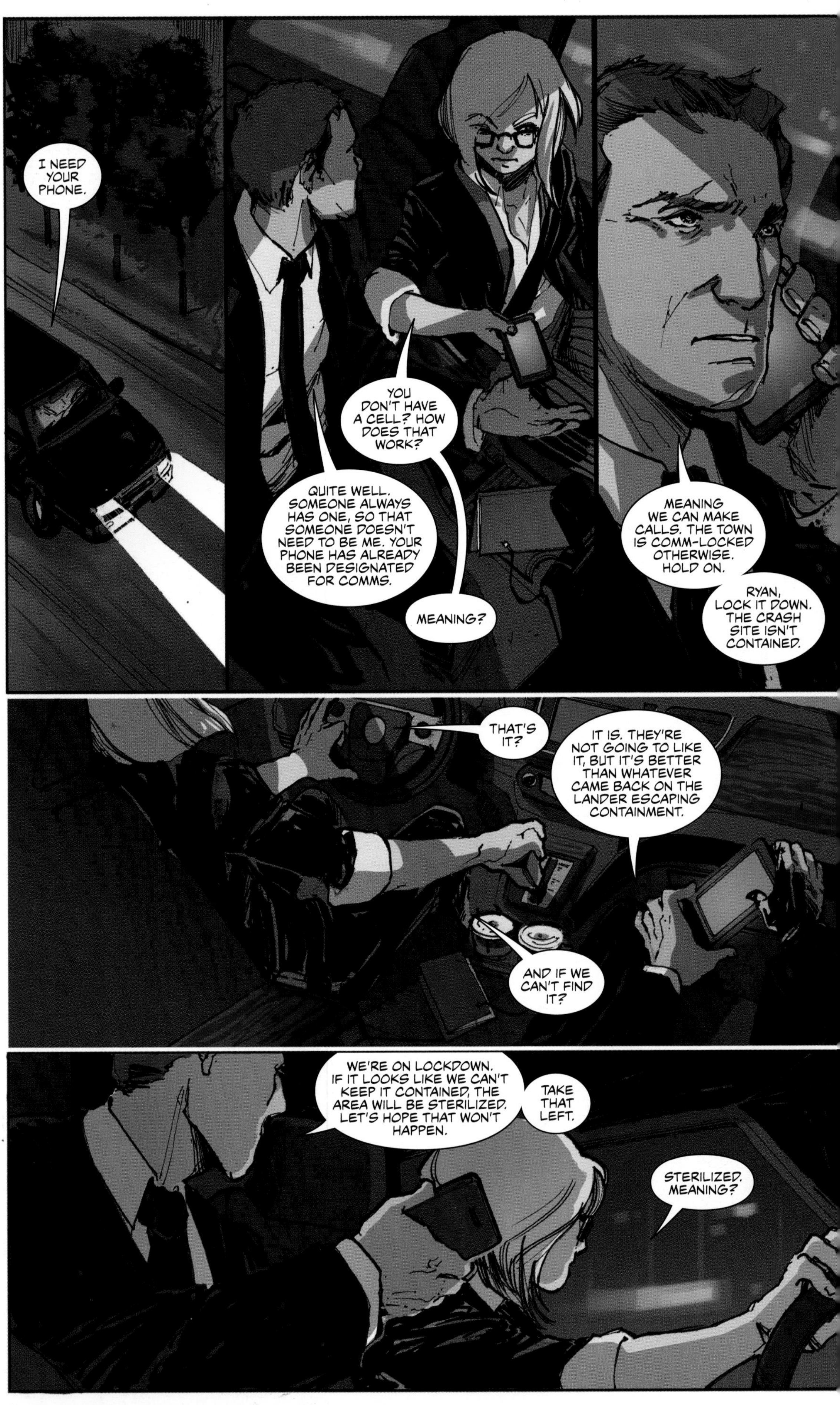
I NEED YOUR PHONE.
YOU DON'T HAVE A CELL? HOW DOES THAT WORK?
QUITE WELL. SOMEONE ALWAYS HAS ONE, SO THAT SOMEONE DOESN'T NEED TO BE ME. YOUR PHONE HAS ALREADY BEEN DESIGNATED FOR COMMS.
MEANING?
MEANING WE CAN MAKE CALLS. THE TOWN IS COMM-LOCKED OTHERWISE. HOLD ON.
RYAN, LOCK IT DOWN. THE CRASH SITE ISN'T CONTAINED.
THAT'S IT?
IT IS. THEY'RE NOT GOING TO LIKE IT, BUT IT'S BETTER THAN WHATEVER CAME BACK ON THE LANDER ESCAPING CONTAINMENT.
AND IF WE CAN'T FIND IT?
WE'RE ON LOCKDOWN. IF IT LOOKS LIKE WE CAN'T KEEP IT CONTAINED, THE AREA WILL BE STERILIZED. LET'S HOPE THAT WON'T HAPPEN.
TAKE THAT LEFT.
STERILIZED. MEANING?

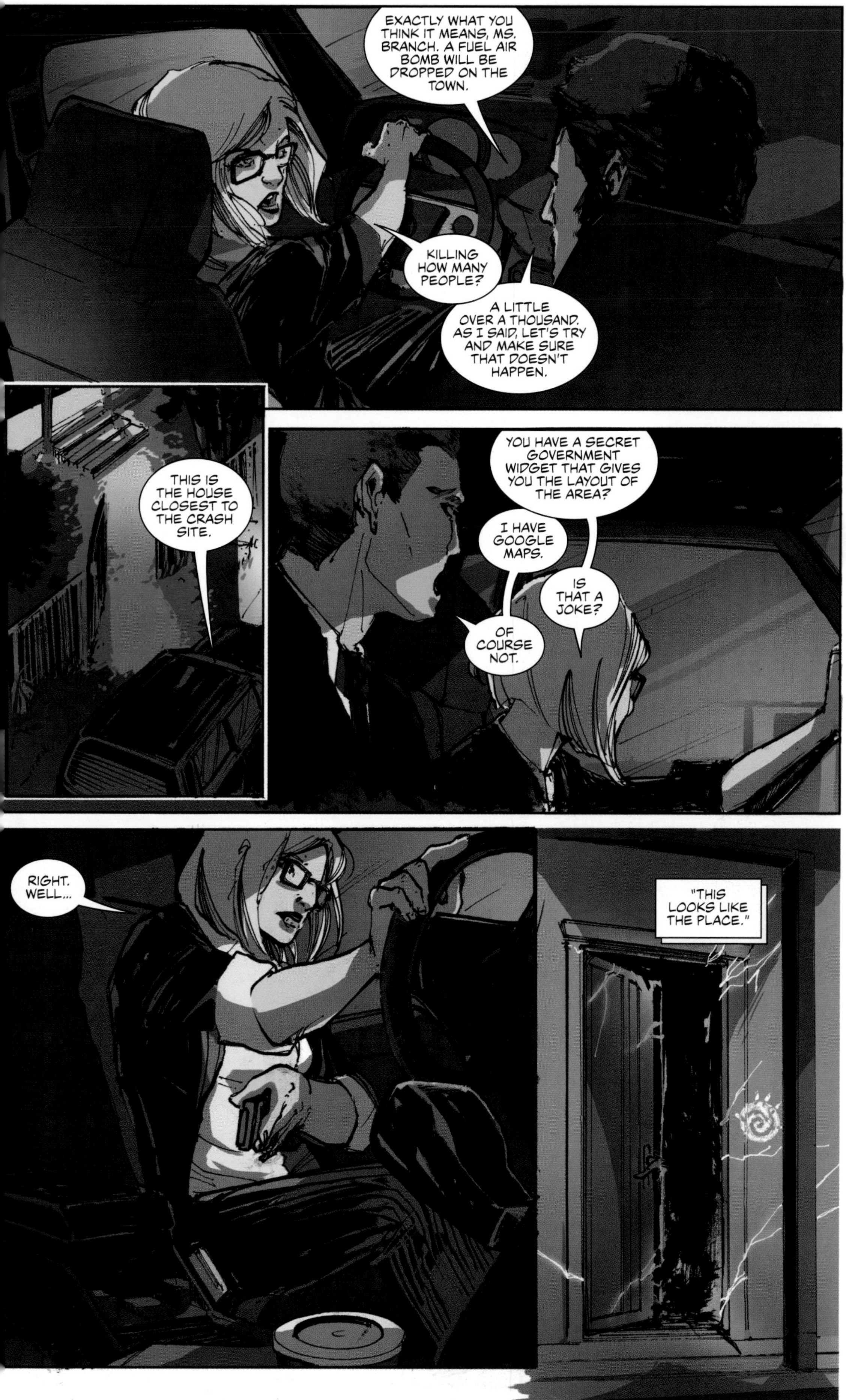
EXACTLY WHAT YOU THINK IT MEANS, MS. BRANCH. A FUEL AIR BOMB WILL BE DROPPED ON THE TOWN.
KILLING HOW MANY PEOPLE?
A LITTLE OVER A THOUSAND. AS I SAID, LET'S TRY AND MAKE SURE THAT DOESN'T HAPPEN.
THIS IS THE HOUSE CLOSEST TO THE CRASH SITE.
YOU HAVE A SECRET GOVERNMENT WIDGET THAT GIVES YOU THE LAYOUT OF THE AREA?
I HAVE GOOGLE MAPS.
IS THAT A JOKE?
OF COURSE NOT.
RIGHT. WELL...
"THIS LOOKS LIKE THE PLACE."

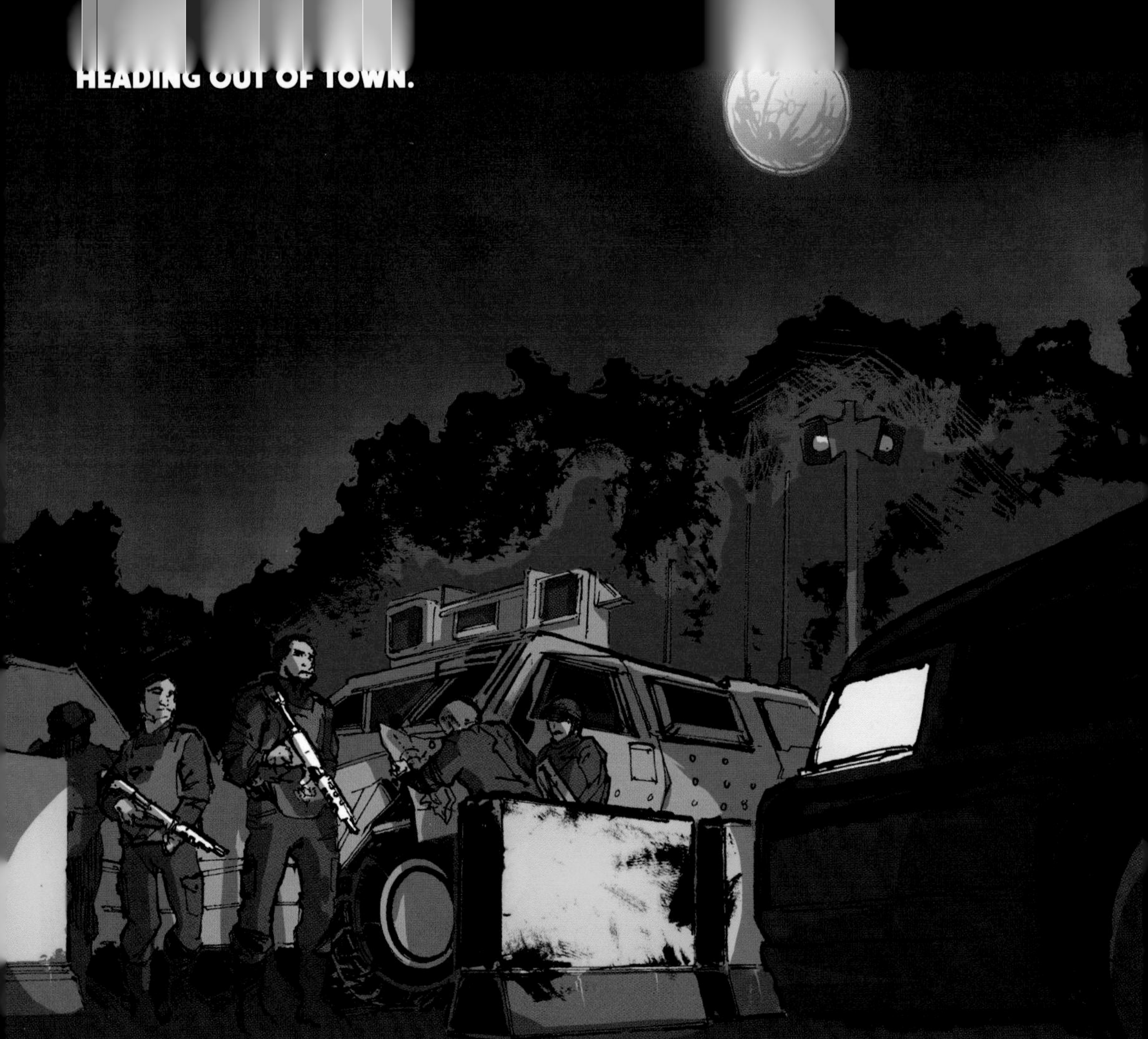
HEADING OUT OF TOWN.

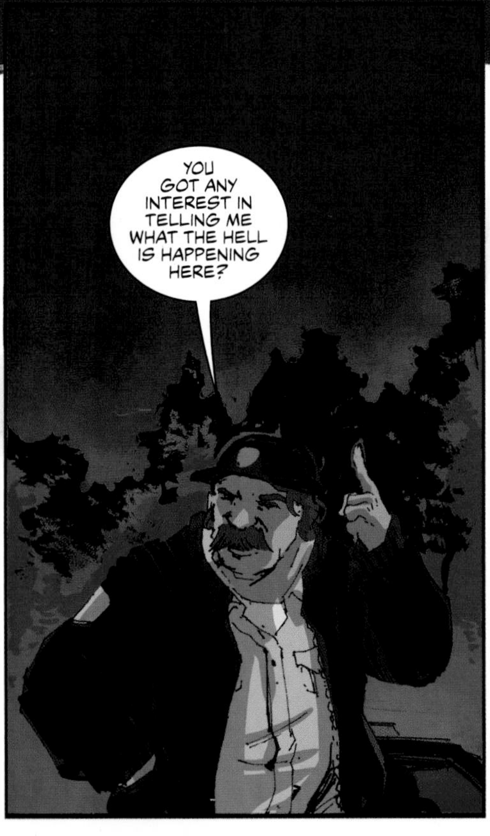
YOU GOT ANY INTEREST IN TELLING ME WHAT THE HELL IS HAPPENING HERE?

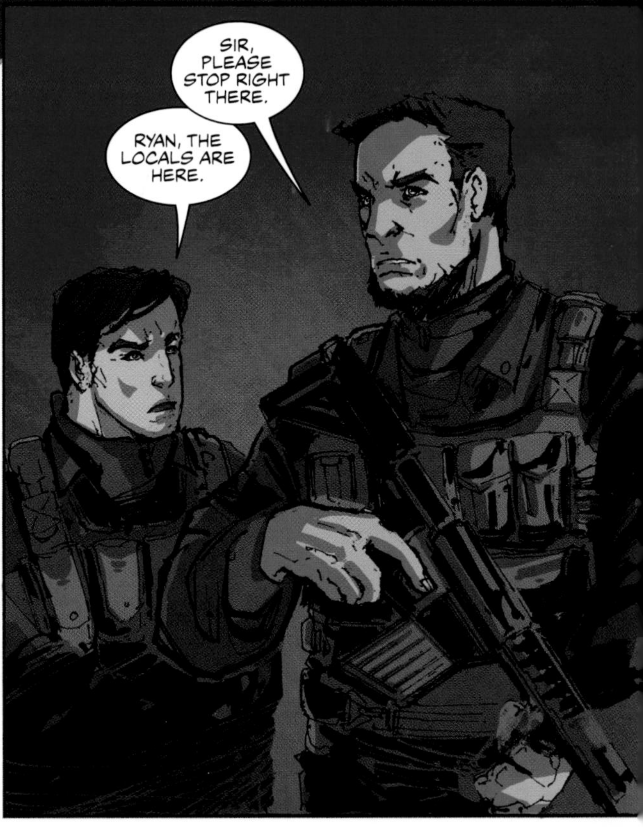
SIR, PLEASE STOP RIGHT THERE.
RYAN, THE LOCALS ARE HERE.

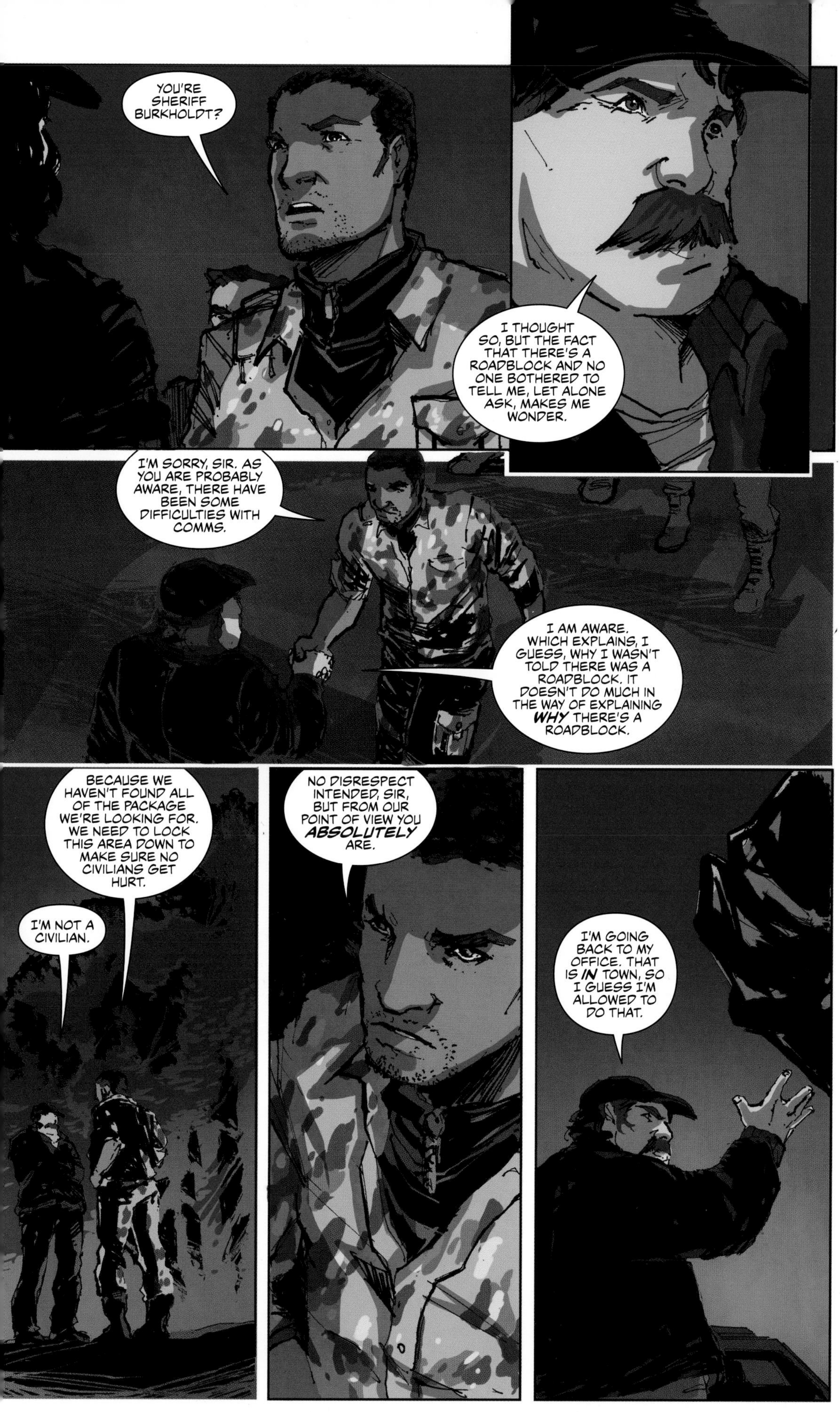

YOU'RE SHERIFF BURKHOLDT?
I THOUGHT SO, BUT THE FACT THAT THERE'S A ROADBLOCK AND NO ONE BOTHERED TO TELL ME, LET ALONE ASK, MAKES ME WONDER.
I'M SORRY, SIR. AS YOU ARE PROBABLY AWARE, THERE HAVE BEEN SOME DIFFICULTIES WITH COMMS.
I AM AWARE. WHICH EXPLAINS, I GUESS, WHY I WASN'T TOLD THERE WAS A ROADBLOCK. IT DOESN'T DO MUCH IN THE WAY OF EXPLAINING WHY THERE'S A ROADBLOCK.
BECAUSE WE HAVEN'T FOUND ALL OF THE PACKAGE WE'RE LOOKING FOR. WE NEED TO LOCK THIS AREA DOWN TO MAKE SURE NO CIVILIANS GET HURT.
I'M NOT A CIVILIAN.
NO DISRESPECT INTENDED, SIR, BUT FROM OUR POINT OF VIEW YOU ABSOLUTELY ARE.
I'M GOING BACK TO MY OFFICE. THAT IS IN TOWN, SO I GUESS I'M ALLOWED TO DO THAT.

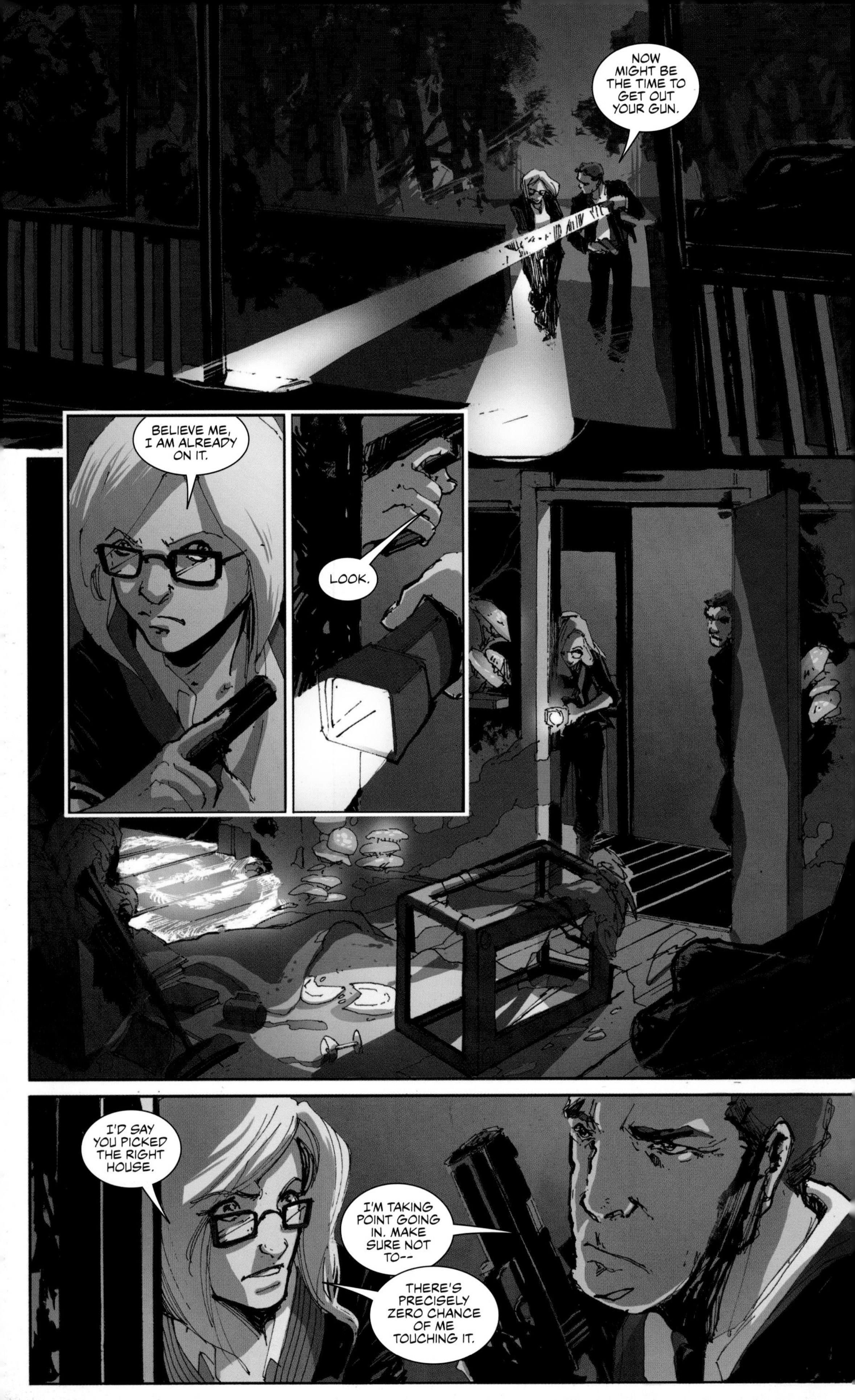
NOW MIGHT BE THE TIME TO GET OUT YOUR GUN.
BELIEVE ME, I AM ALREADY ON IT.
LOOK.
I'D SAY YOU PICKED THE RIGHT HOUSE.
I'M TAKING POINT GOING IN. MAKE SURE NOT TO--
THERE'S PRECISELY ZERO CHANCE OF ME TOUCHING IT.

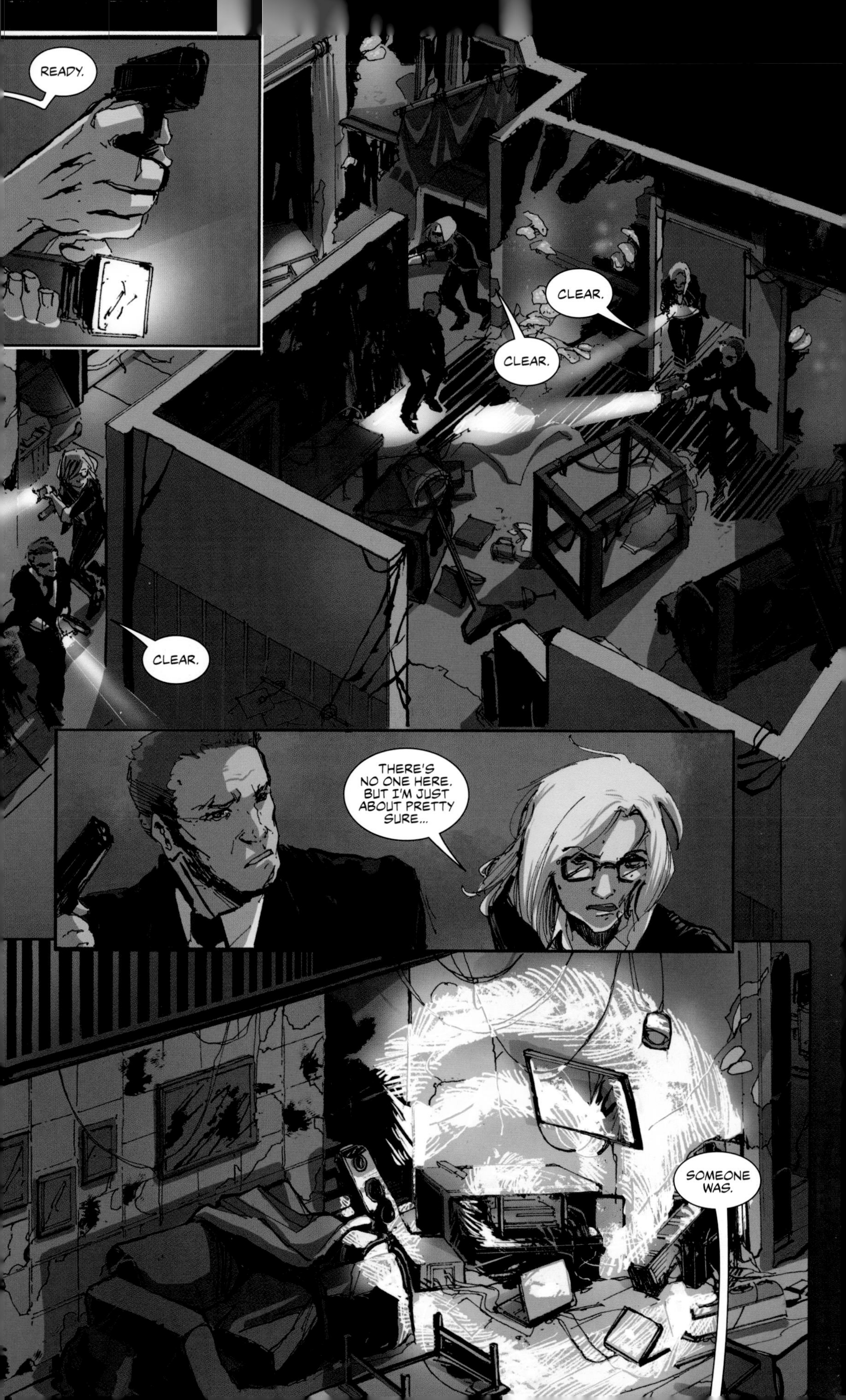
READY.
CLEAR.
CLEAR.
CLEAR.
THERE'S NO ONE HERE. BUT I'M JUST ABOUT PRETTY SURE...
SOMEONE WAS.

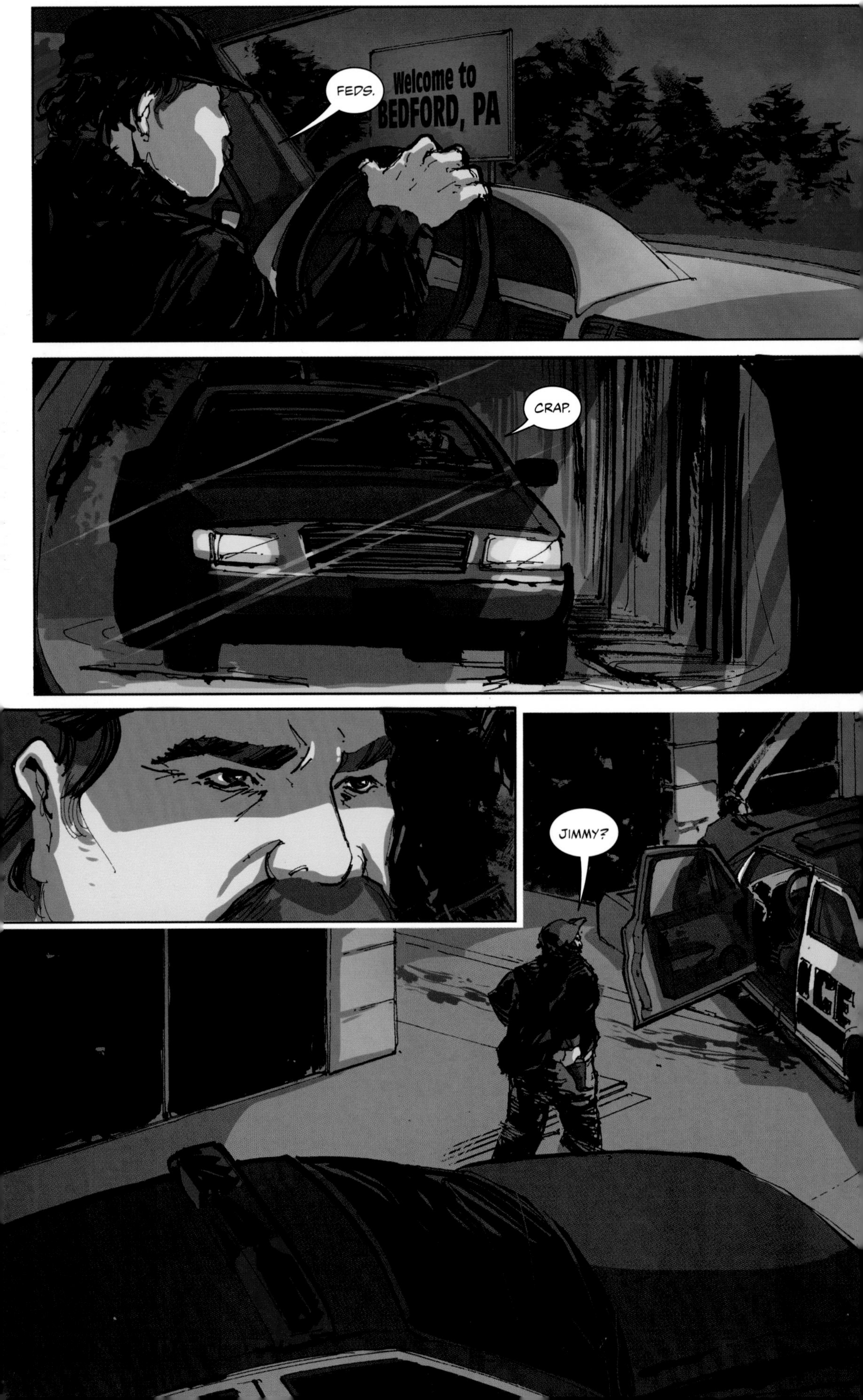
Welcome to
BEDFORD, PA
FEDS.
CRAP.
JIMMY?

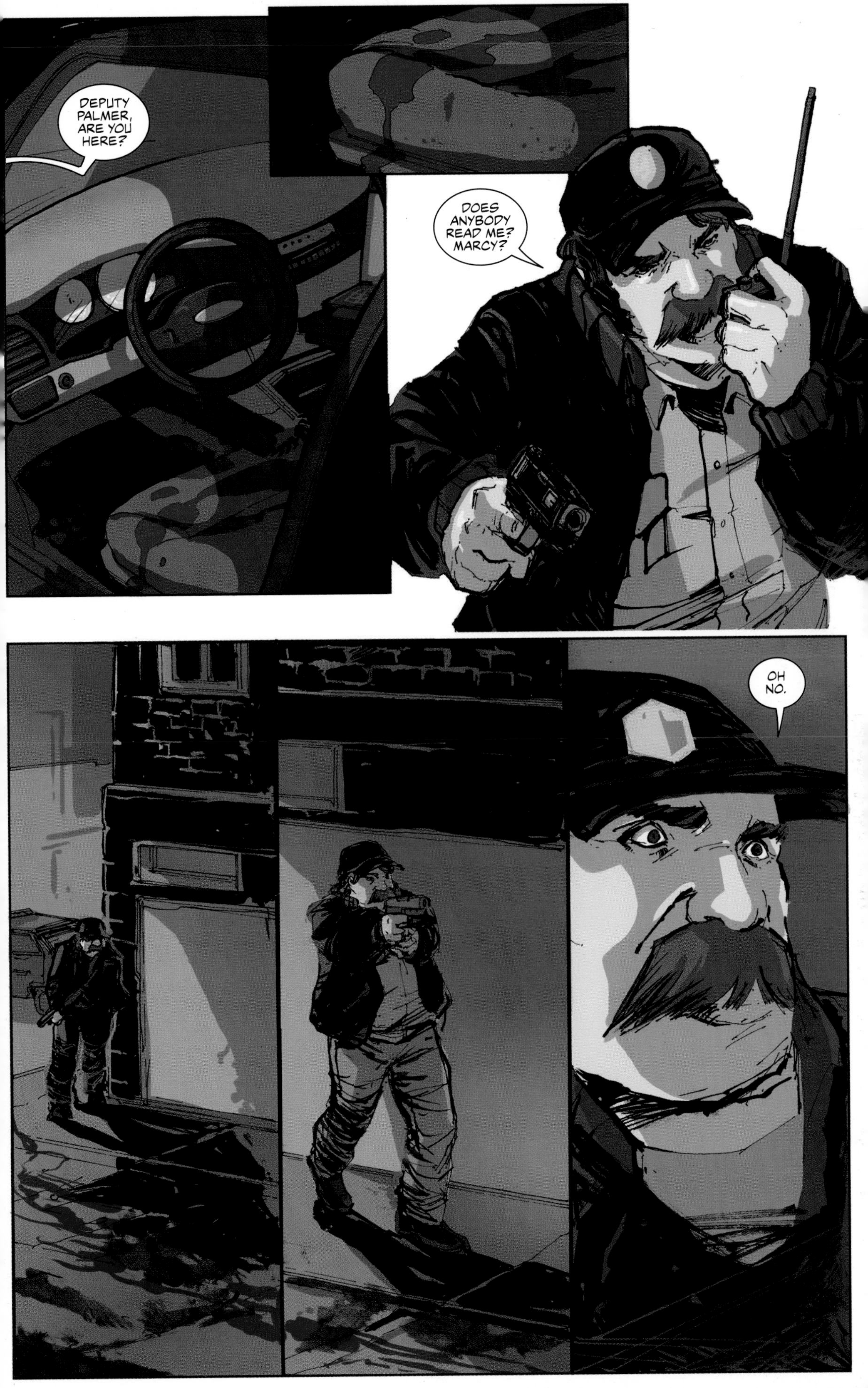
DEPUTY PALMER, ARE YOU HERE?
DOES ANYBODY READ ME? MARCY?
OH NO.

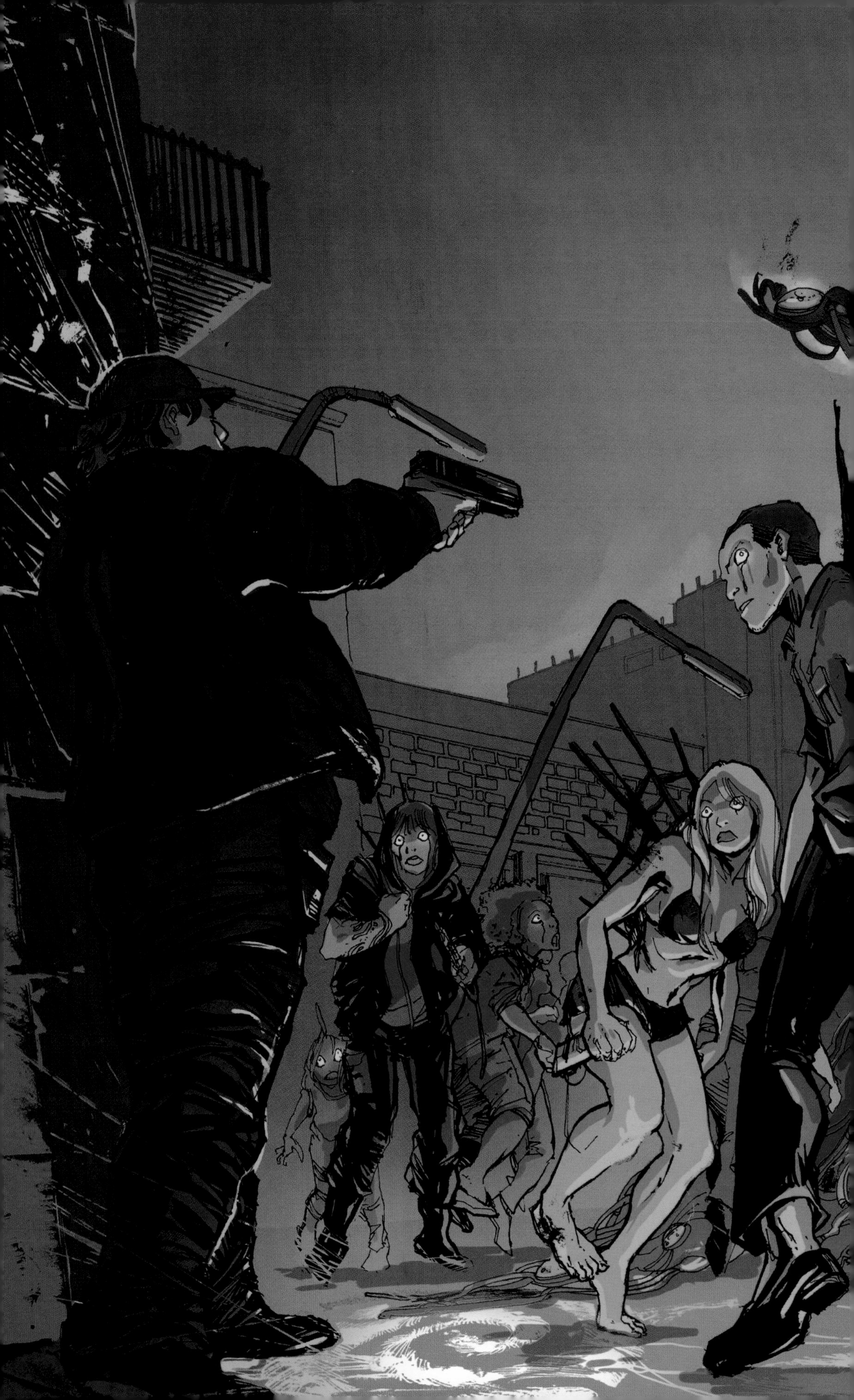

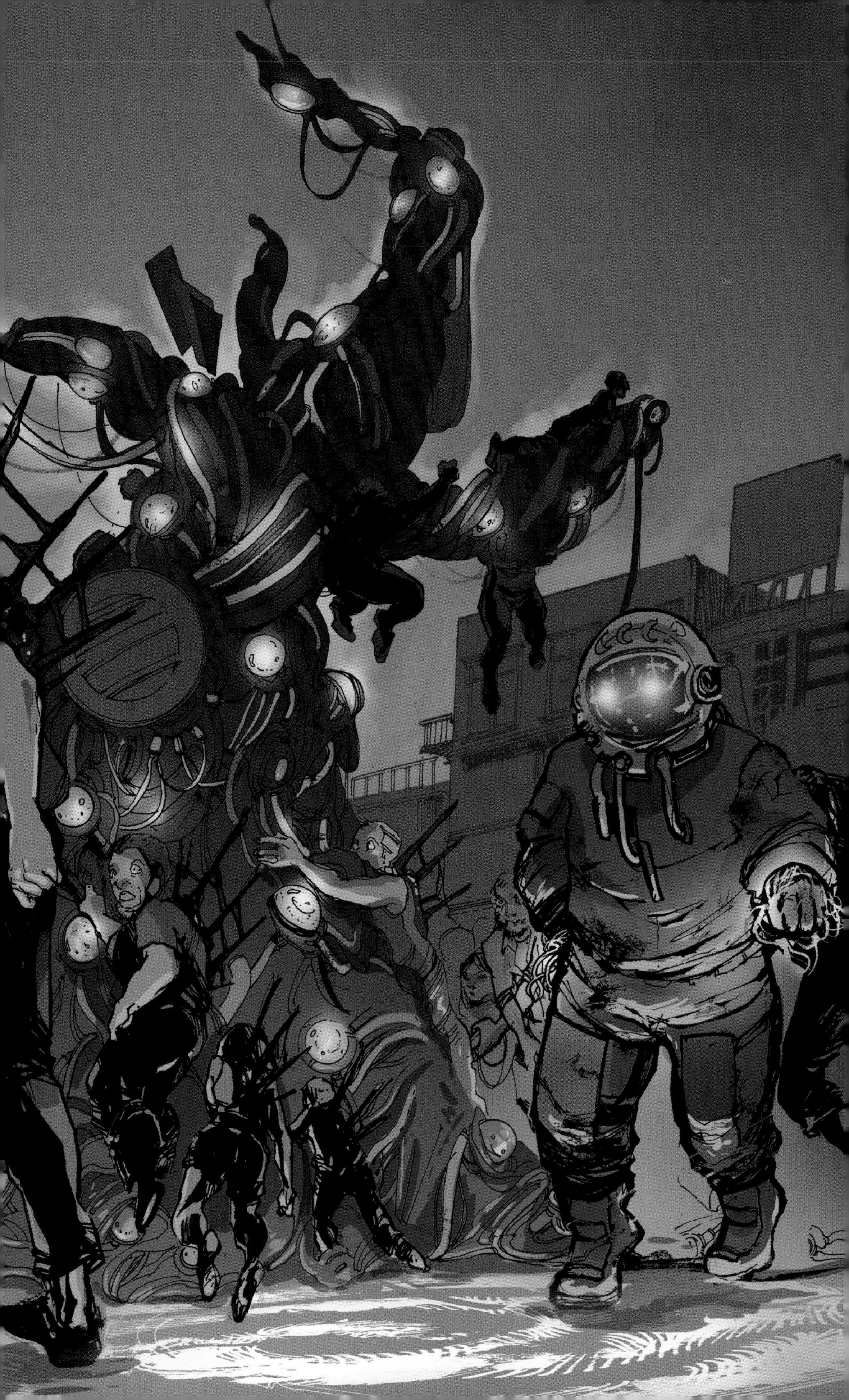

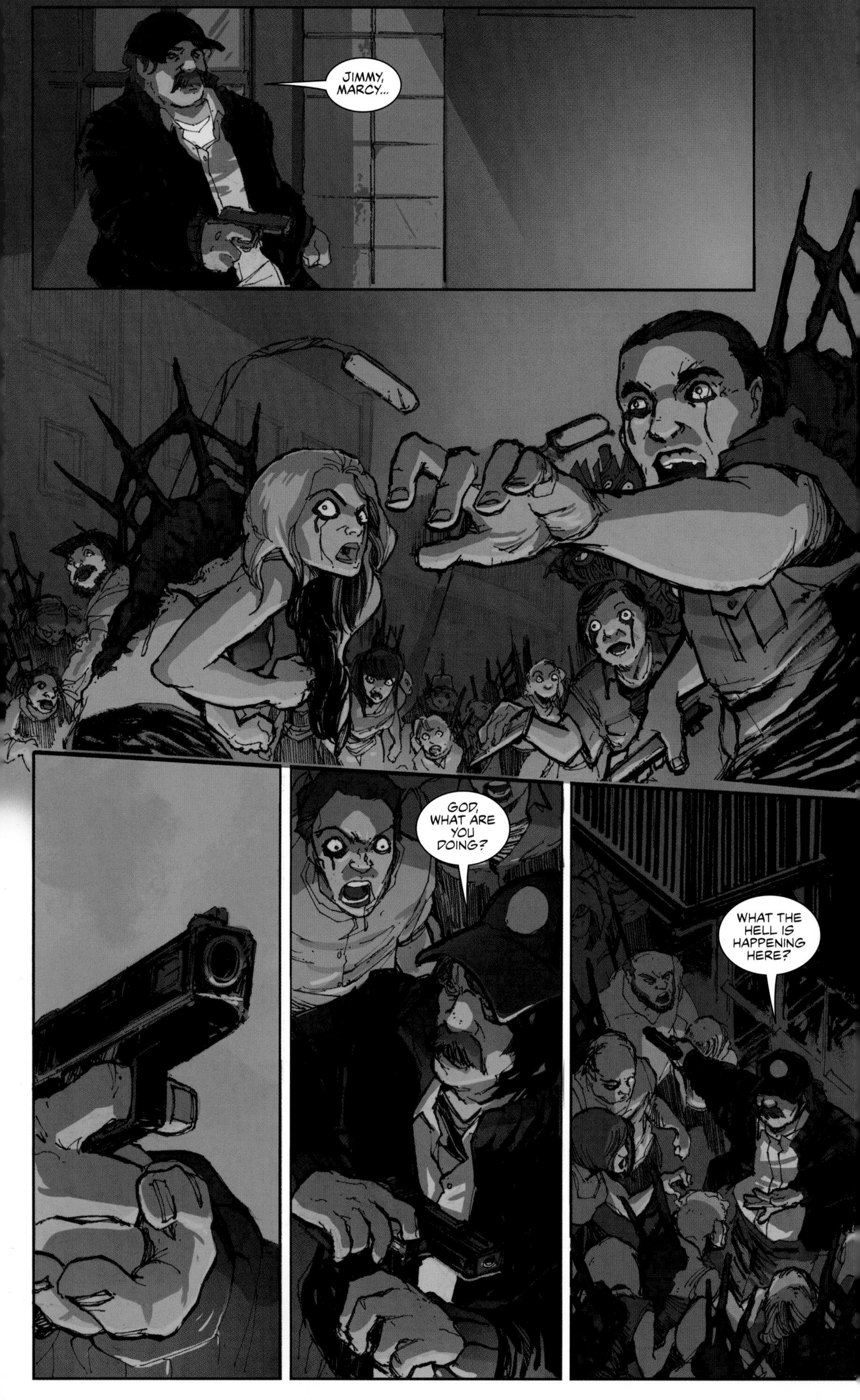
JIMMY, MARCY...
GOD, WHAT ARE YOU DOING?
WHAT THE HELL IS HAPPENING HERE?

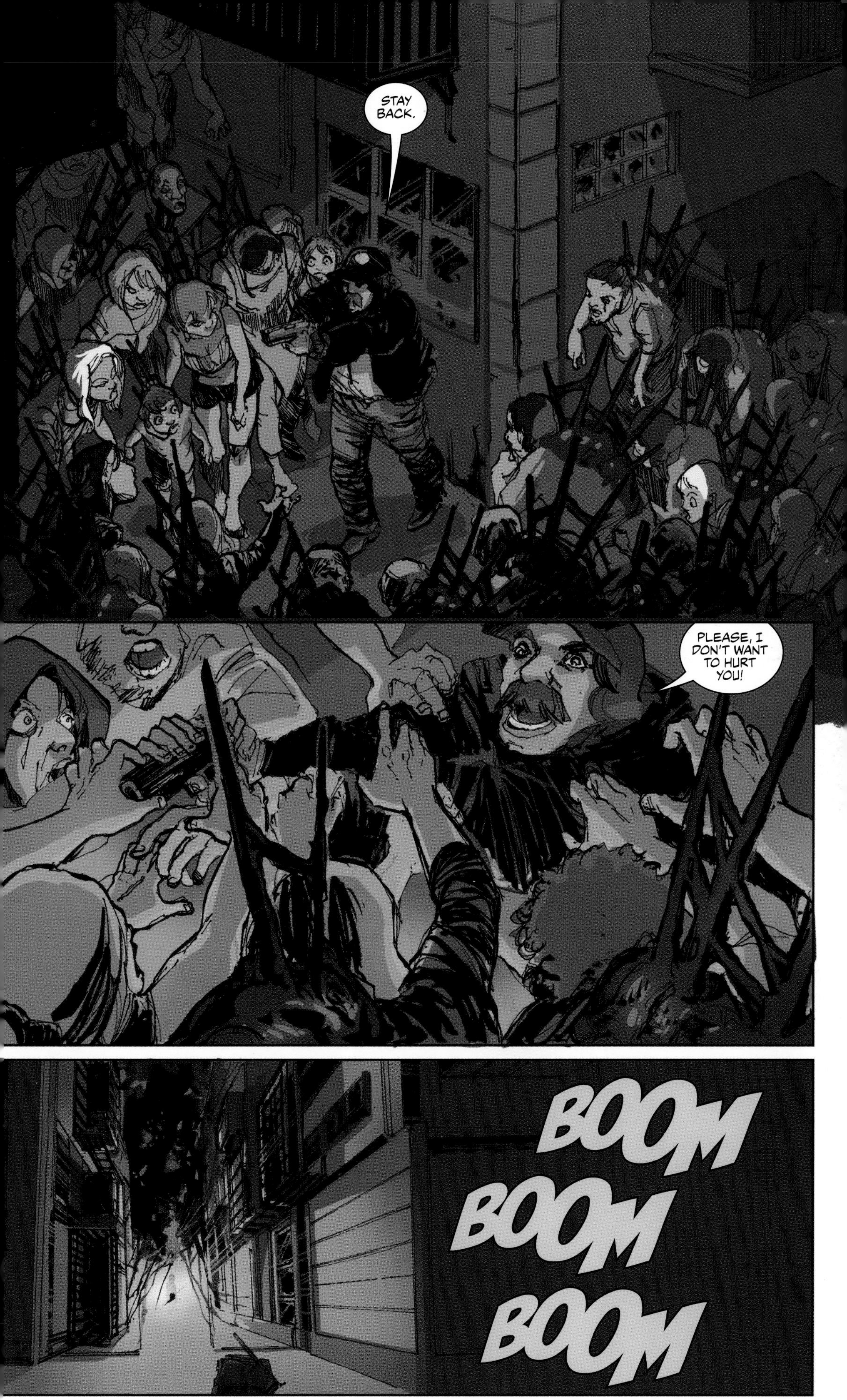
STAY BACK.
PLEASE, I DON'T WANT TO HURT YOU!
BOOM
BOOM
BOOM

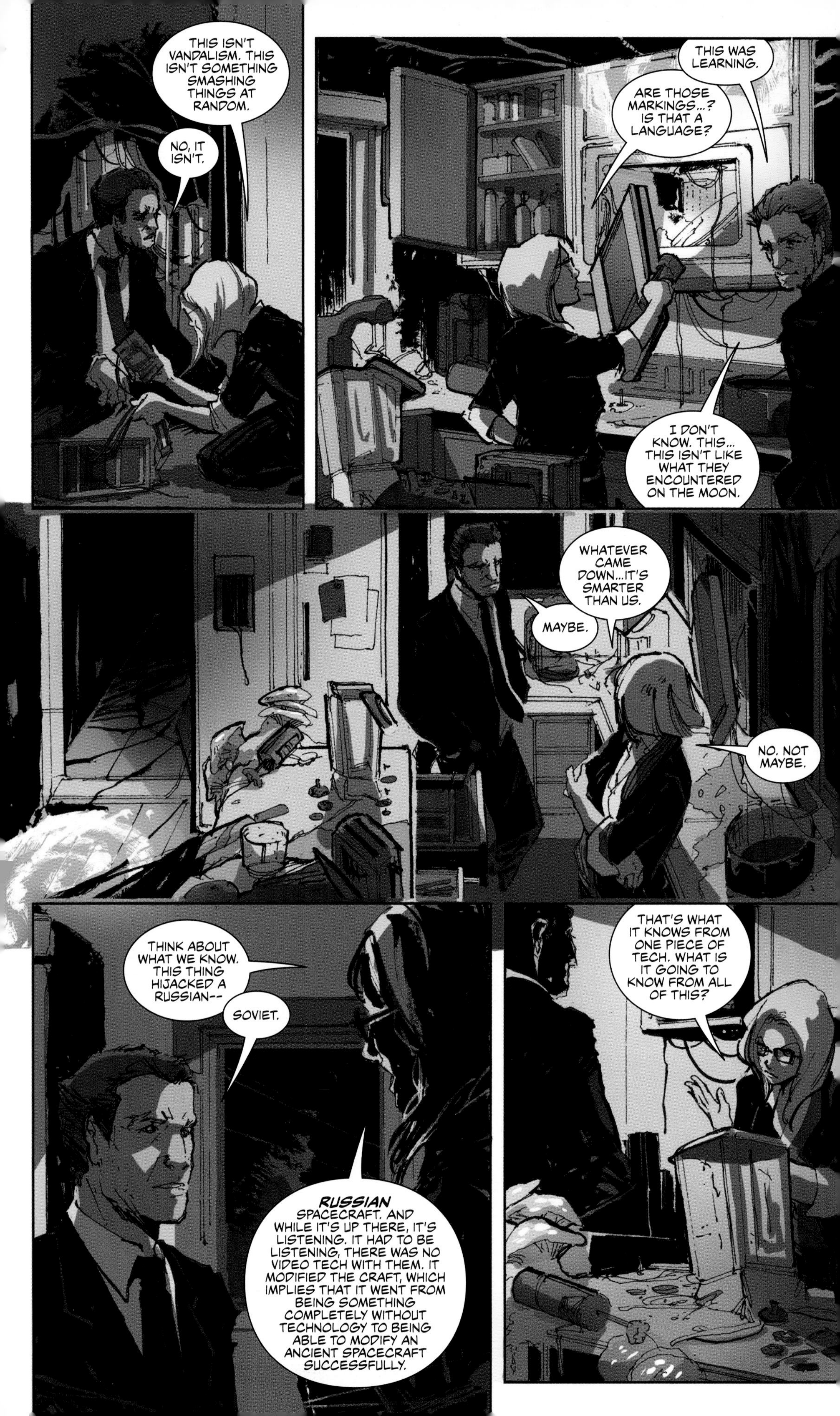
THIS ISN'T VANDALISM. THIS ISN'T SOMETHING SMASHING THINGS AT RANDOM.
NO, IT ISN'T.
ARE THOSE MARKINGS...? IS THAT A LANGUAGE?
THIS WAS LEARNING.
I DON'T KNOW. THIS... THIS ISN'T LIKE WHAT THEY ENCOUNTERED ON THE MOON.
WHATEVER CAME DOWN...IT'S SMARTER THAN US.
MAYBE.
NO. NOT MAYBE.
THINK ABOUT WHAT WE KNOW. THIS THING HIJACKED A RUSSIAN--
SOVIET.
RUSSIAN SPACECRAFT. AND WHILE IT'S UP THERE, IT'S LISTENING. IT HAD TO BE LISTENING, THERE WAS NO VIDEO TECH WITH THEM. IT MODIFIED THE CRAFT, WHICH IMPLIES THAT IT WENT FROM BEING SOMETHING COMPLETELY WITHOUT TECHNOLOGY TO BEING ABLE TO MODIFY AN ANCIENT SPACECRAFT SUCCESSFULLY.
THAT'S WHAT IT KNOWS FROM ONE PIECE OF TECH. WHAT IS IT GOING TO KNOW FROM ALL OF THIS?

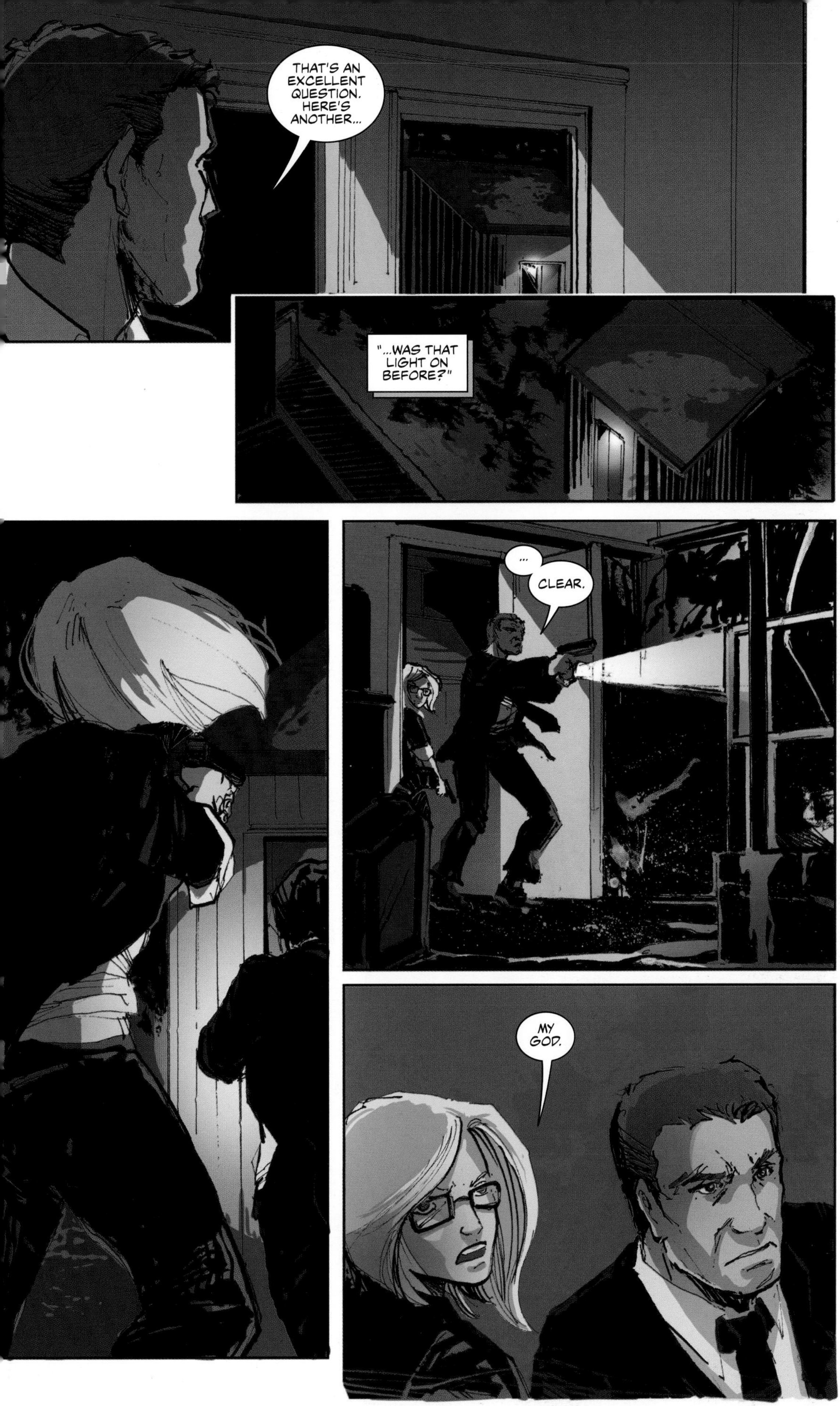
THAT'S AN EXCELLENT QUESTION. HERE'S ANOTHER...
"...WAS THAT LIGHT ON BEFORE?"
...
CLEAR.
MY GOD.

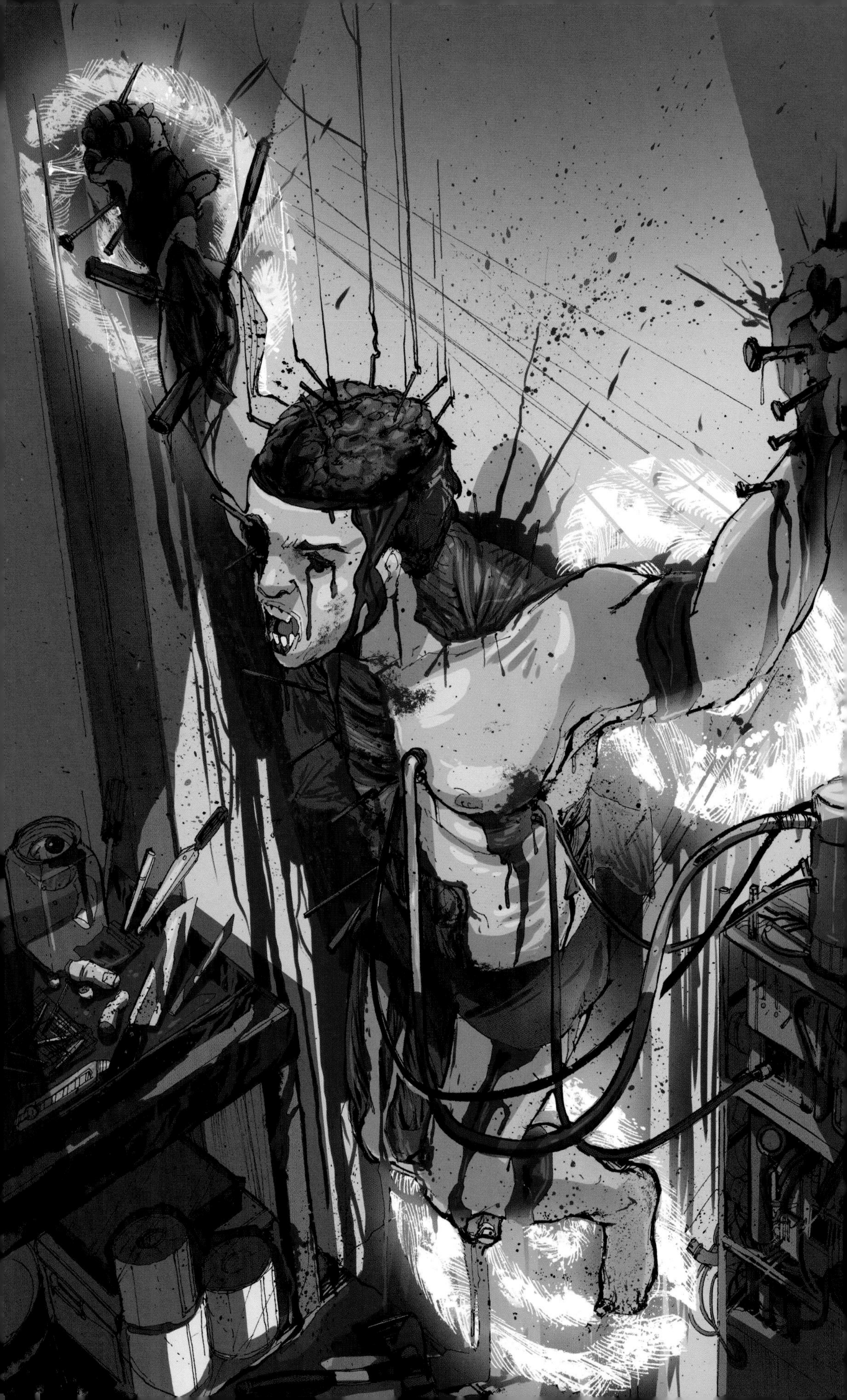

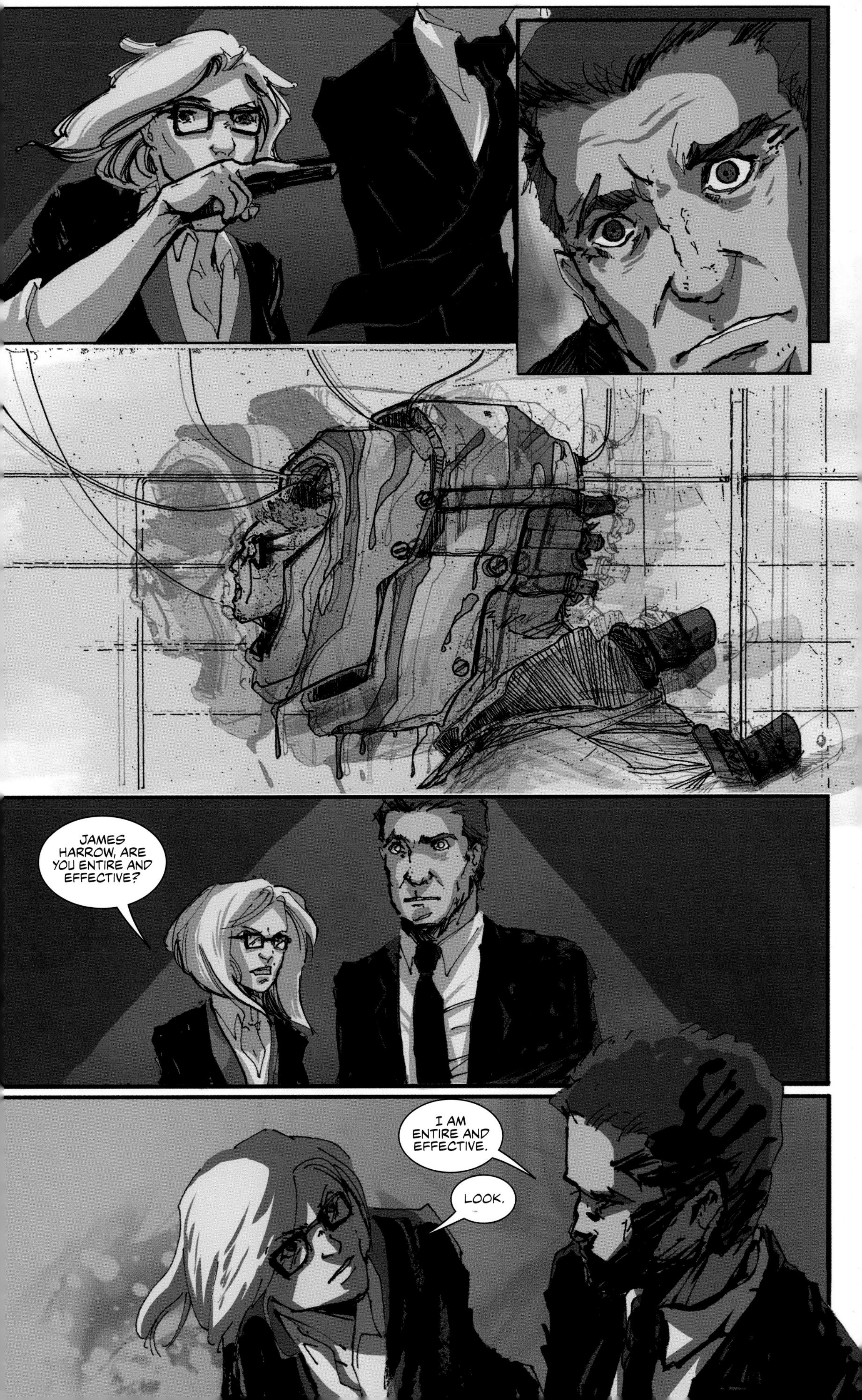
JAMES HARROW, ARE YOU ENTIRE AND EFFECTIVE?
I AM ENTIRE AND EFFECTIVE.
LOOK.

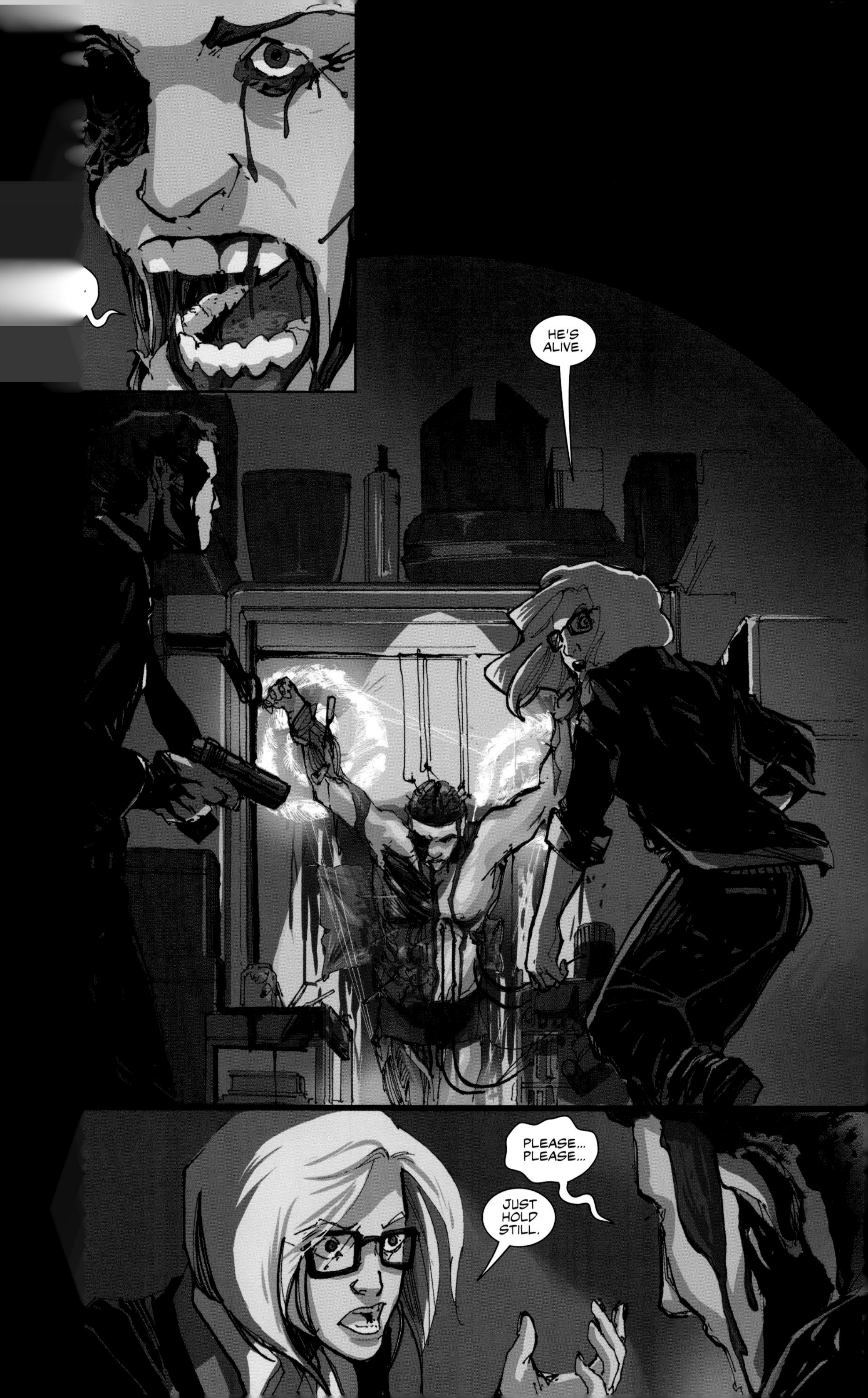
HE'S ALIVE.
PLEASE... PLEASE...
JUST HOLD STILL.

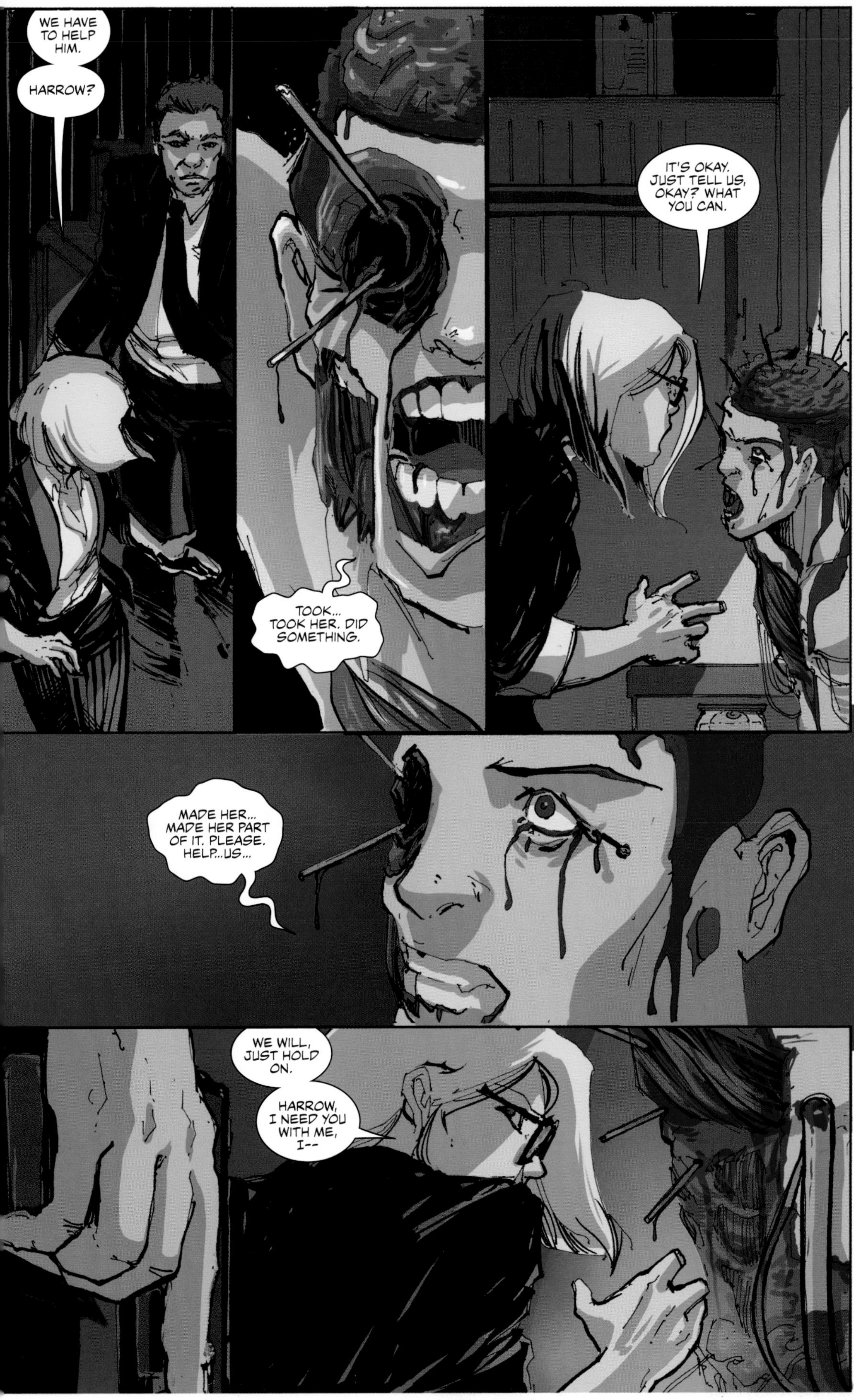
WE HAVE TO HELP HIM.
HARROW?
TOOK... TOOK HER. DID SOMETHING.
IT'S OKAY. JUST TELL US, OKAY? WHAT YOU CAN.
MADE HER... MADE HER PART OF IT. PLEASE. HELP...US...
WE WILL, JUST HOLD ON.
HARROW, I NEED YOU WITH ME, I--

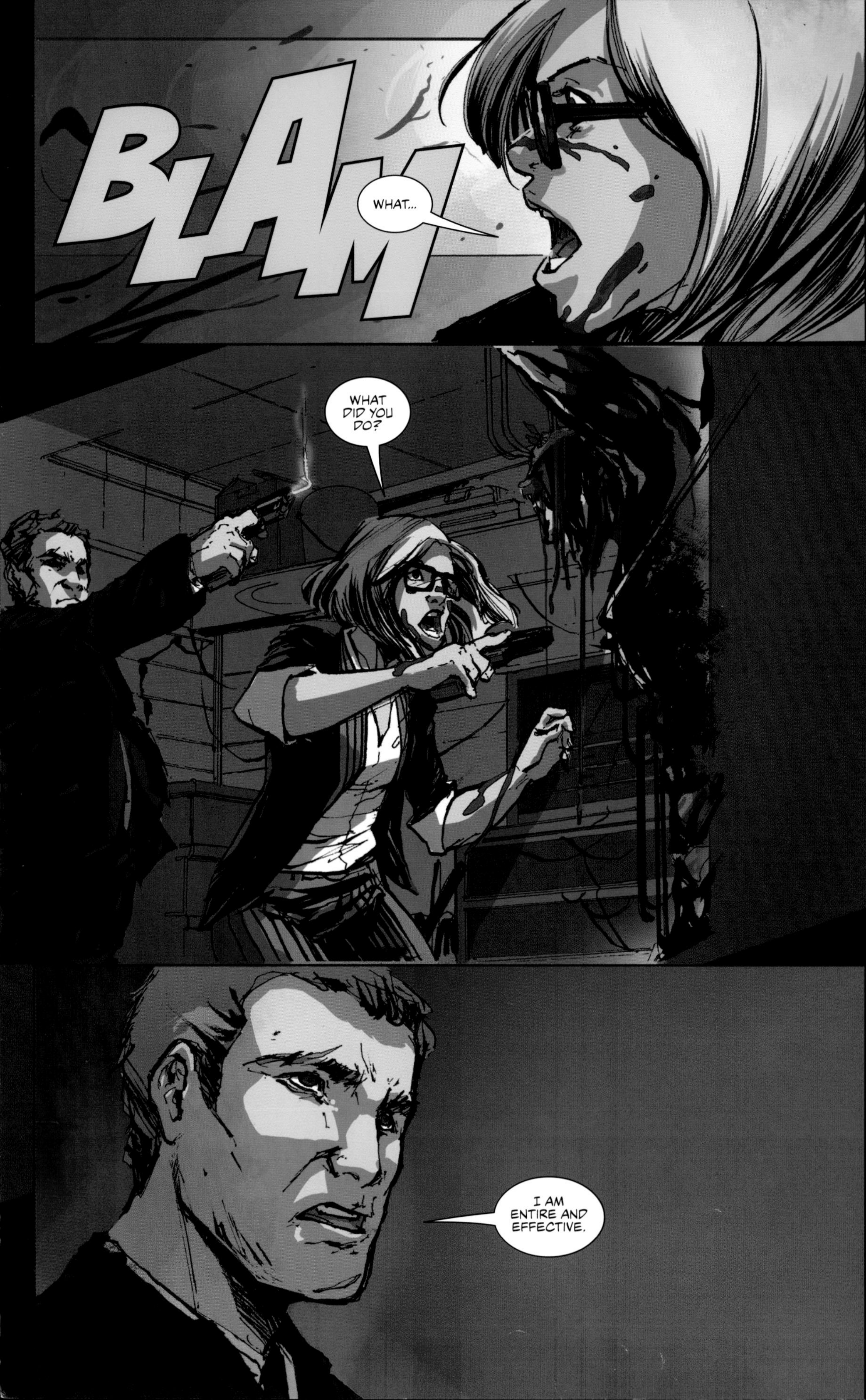
BLAM
WHAT...
WHAT DID YOU DO?
I AM ENTIRE AND EFFECTIVE.

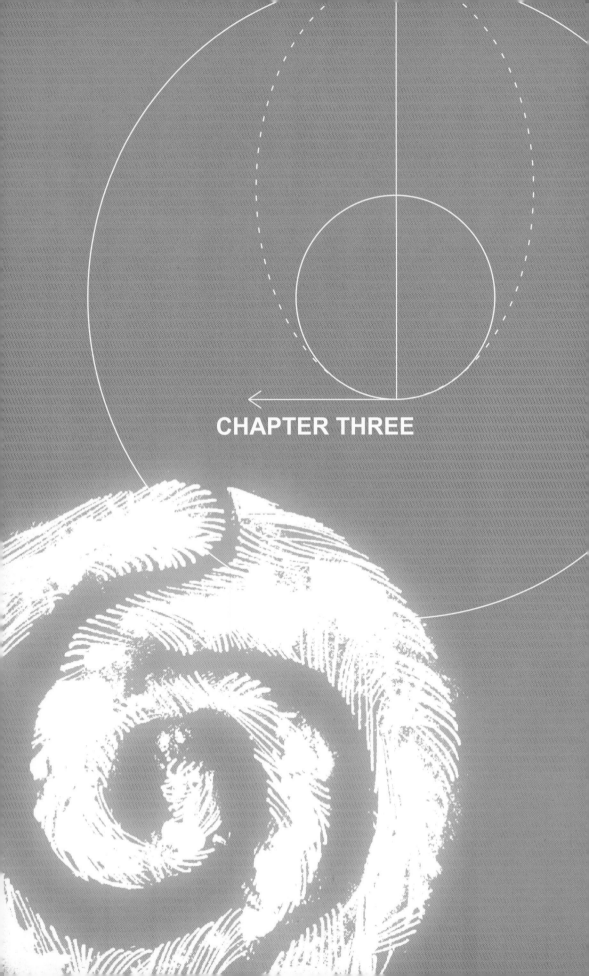

CHAPTER THREE

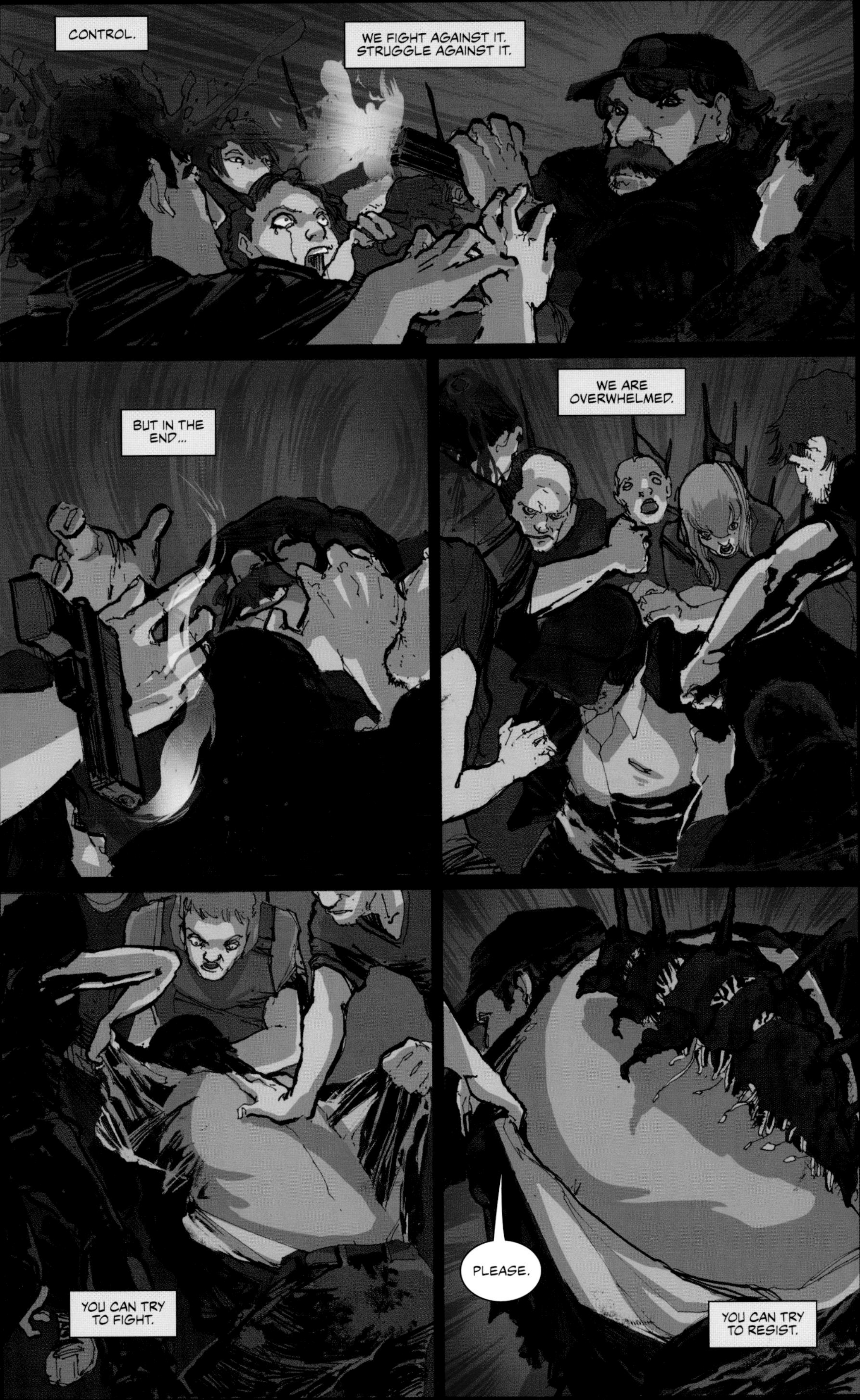
CONTROL.
WE FIGHT AGAINST IT. STRUGGLE AGAINST IT.
BUT IN THE END...
WE ARE OVERWHELMED.
YOU CAN TRY TO FIGHT.
PLEASE.
YOU CAN TRY TO RESIST.

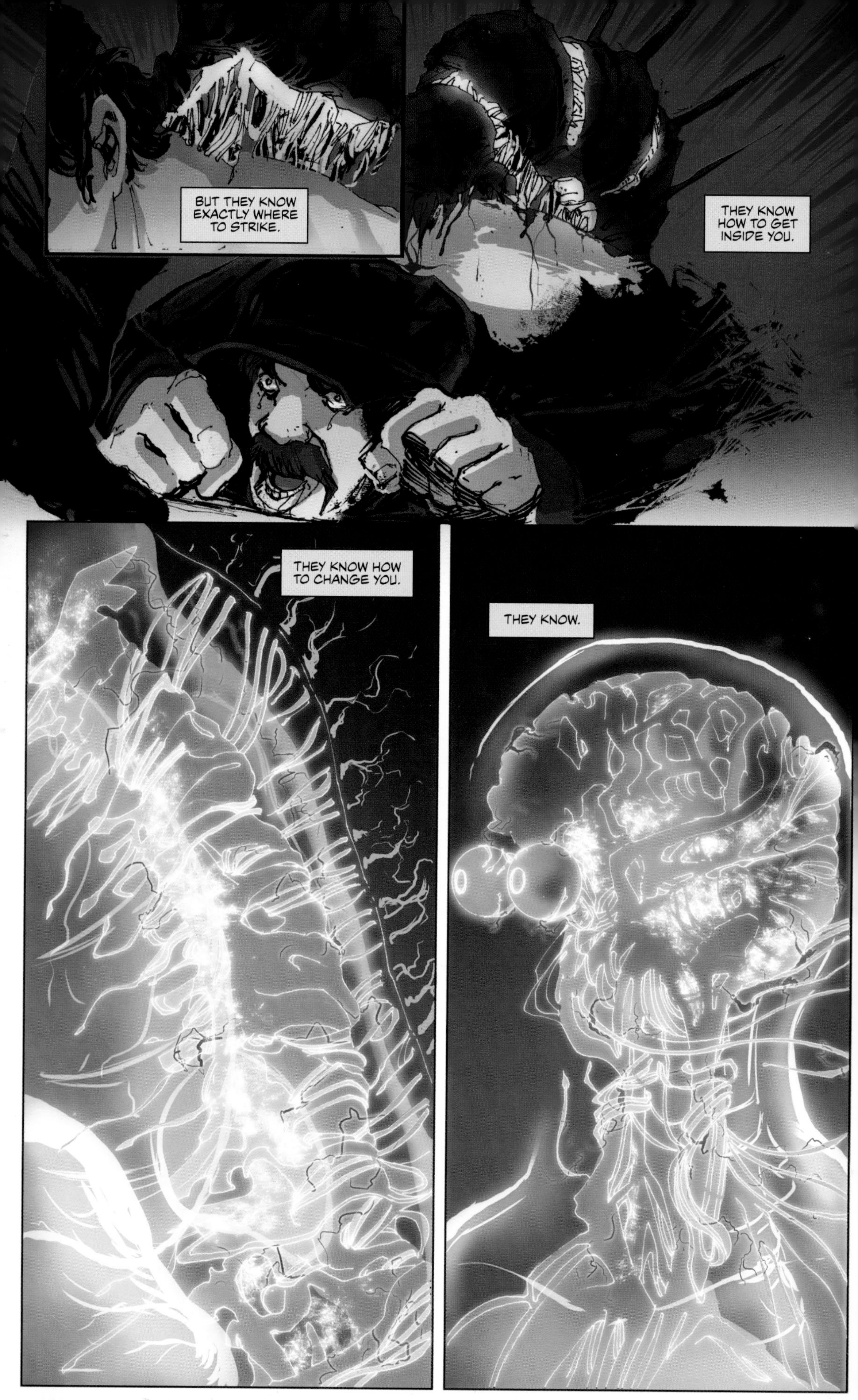
BUT THEY KNOW EXACTLY WHERE TO STRIKE.
THEY KNOW HOW TO GET INSIDE YOU.
THEY KNOW HOW TO CHANGE YOU.
THEY KNOW.

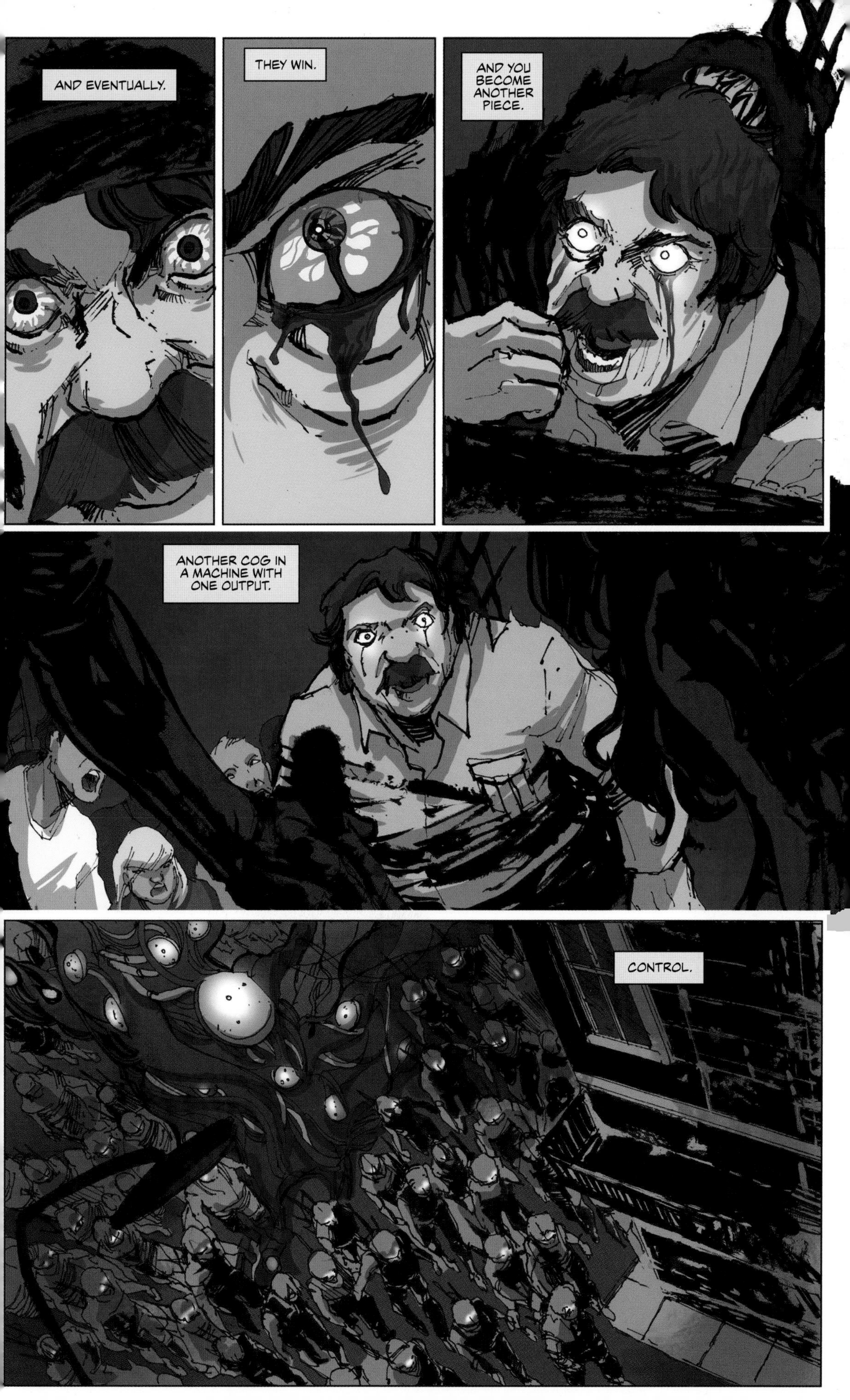
AND EVENTUALLY.
THEY WIN.
AND YOU BECOME ANOTHER PIECE.
ANOTHER COG IN A MACHINE WITH ONE OUTPUT.
CONTROL.

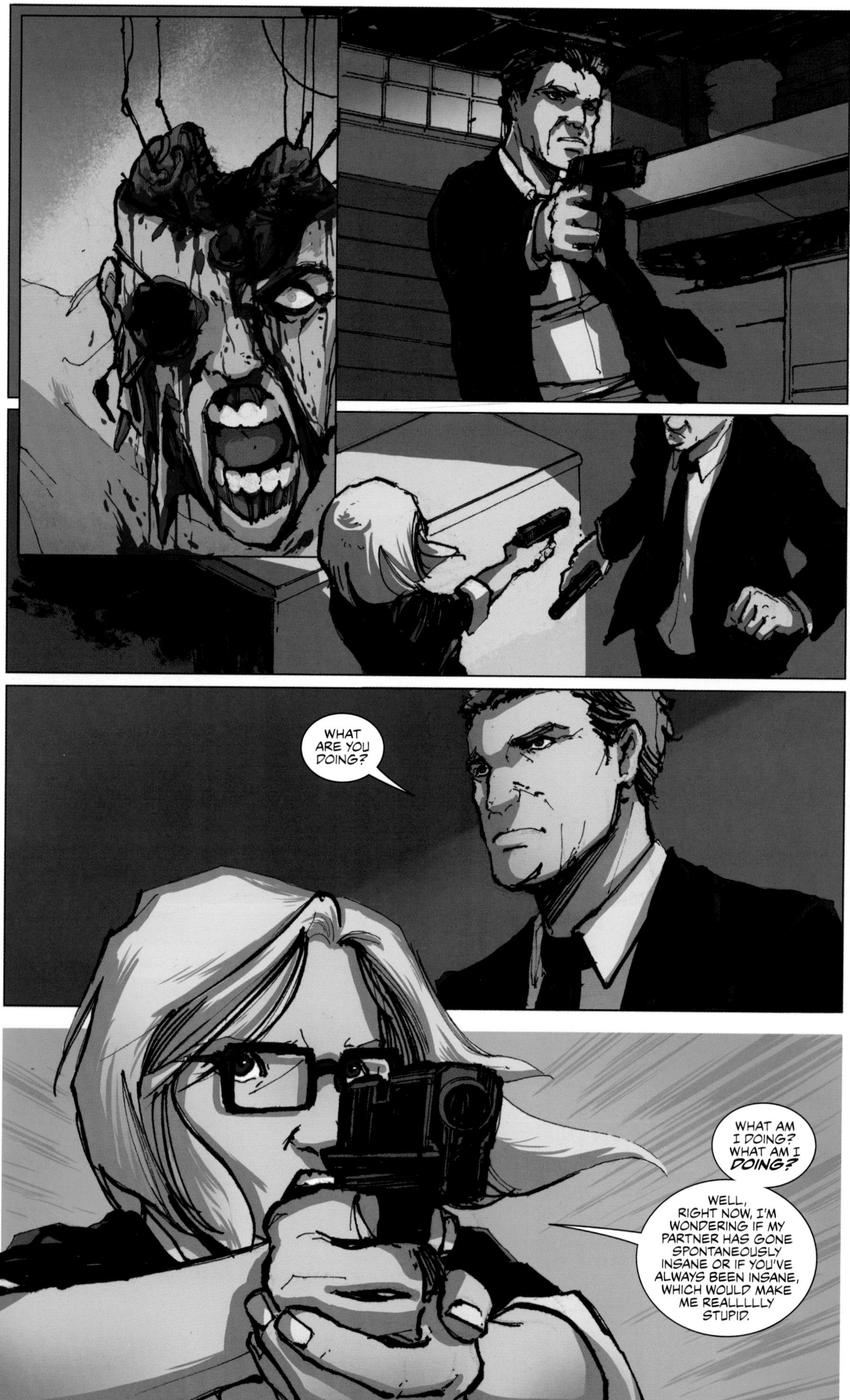
WHAT ARE YOU DOING?
WHAT AM I DOING? WHAT AM I DOING?
WELL, RIGHT NOW, I'M WONDERING IF MY PARTNER HAS GONE SPONTANEOUSLY INSANE OR IF YOU'VE ALWAYS BEEN INSANE, WHICH WOULD MAKE ME REALLLLLY STUPID.

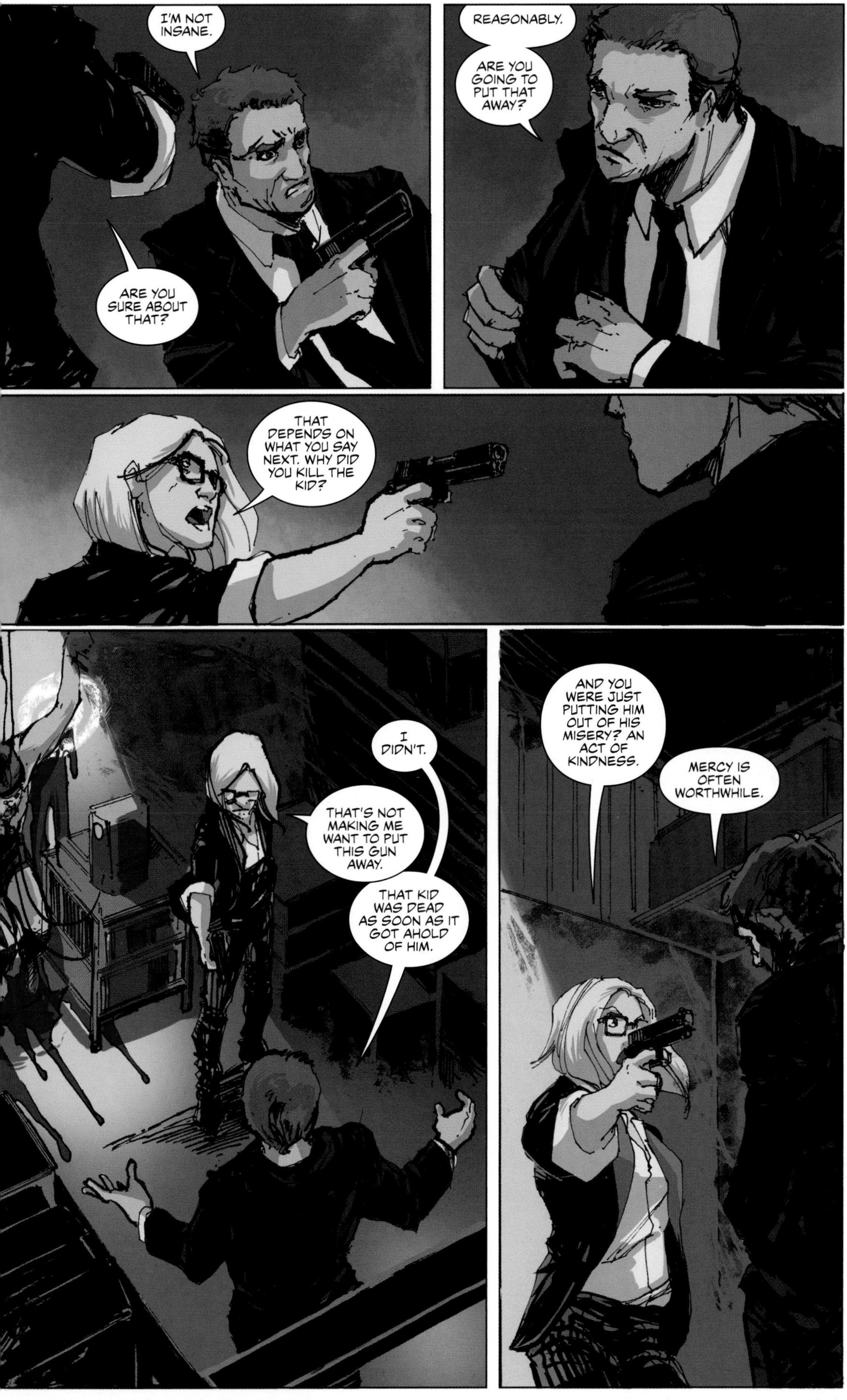
I'M NOT INSANE.
ARE YOU SURE ABOUT THAT?
REASONABLY.
ARE YOU GOING TO PUT THAT AWAY?
THAT DEPENDS ON WHAT YOU SAY NEXT. WHY DID YOU KILL THE KID?
I DIDN'T.
THAT'S NOT MAKING ME WANT TO PUT THIS GUN AWAY.
THAT KID WAS DEAD AS SOON AS IT GOT AHOLD OF HIM.
AND YOU WERE JUST PUTTING HIM OUT OF HIS MISERY? AN ACT OF KINDNESS.
MERCY IS OFTEN WORTHWHILE.

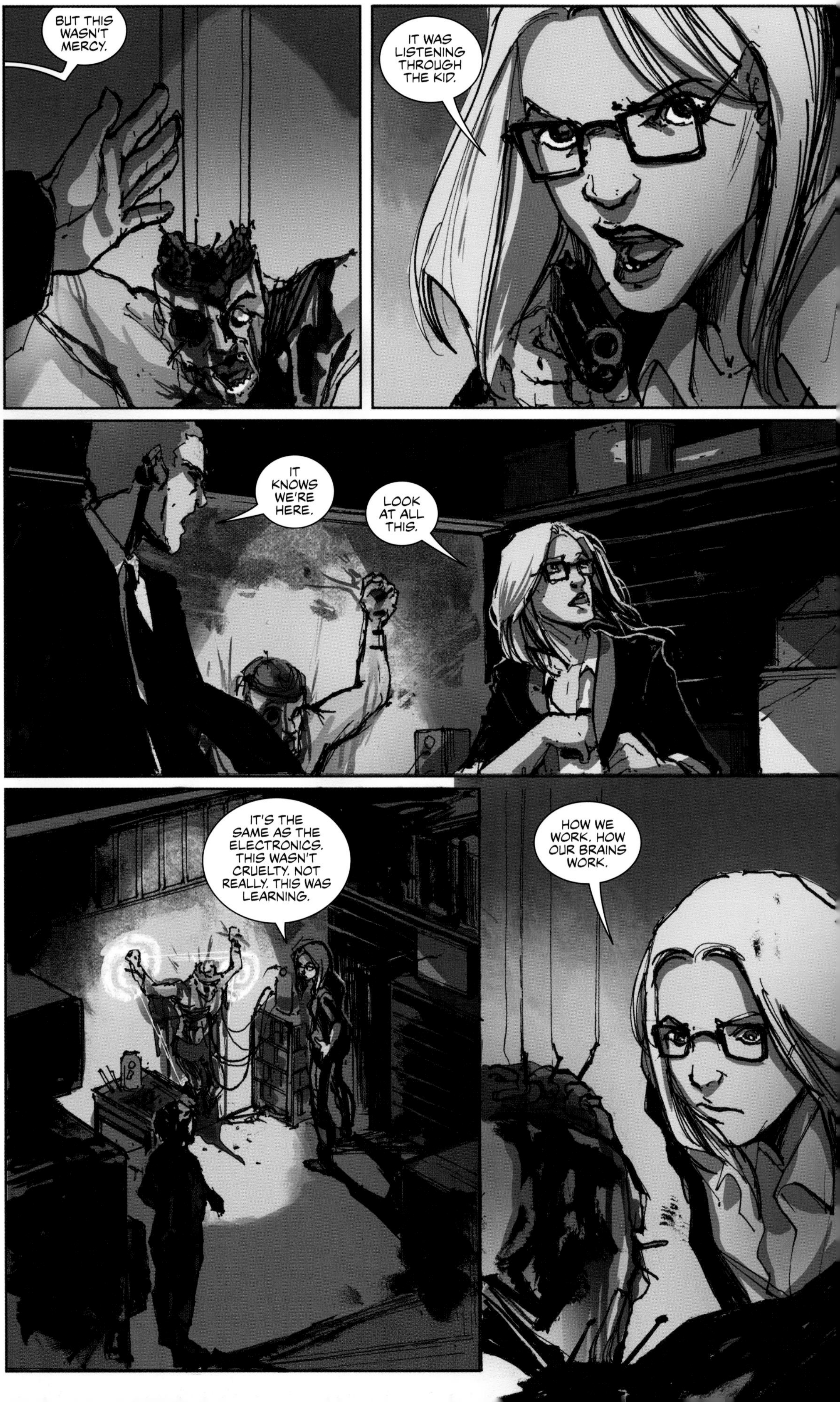

BUT THIS WASN'T MERCY.
IT WAS LISTENING THROUGH THE KID.
IT KNOWS WE'RE HERE.
LOOK AT ALL THIS.
IT'S THE SAME AS THE ELECTRONICS. THIS WASN'T CRUELTY. NOT REALLY. THIS WAS LEARNING.
HOW WE WORK. HOW OUR BRAINS WORK.

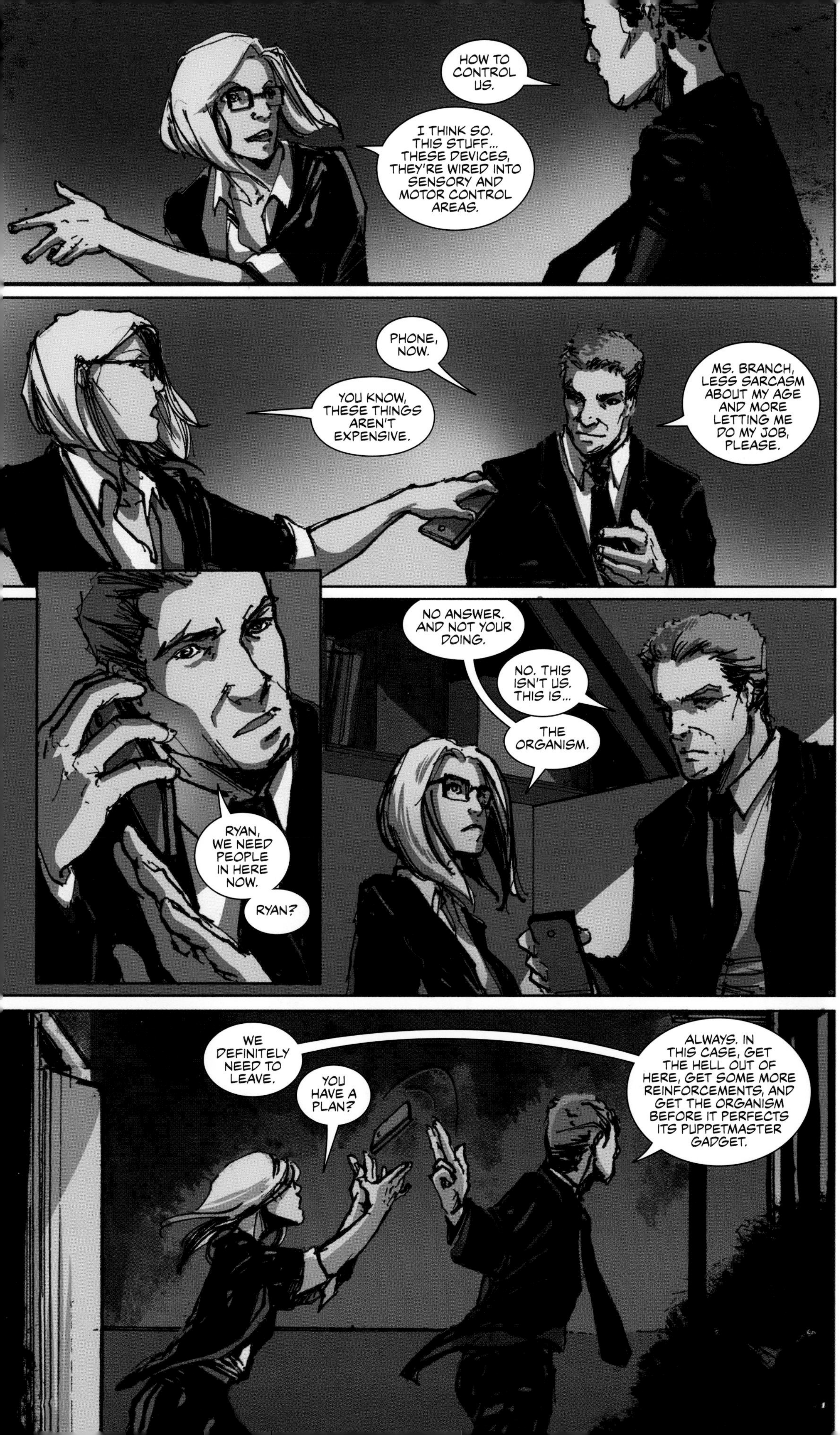
HOW TO CONTROL US.
I THINK SO. THIS STUFF... THESE DEVICES, THEY'RE WIRED INTO SENSORY AND MOTOR CONTROL AREAS.
PHONE, NOW.
YOU KNOW, THESE THINGS AREN'T EXPENSIVE.
MS. BRANCH, LESS SARCASM ABOUT MY AGE AND MORE LETTING ME DO MY JOB, PLEASE.
RYAN, WE NEED PEOPLE IN HERE NOW.
RYAN?
NO ANSWER. AND NOT YOUR DOING.
NO. THIS ISN'T US. THIS IS...
THE ORGANISM.
WE DEFINITELY NEED TO LEAVE.
YOU HAVE A PLAN?
ALWAYS. IN THIS CASE, GET THE HELL OUT OF HERE, GET SOME MORE REINFORCEMENTS, AND GET THE ORGANISM BEFORE IT PERFECTS ITS PUPPETMASTER GADGET.

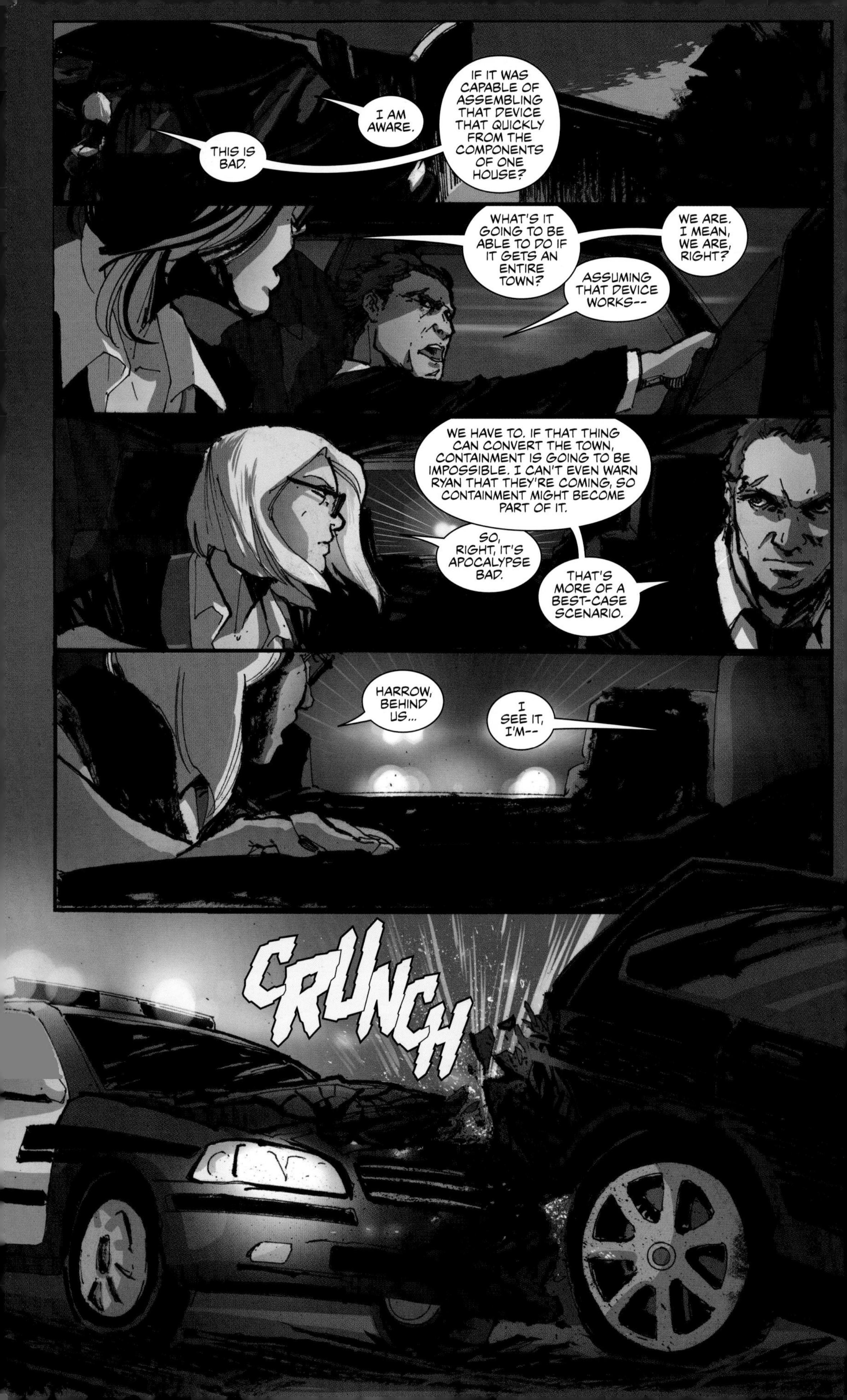
THIS IS BAD.
I AM AWARE.
IF IT WAS CAPABLE OF ASSEMBLING THAT DEVICE THAT QUICKLY FROM THE COMPONENTS OF ONE HOUSE?
WHAT'S IT GOING TO BE ABLE TO DO IF IT GETS AN ENTIRE TOWN?
WE ARE. I MEAN, WE ARE, RIGHT?
ASSUMING THAT DEVICE WORKS--
WE HAVE TO. IF THAT THING CAN CONVERT THE TOWN, CONTAINMENT IS GOING TO BE IMPOSSIBLE. I CAN'T EVEN WARN RYAN THAT THEY'RE COMING, SO CONTAINMENT MIGHT BECOME PART OF IT.
SO, RIGHT, IT'S APOCALYPSE BAD.
THAT'S MORE OF A BEST-CASE SCENARIO.
HARROW, BEHIND US...
I SEE IT, I'M--
CRUNCH

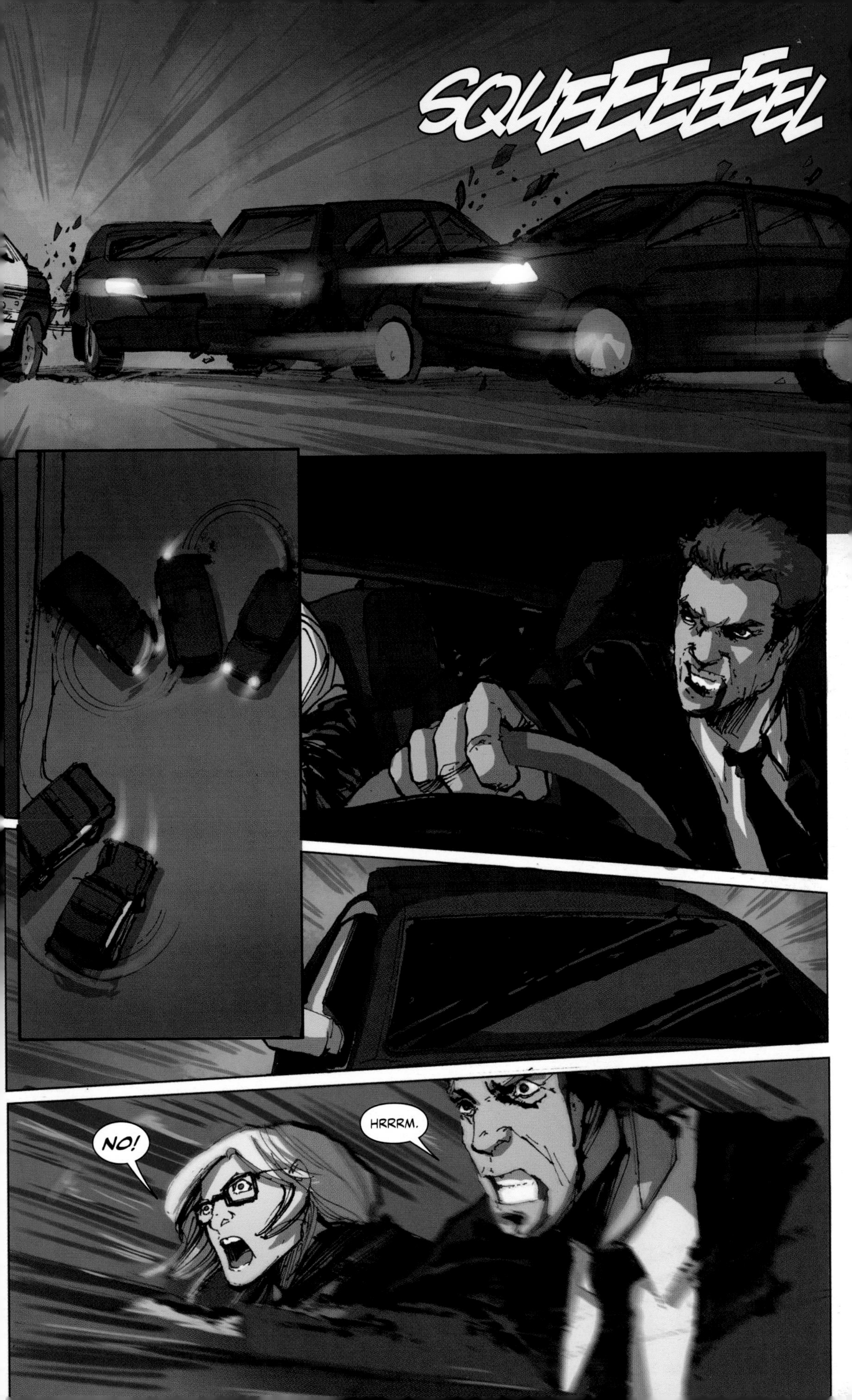
SQUEEEEEEL
NO!
HRRRM.

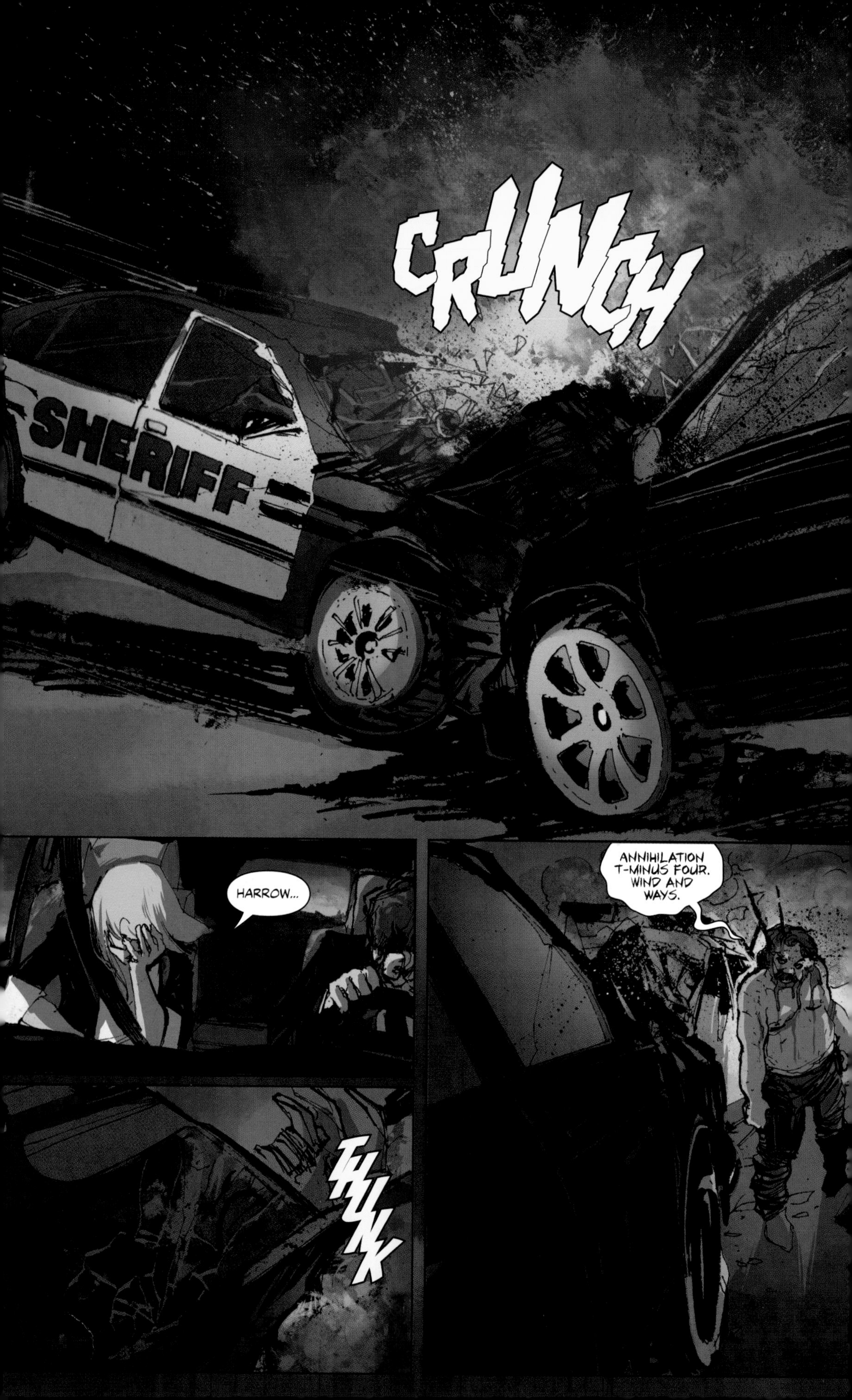
CRUNCH
SHERIFF
HARROW...
ANNIHILATION T-MINUS FOUR. WIND AND WAYS.
THUNK

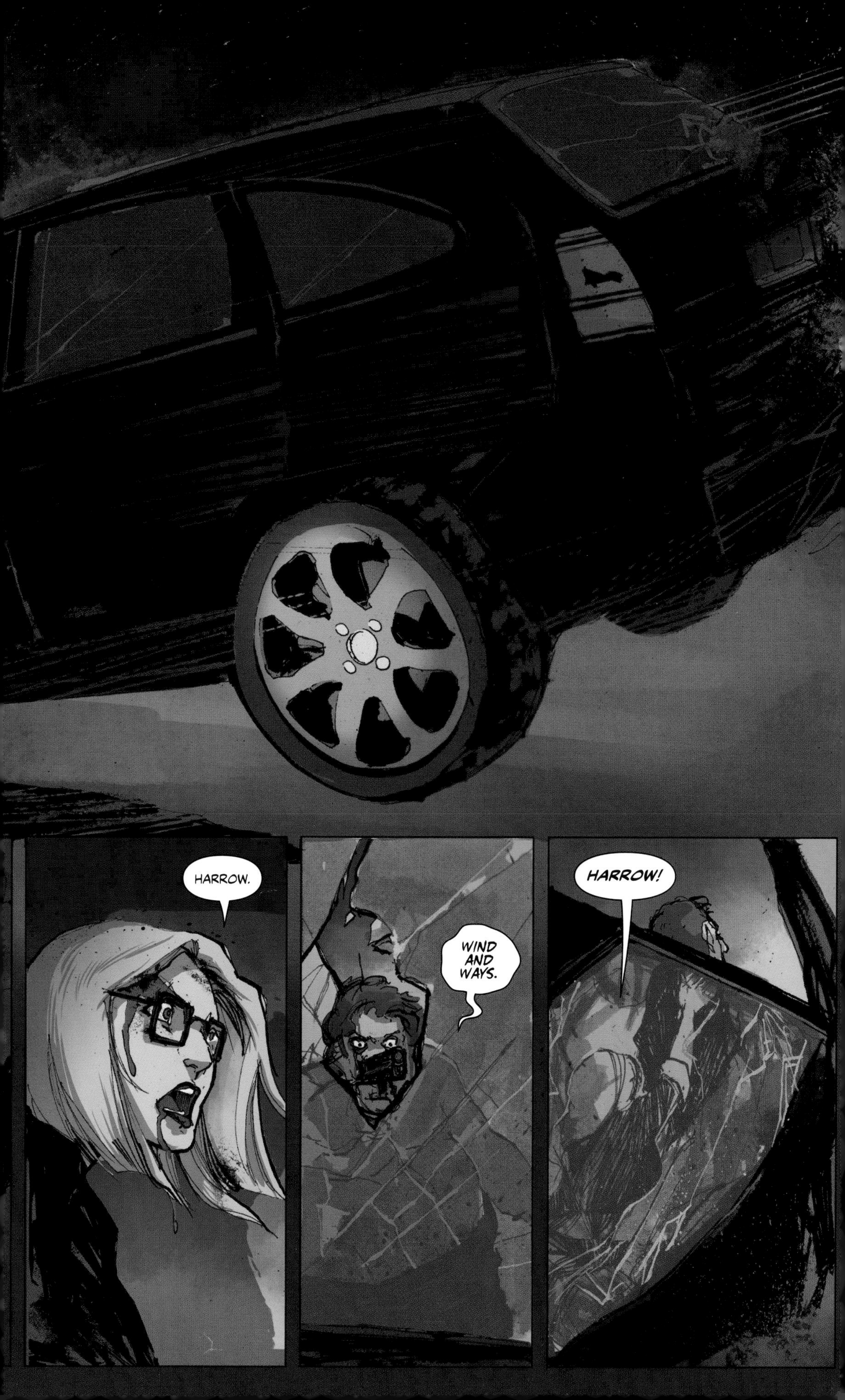
HARROW.
WIND AND WAYS.
HARROW!

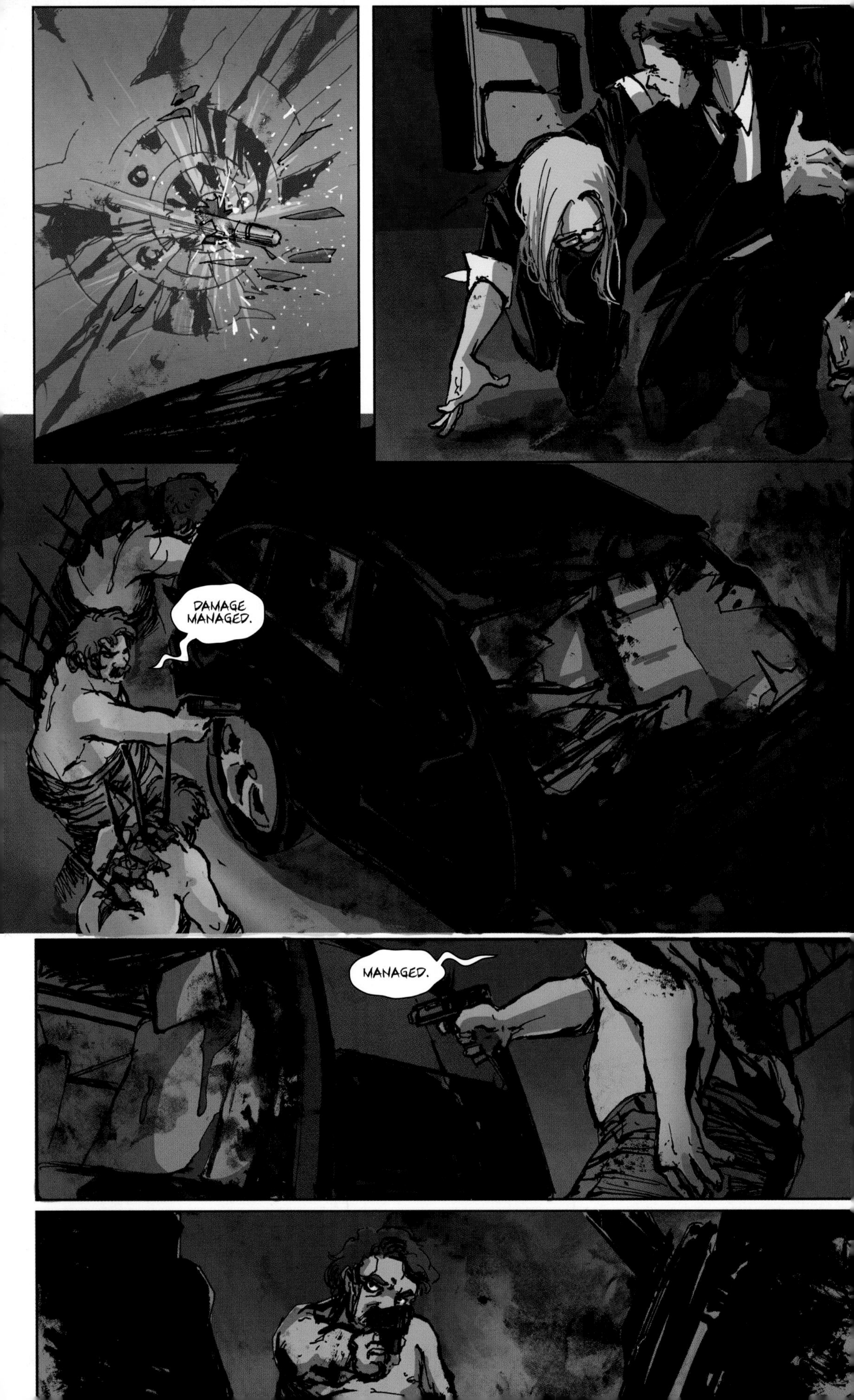
DAMAGE MANAGED.
MANAGED.

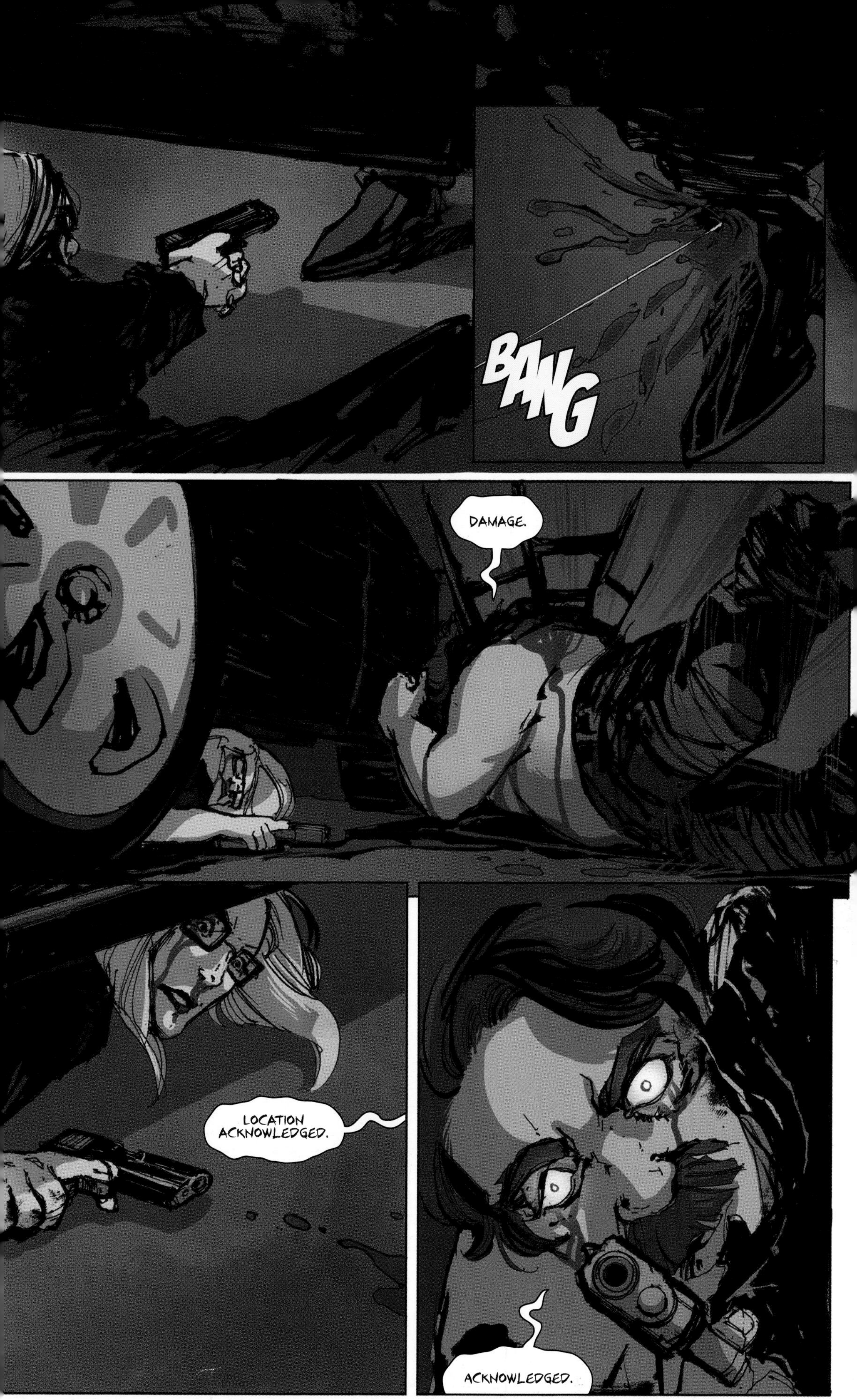
BANG
DAMAGE.
LOCATION ACKNOWLEDGED.
ACKNOWLEDGED.

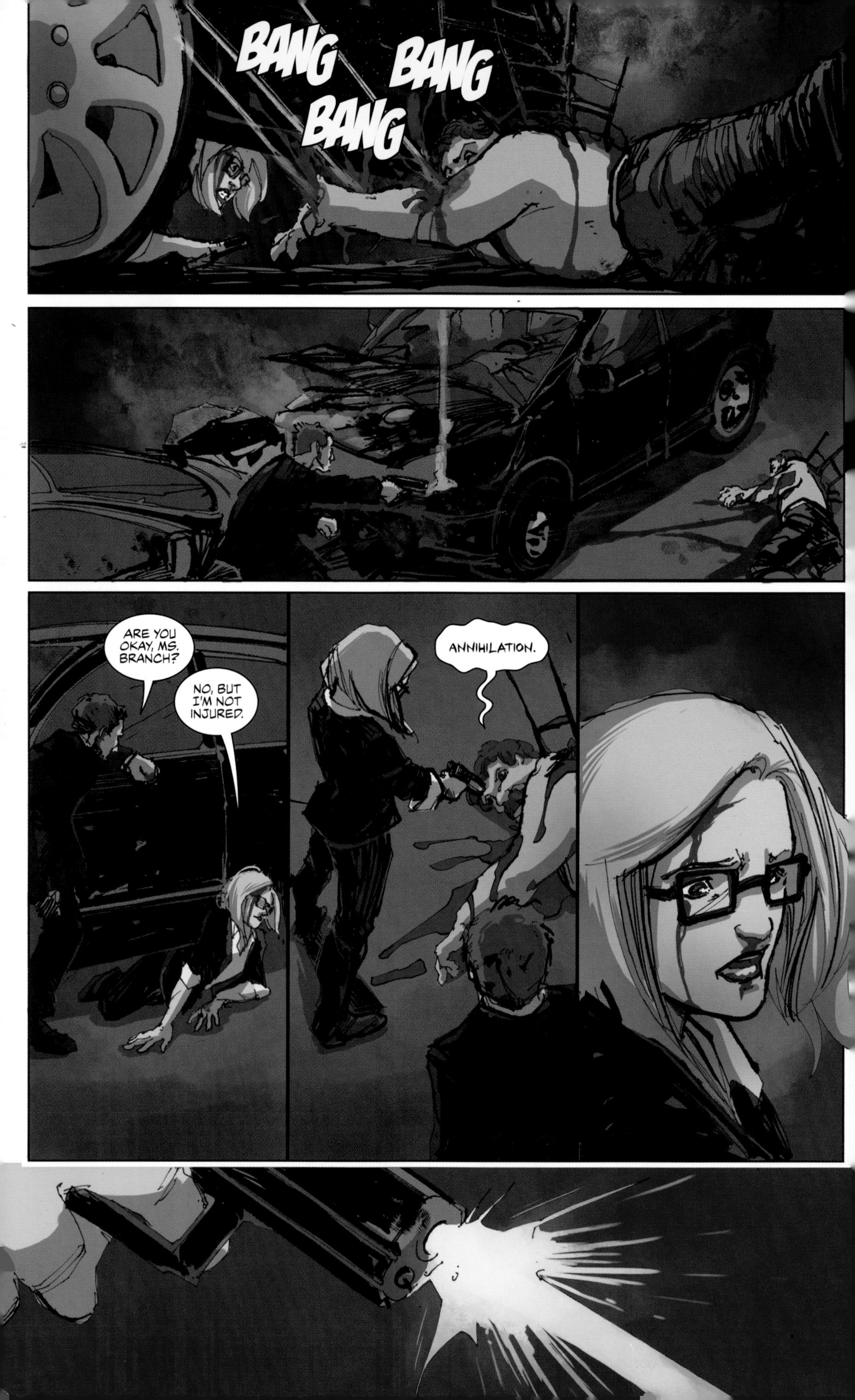
BANG
BANG
BANG
ARE YOU OKAY, MS. BRANCH?
NO, BUT I'M NOT INJURED.
ANNIHILATION.

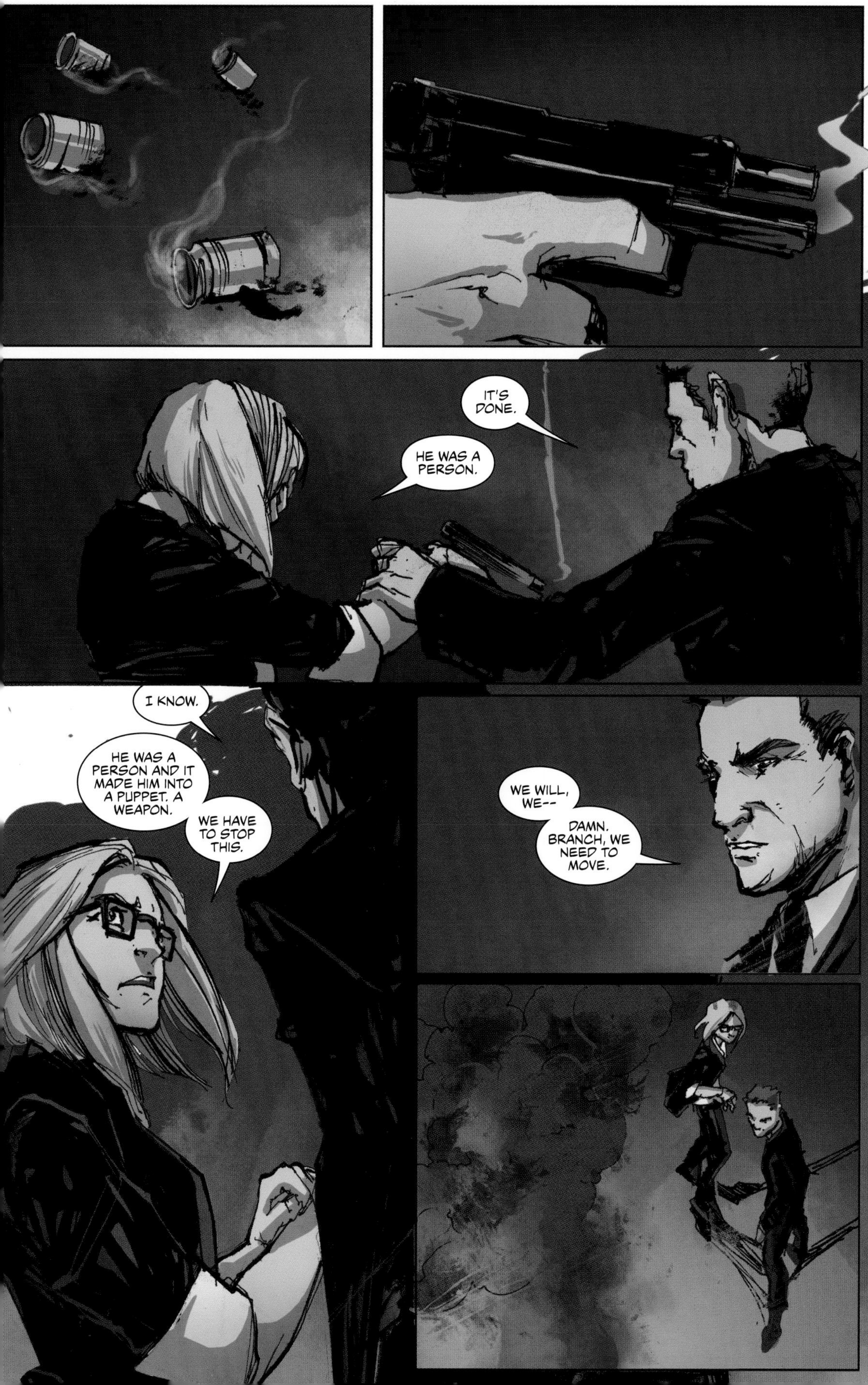
IT'S DONE.
HE WAS A PERSON.
I KNOW.
HE WAS A PERSON AND IT MADE HIM INTO A PUPPET. A WEAPON.
WE HAVE TO STOP THIS.
WE WILL, WE--
DAMN. BRANCH, WE NEED TO MOVE.

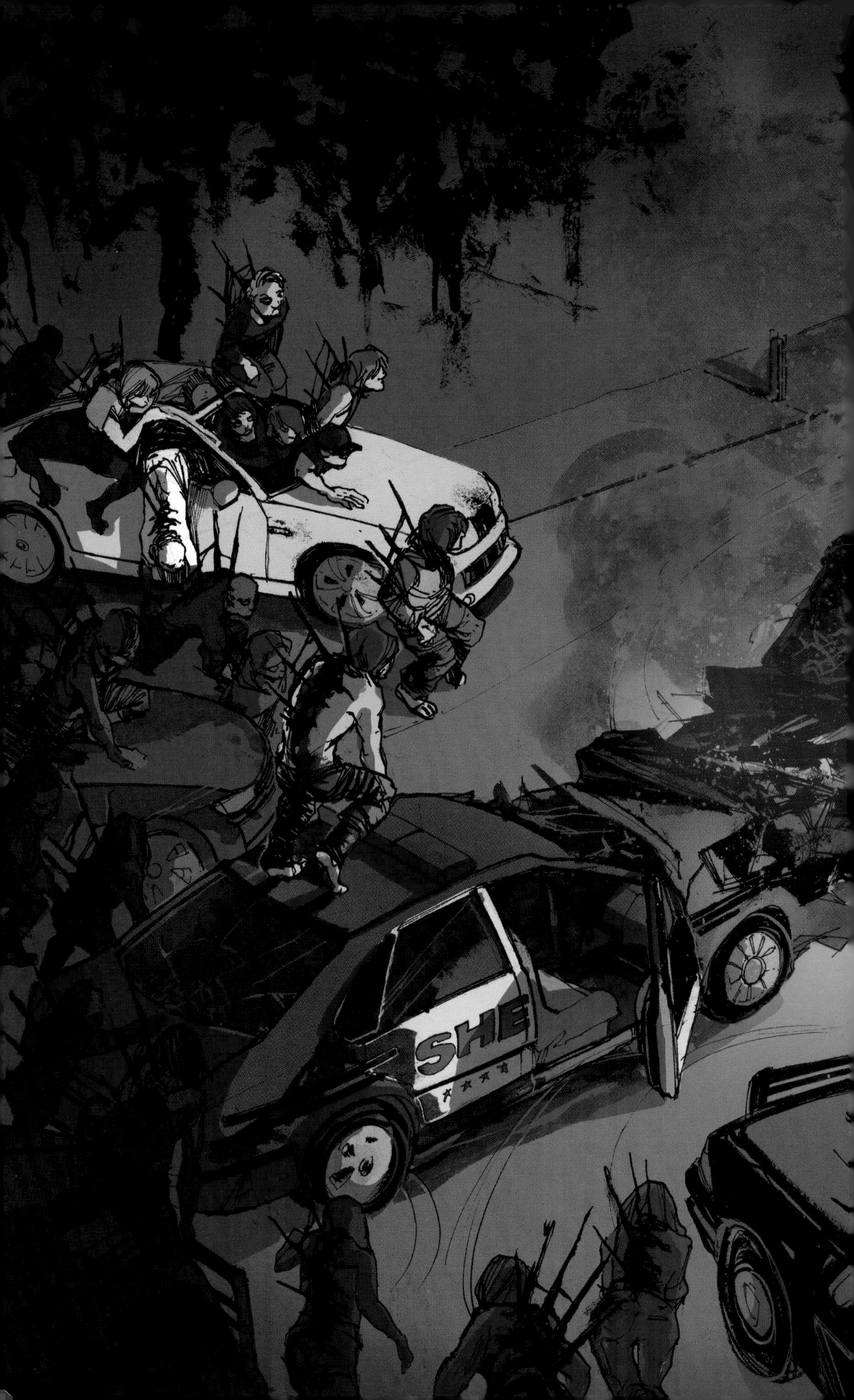
SHE

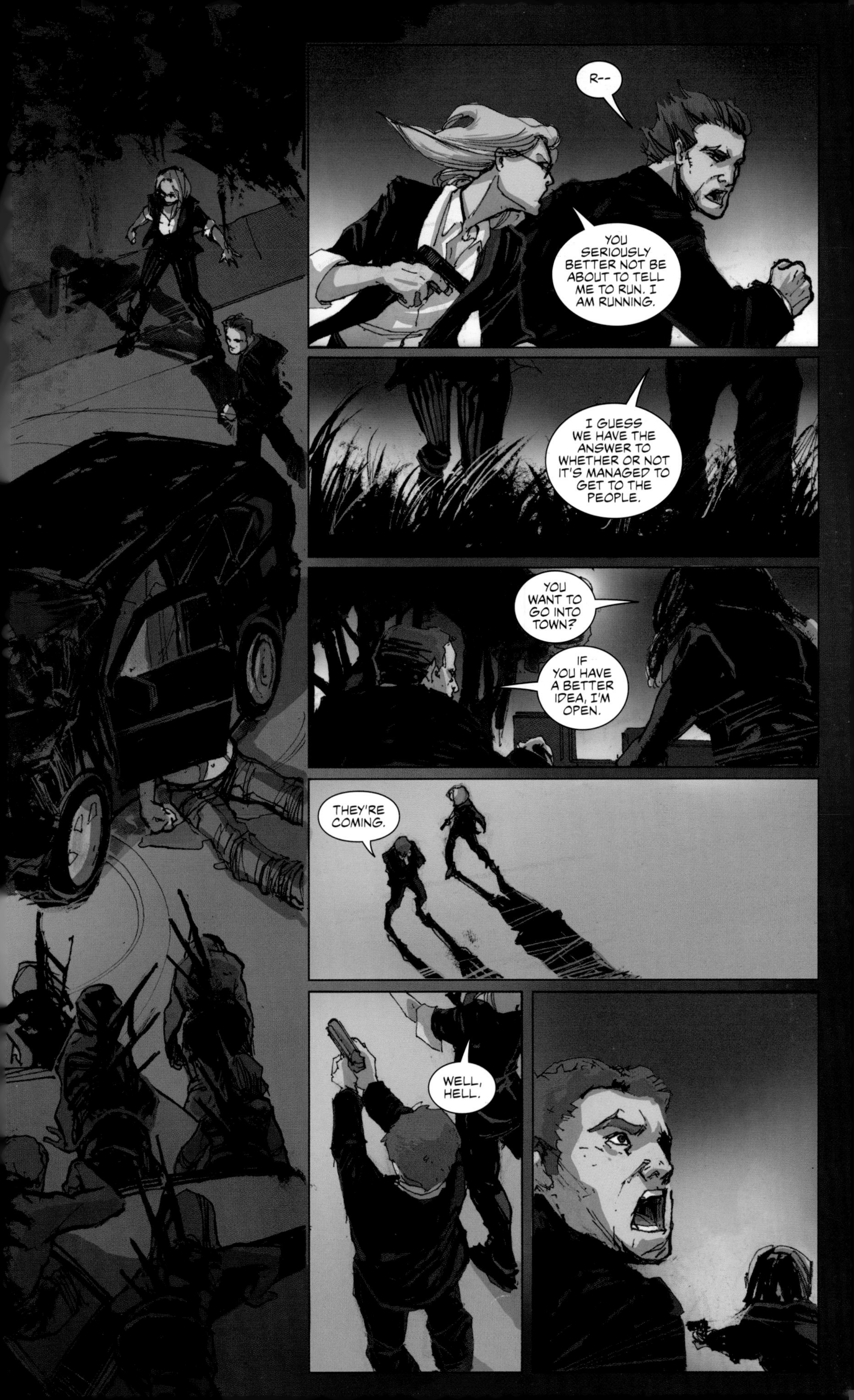
R--
YOU SERIOUSLY BETTER NOT BE ABOUT TO TELL ME TO RUN. I AM RUNNING.
I GUESS WE HAVE THE ANSWER TO WHETHER OR NOT IT'S MANAGED TO GET TO THE PEOPLE.
YOU WANT TO GO INTO TOWN?
IF YOU HAVE A BETTER IDEA, I'M OPEN.
THEY'RE COMING.
WELL, HELL.

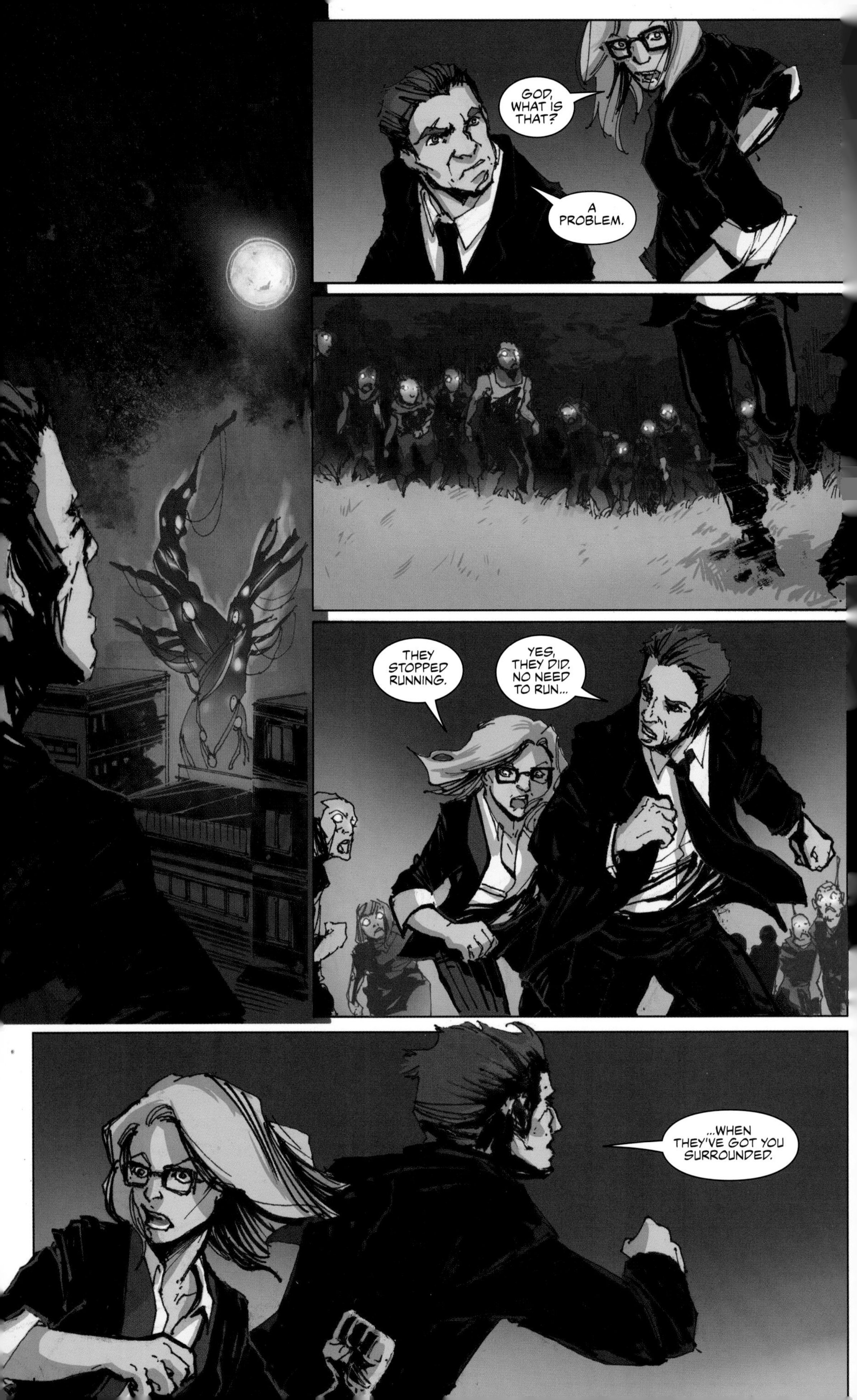
GOD, WHAT IS THAT?
A PROBLEM.
THEY STOPPED RUNNING.
YES, THEY DID. NO NEED TO RUN...
...WHEN THEY'VE GOT YOU SURROUNDED.

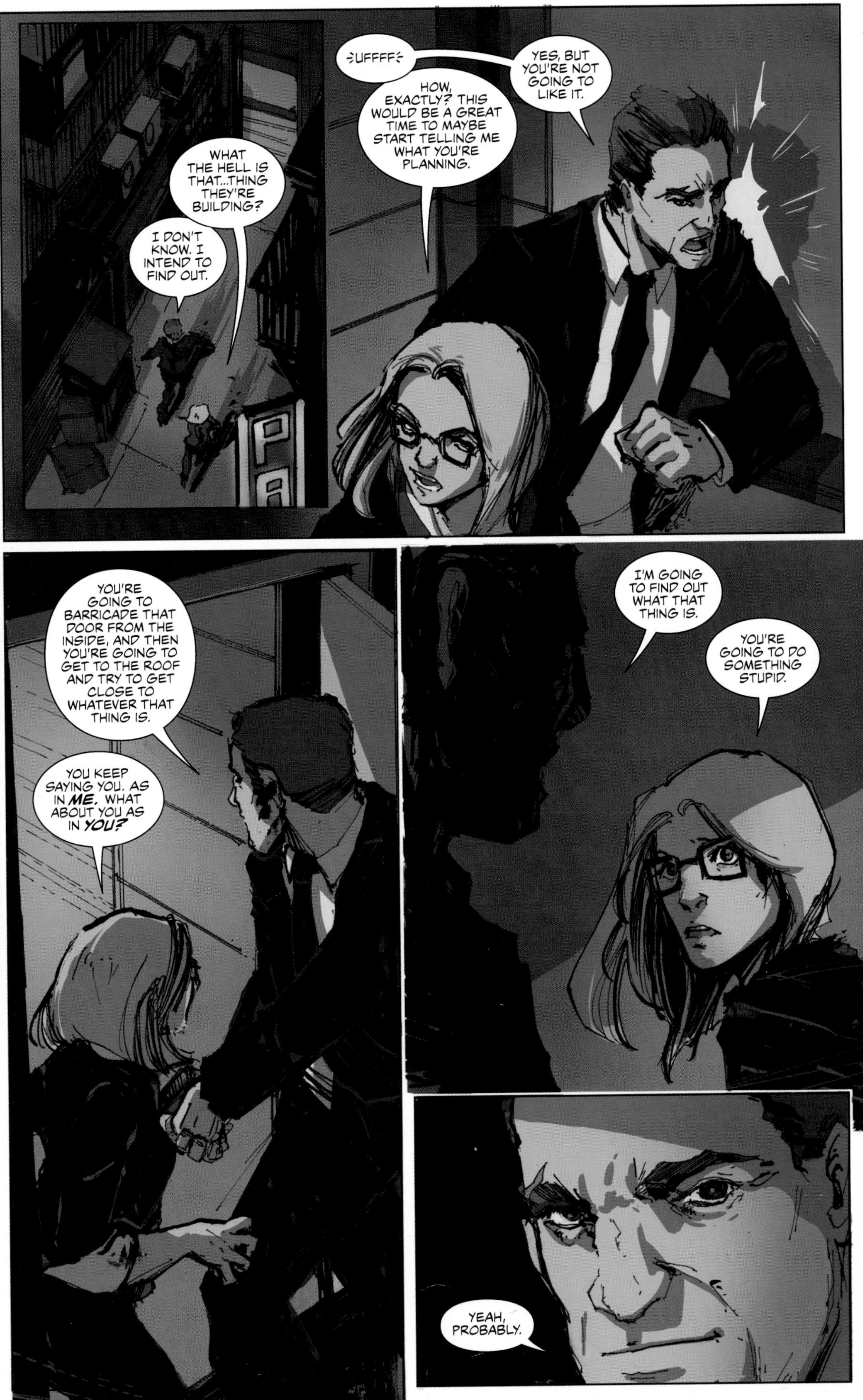
WHAT THE HELL IS THAT...THING THEY'RE BUILDING?
I DON'T KNOW. I INTEND TO FIND OUT.
UFFFF
HOW, EXACTLY? THIS WOULD BE A GREAT TIME TO MAYBE START TELLING ME WHAT YOU'RE PLANNING.
YES, BUT YOU'RE NOT GOING TO LIKE IT.
YOU'RE GOING TO BARRICADE THAT DOOR FROM THE INSIDE, AND THEN YOU'RE GOING TO GET TO THE ROOF AND TRY TO GET CLOSE TO WHATEVER THAT THING IS.
YOU KEEP SAYING YOU. AS IN ME. WHAT ABOUT YOU AS IN YOU?
I'M GOING TO FIND OUT WHAT THAT THING IS.
YOU'RE GOING TO DO SOMETHING STUPID.
YEAH, PROBABLY.

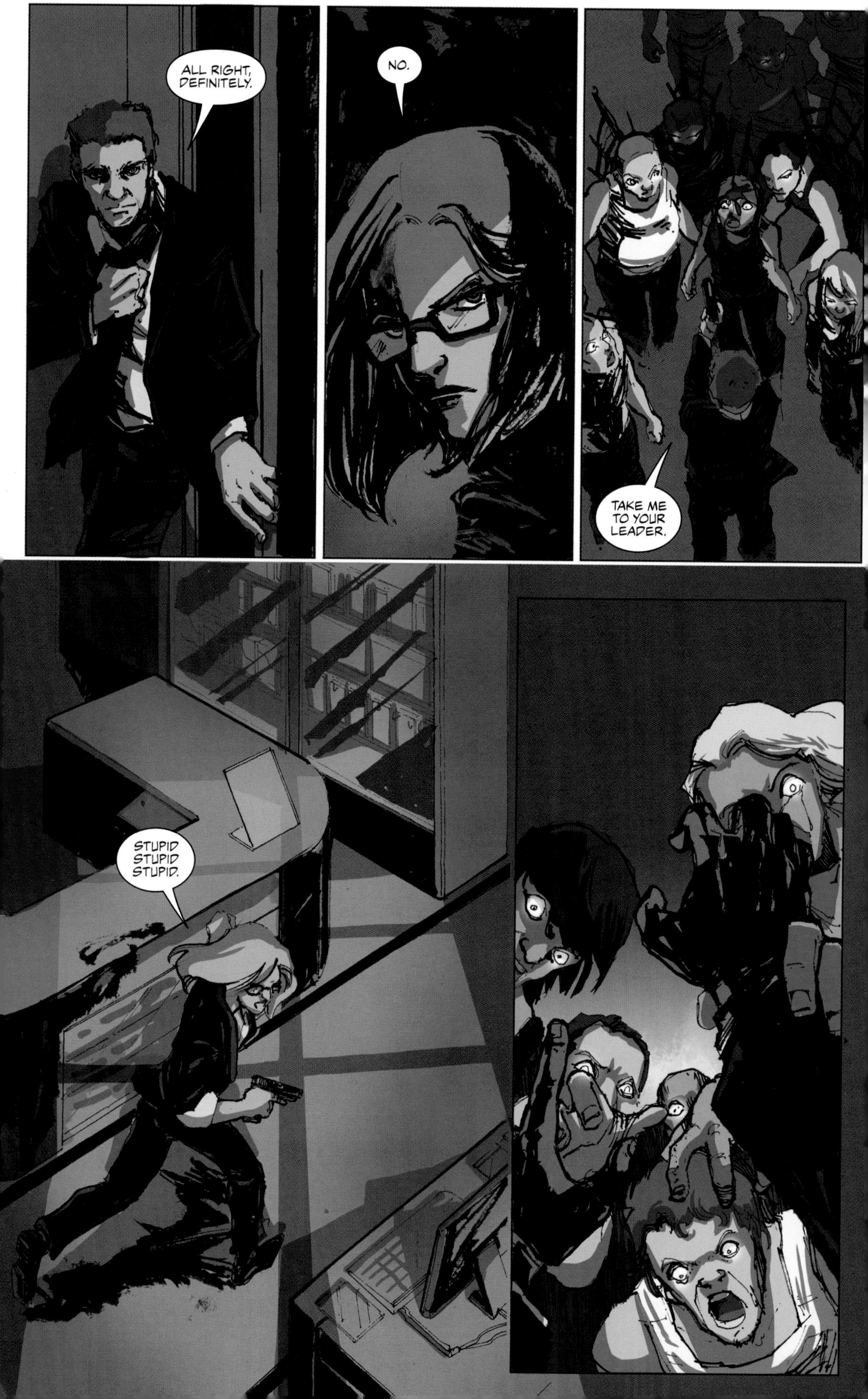
ALL RIGHT, DEFINITELY.
NO.
TAKE ME TO YOUR LEADER.
STUPID STUPID STUPID.

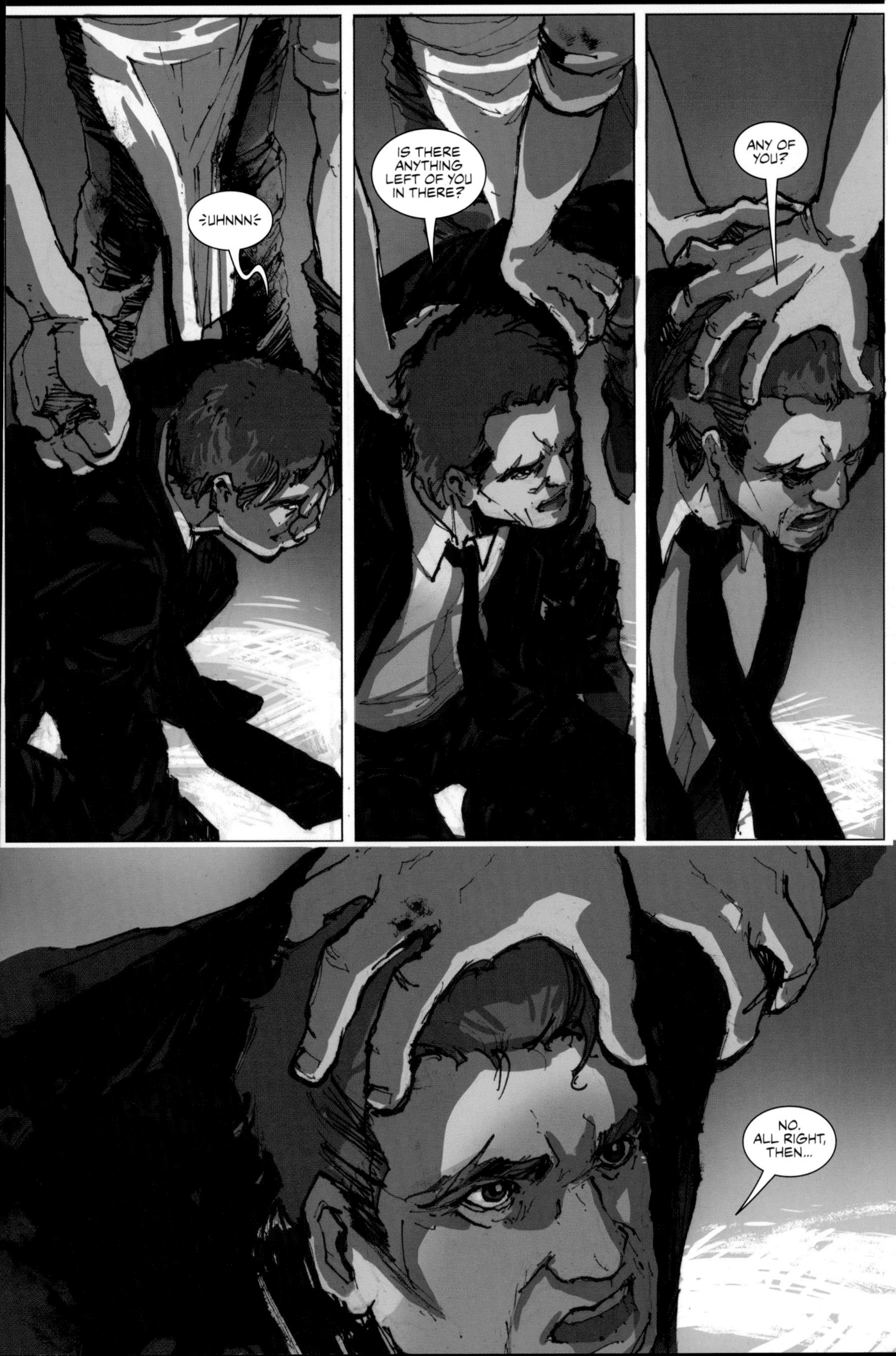

UHNNN
IS THERE ANYTHING LEFT OF YOU IN THERE?
ANY OF YOU?
NO. ALL RIGHT, THEN...

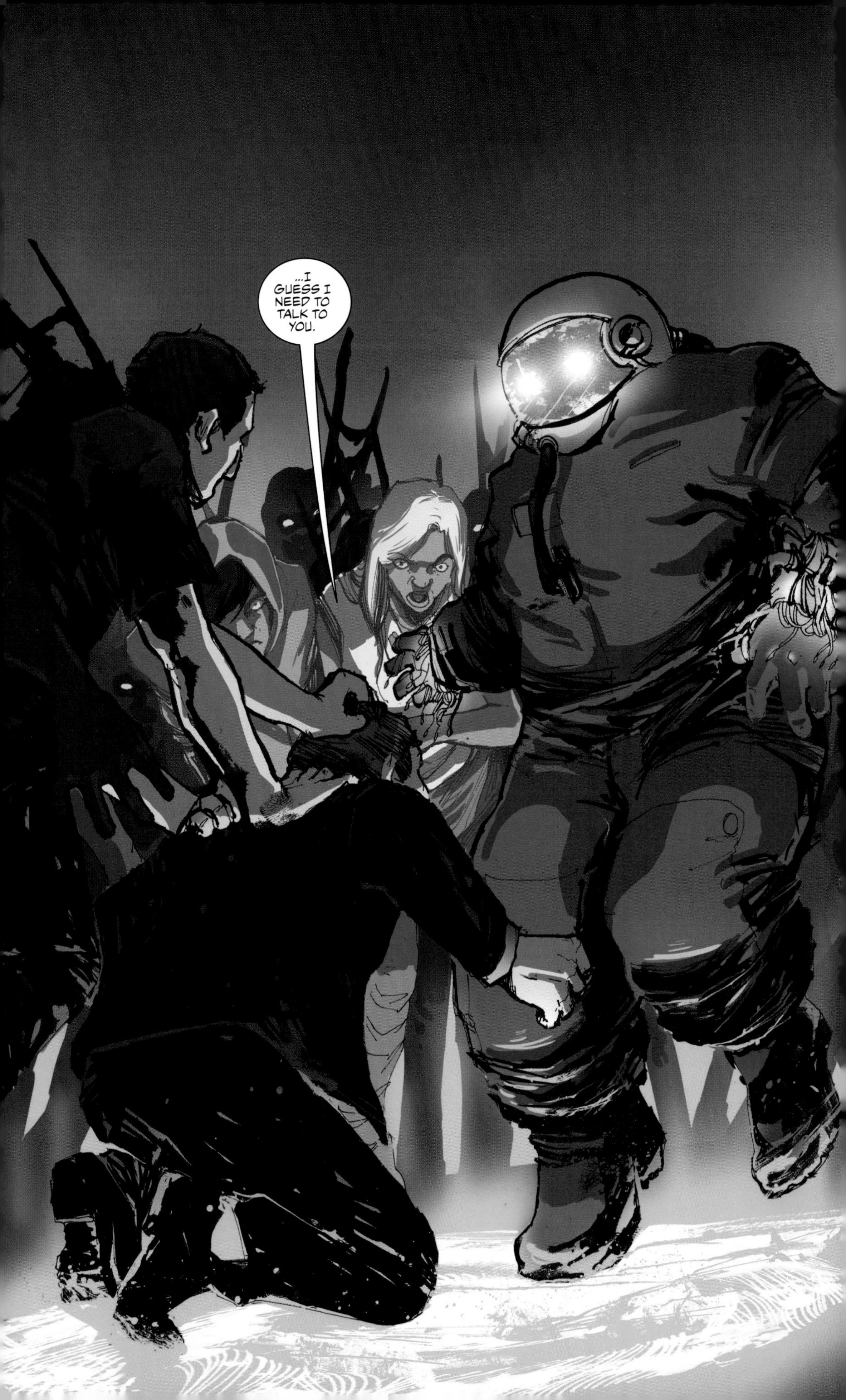
...I GUESS I NEED TO TALK TO YOU.

CHAPTER FOUR

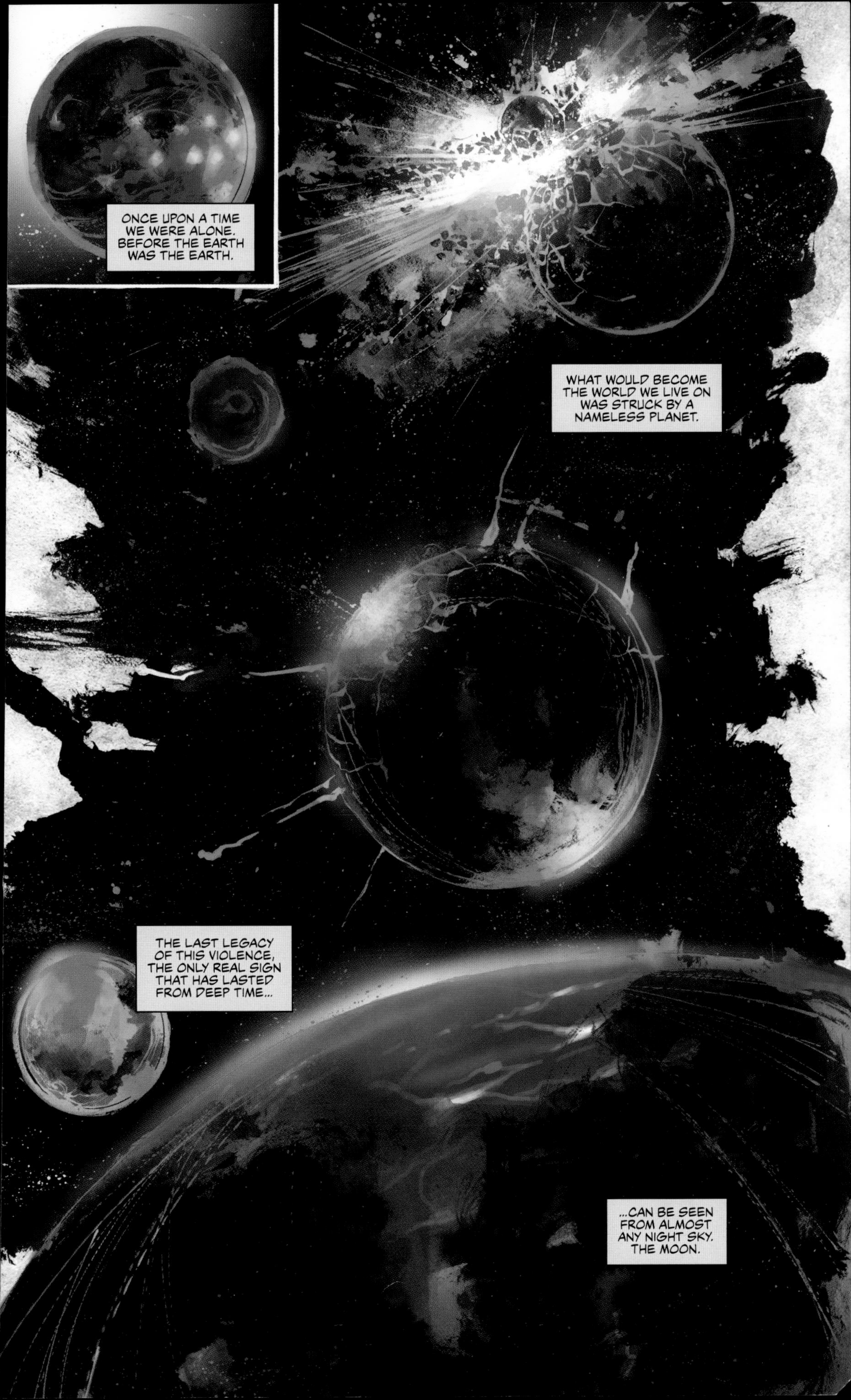
ONCE UPON A TIME WE WERE ALONE. BEFORE THE EARTH WAS THE EARTH.
WHAT WOULD BECOME THE WORLD WE LIVE ON WAS STRUCK BY A NAMELESS PLANET.
THE LAST LEGACY OF THIS VIOLENCE, THE ONLY REAL SIGN THAT HAS LASTED FROM DEEP TIME...
...CAN BE SEEN FROM ALMOST ANY NIGHT SKY. THE MOON.

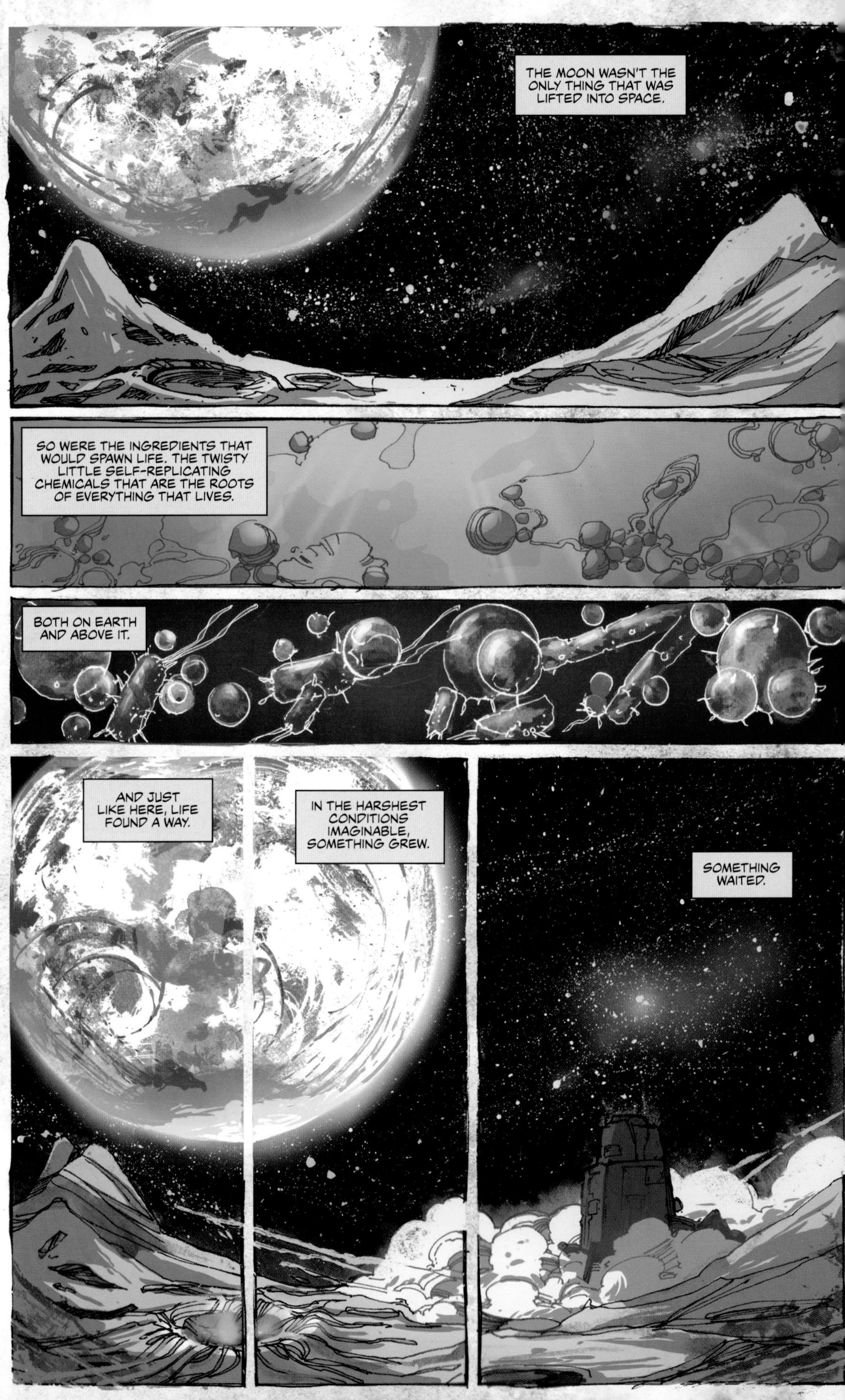
THE MOON WASN'T THE ONLY THING THAT WAS LIFTED INTO SPACE.
SO WERE THE INGREDIENTS THAT WOULD SPAWN LIFE. THE TWISTY LITTLE SELF-REPLICATING CHEMICALS THAT ARE THE ROOTS OF EVERYTHING THAT LIVES.
BOTH ON EARTH AND ABOVE IT.
AND JUST LIKE HERE, LIFE FOUND A WAY.
IN THE HARSHEST CONDITIONS IMAGINABLE, SOMETHING GREW.
SOMETHING WAITED.

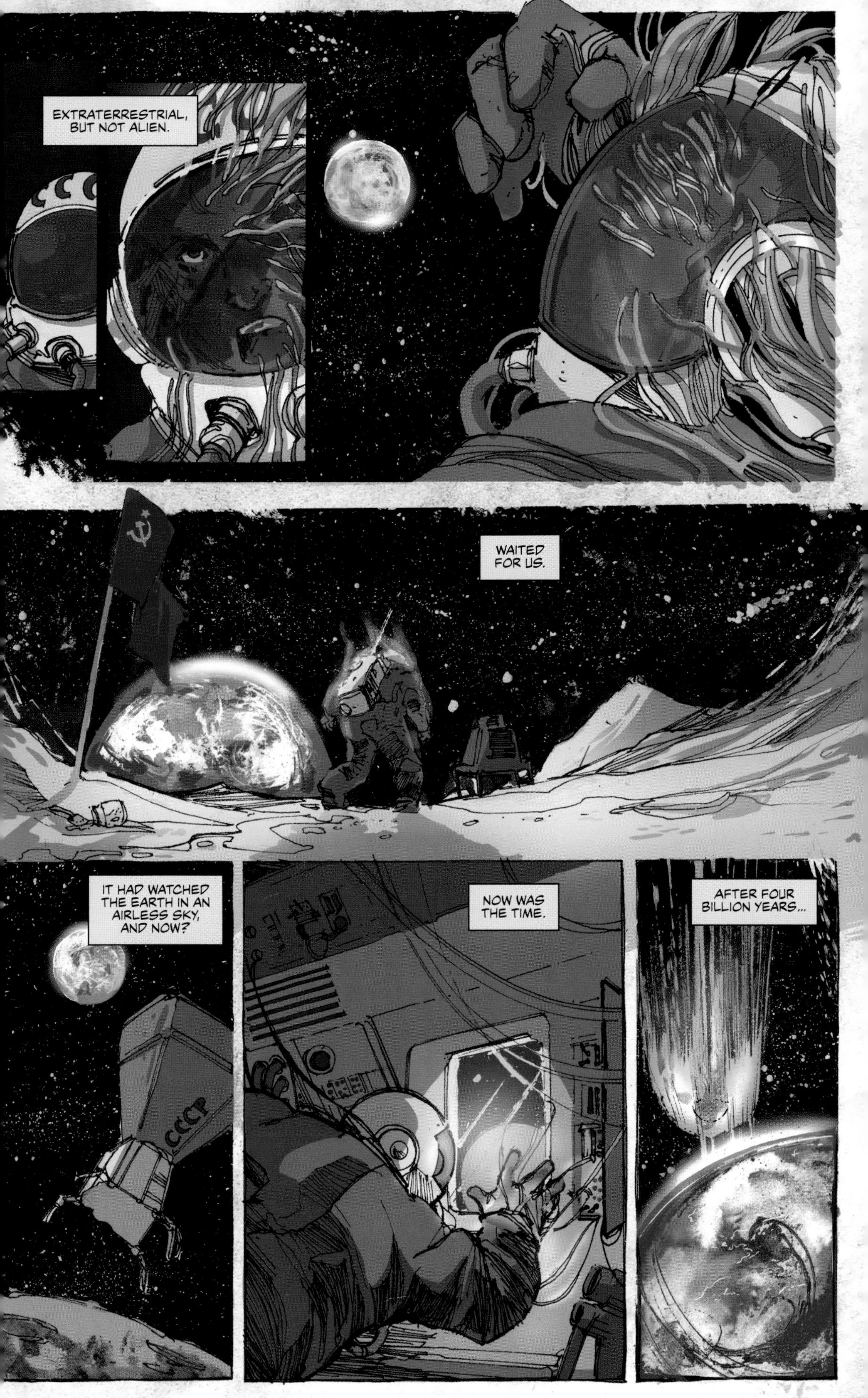
EXTRATERRESTRIAL, BUT NOT ALIEN.
WAITED FOR US.
IT HAD WATCHED THE EARTH IN AN AIRLESS SKY, AND NOW?
NOW WAS THE TIME.
AFTER FOUR BILLION YEARS...

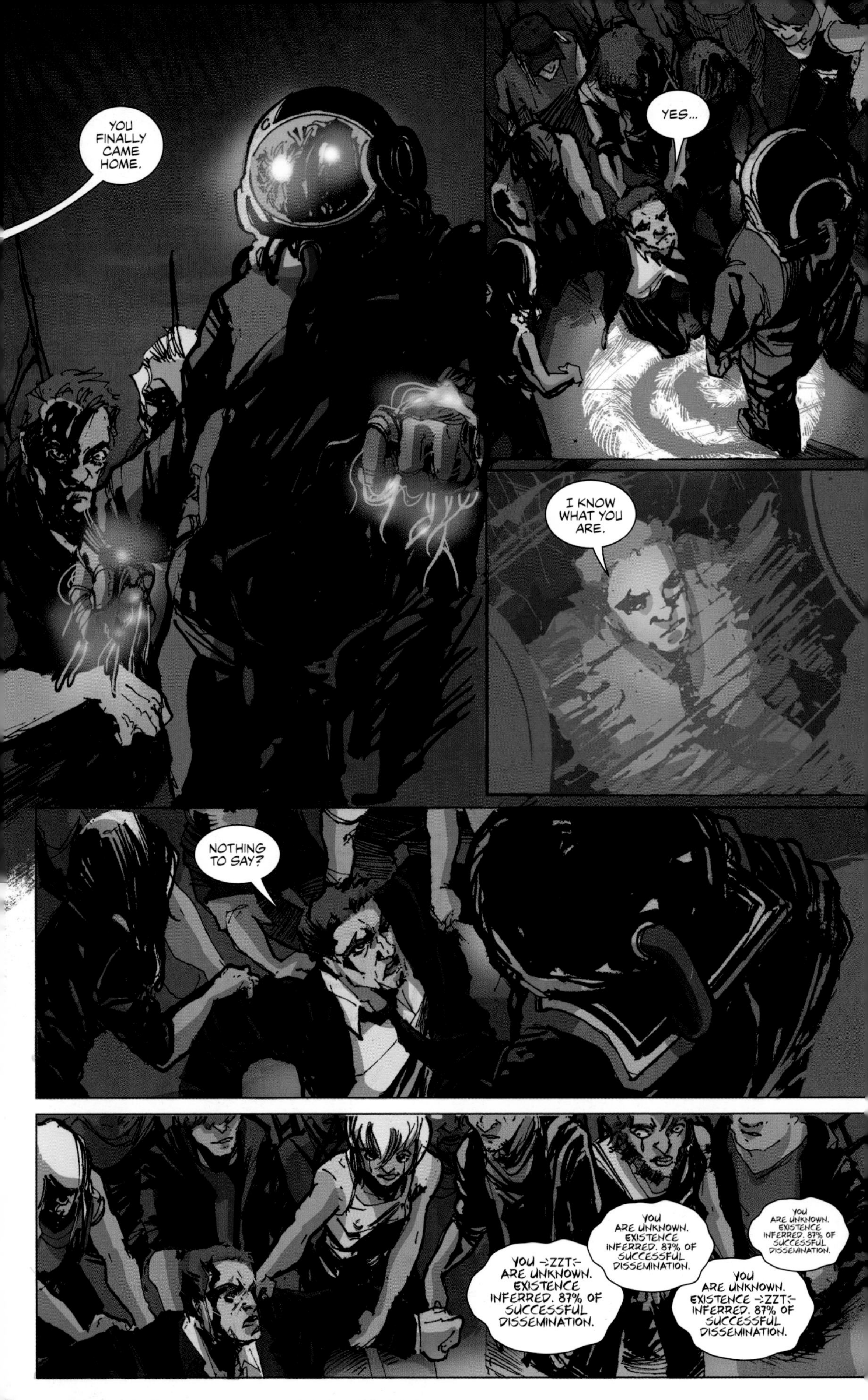
YOU FINALLY CAME HOME.
YES...
I KNOW WHAT YOU ARE.
NOTHING TO SAY?
YOU -ZZT- ARE UNKNOWN. EXISTENCE INFERRED. 87% OF SUCCESSFUL DISSEMINATION.
YOU ARE UNKNOWN. EXISTENCE INFERRED. 87% OF SUCCESSFUL DISSEMINATION.
YOU ARE UNKNOWN. EXISTENCE -ZZT- INFERRED. 87% OF SUCCESSFUL DISSEMINATION.
YOU ARE UNKNOWN. EXISTENCE INFERRED. 87% OF SUCCESSFUL DISSEMINATION.

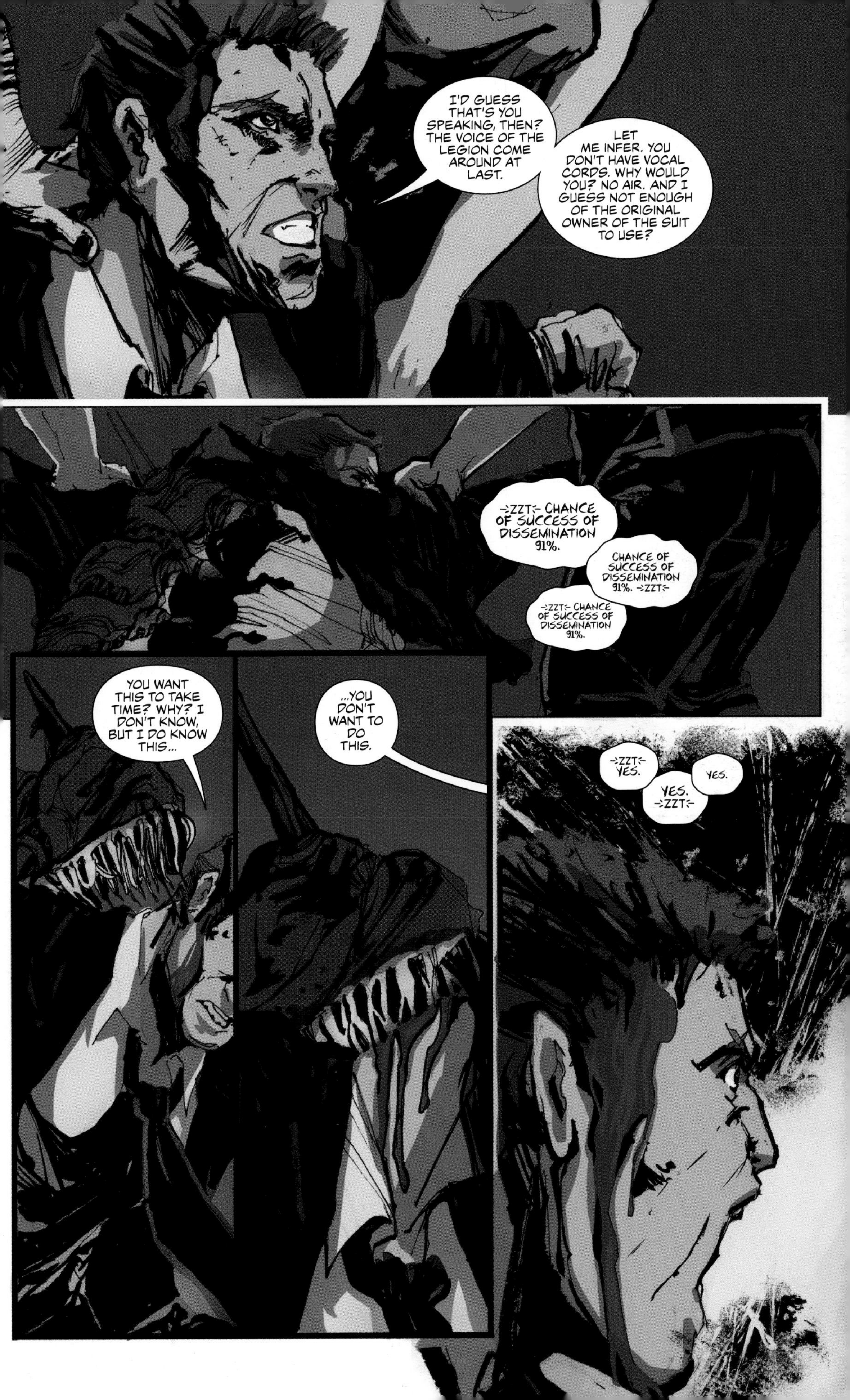

I'D GUESS THAT'S YOU SPEAKING, THEN? THE VOICE OF THE LEGION COME AROUND AT LAST.
LET ME INFER. YOU DON'T HAVE VOCAL CORDS. WHY WOULD YOU? NO AIR. AND I GUESS NOT ENOUGH OF THE ORIGINAL OWNER OF THE SUIT TO USE?
->ZZT<- CHANCE OF SUCCESS OF DISSEMINATION 91%.
CHANCE OF SUCCESS OF DISSEMINATION 91%. ->ZZT<-
->ZZT<- CHANCE OF SUCCESS OF DISSEMINATION 91%.
YOU WANT THIS TO TAKE TIME? WHY? I DON'T KNOW, BUT I DO KNOW THIS...
...YOU DON'T WANT TO DO THIS.
->ZZT<- YES.
YES. ->ZZT<-
YES.

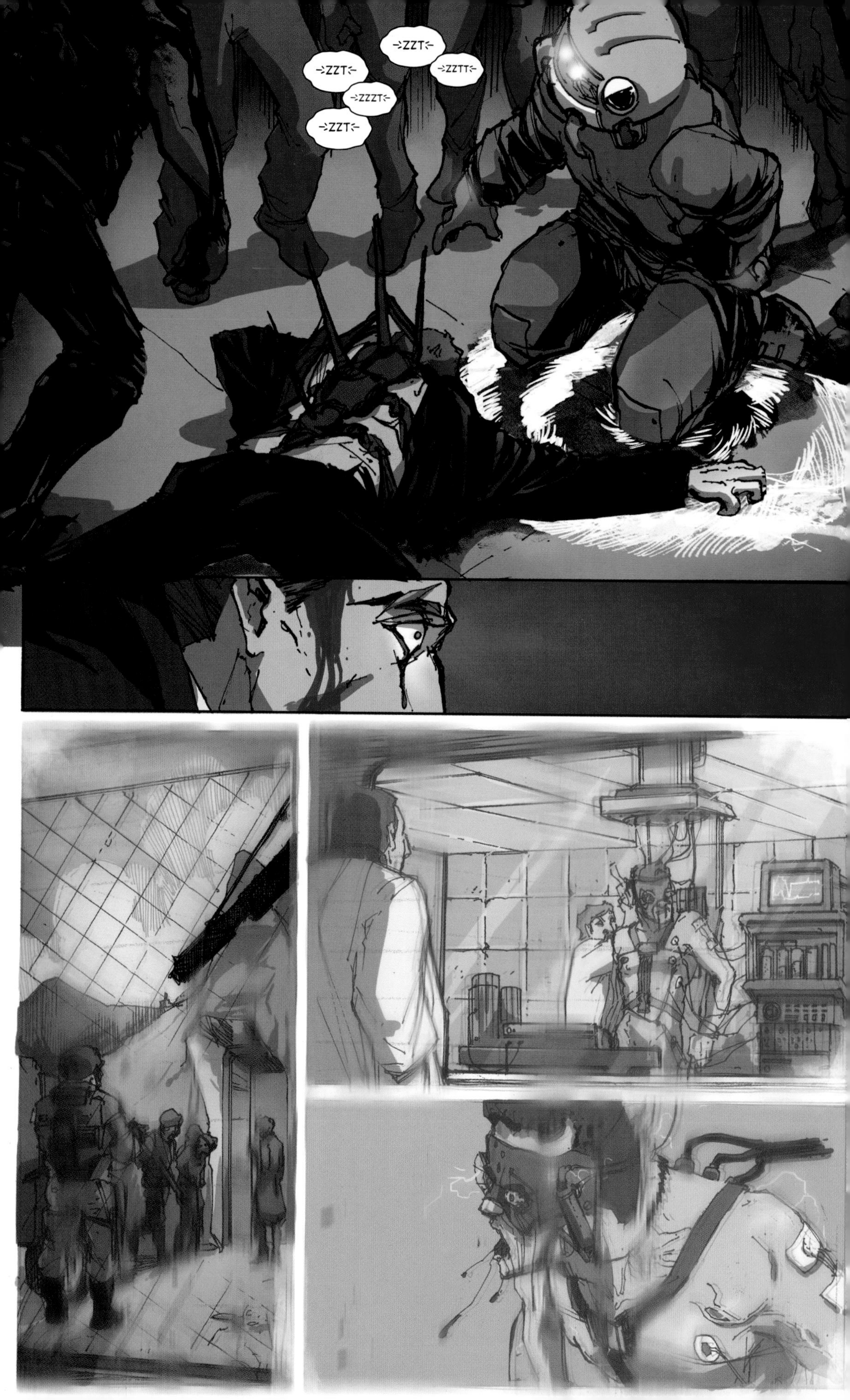
-ZZT-
-ZZT-
-ZZTT-
-ZZZT-
-ZZT-

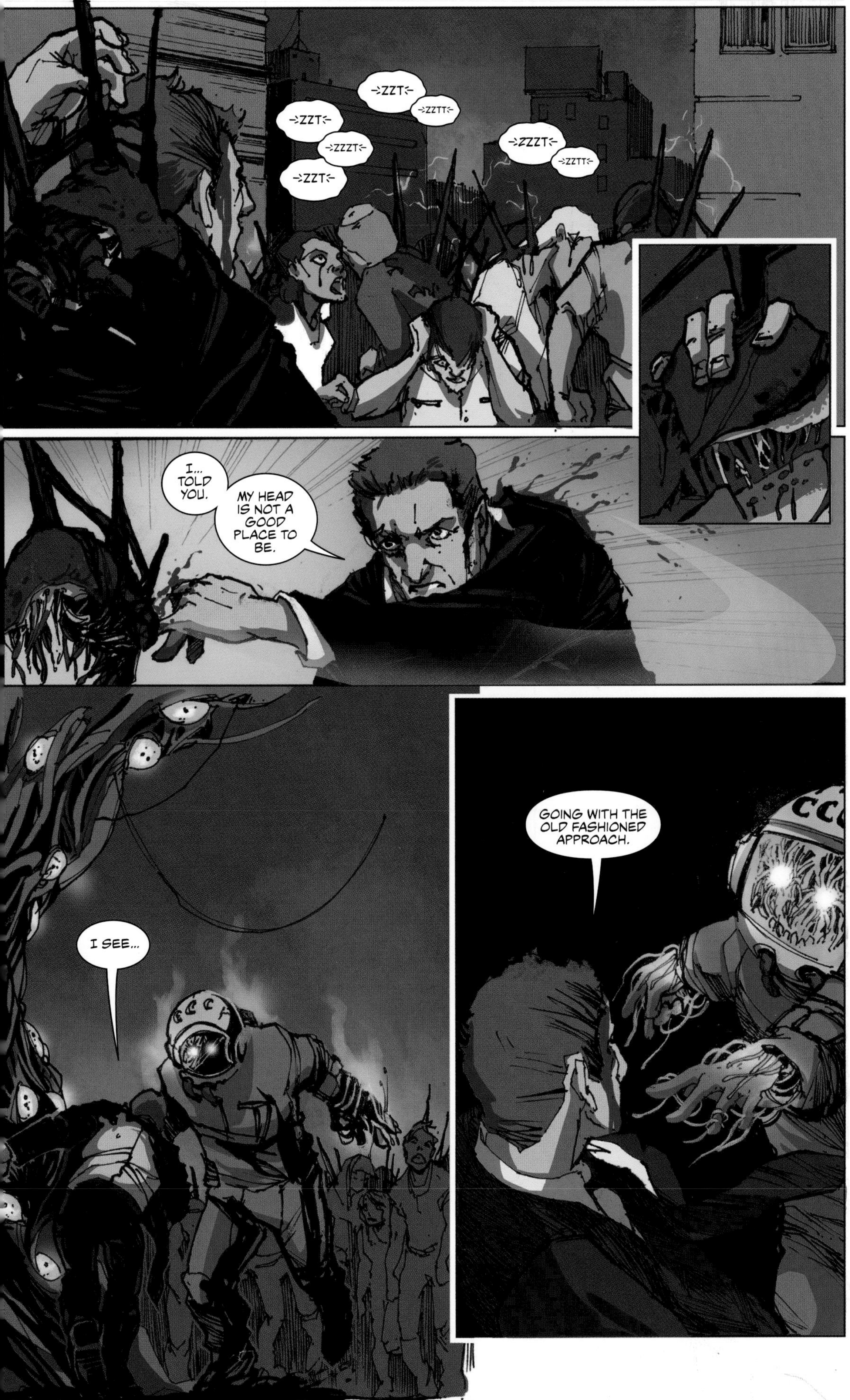

-ZZT-
-ZZTT-
-ZZT-
-ZZZT-
-ZZT-
-ZZZT-
-ZZTT-
I... TOLD YOU.
MY HEAD IS NOT A GOOD PLACE TO BE.
I SEE...
GOING WITH THE OLD FASHIONED APPROACH.

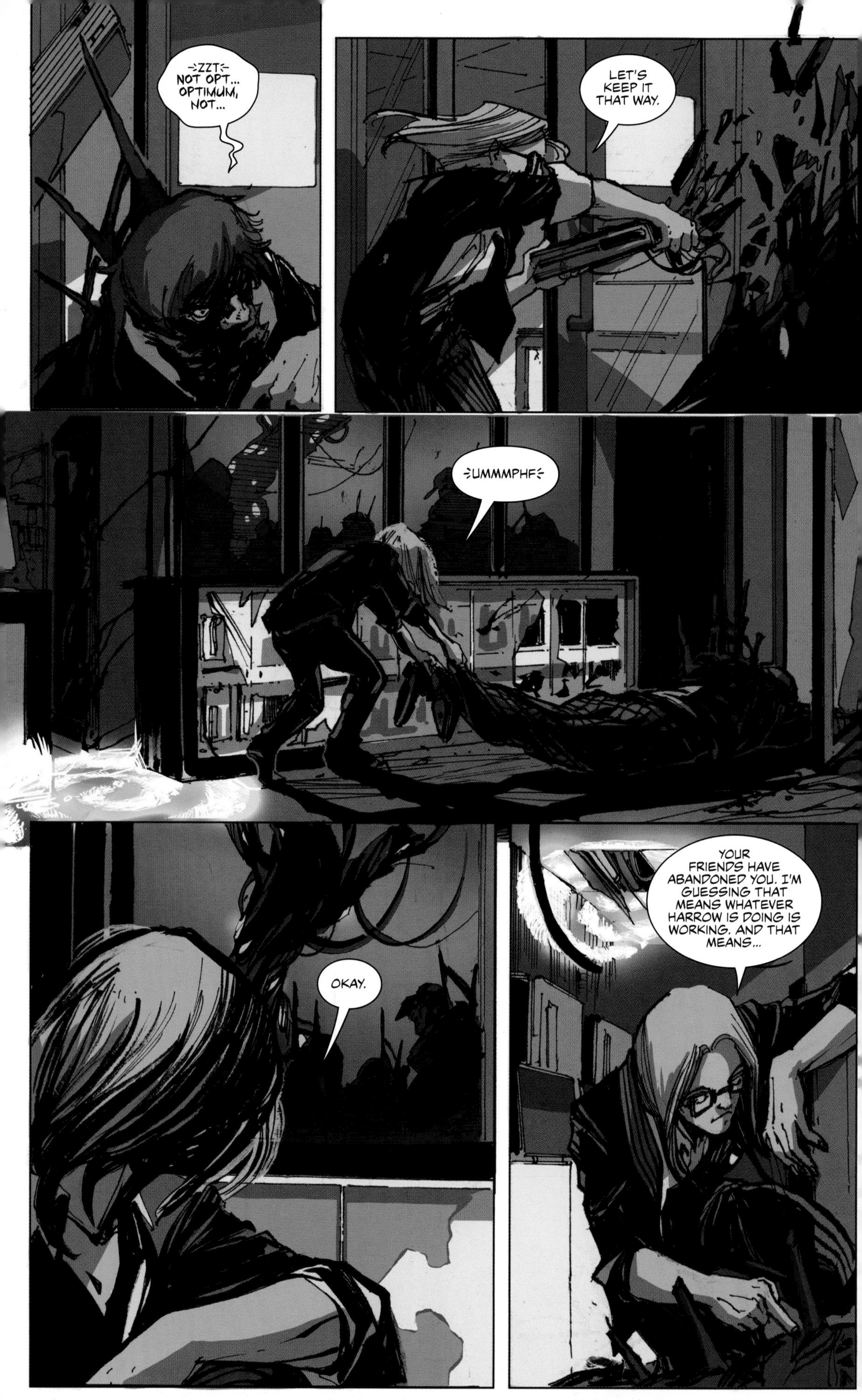
-ZZT- NOT OPT... OPTIMUM, NOT...
LET'S KEEP IT THAT WAY.
-UMMMPHF-
OKAY.
YOUR FRIENDS HAVE ABANDONED YOU. I'M GUESSING THAT MEANS WHATEVER HARROW IS DOING IS WORKING. AND THAT MEANS...

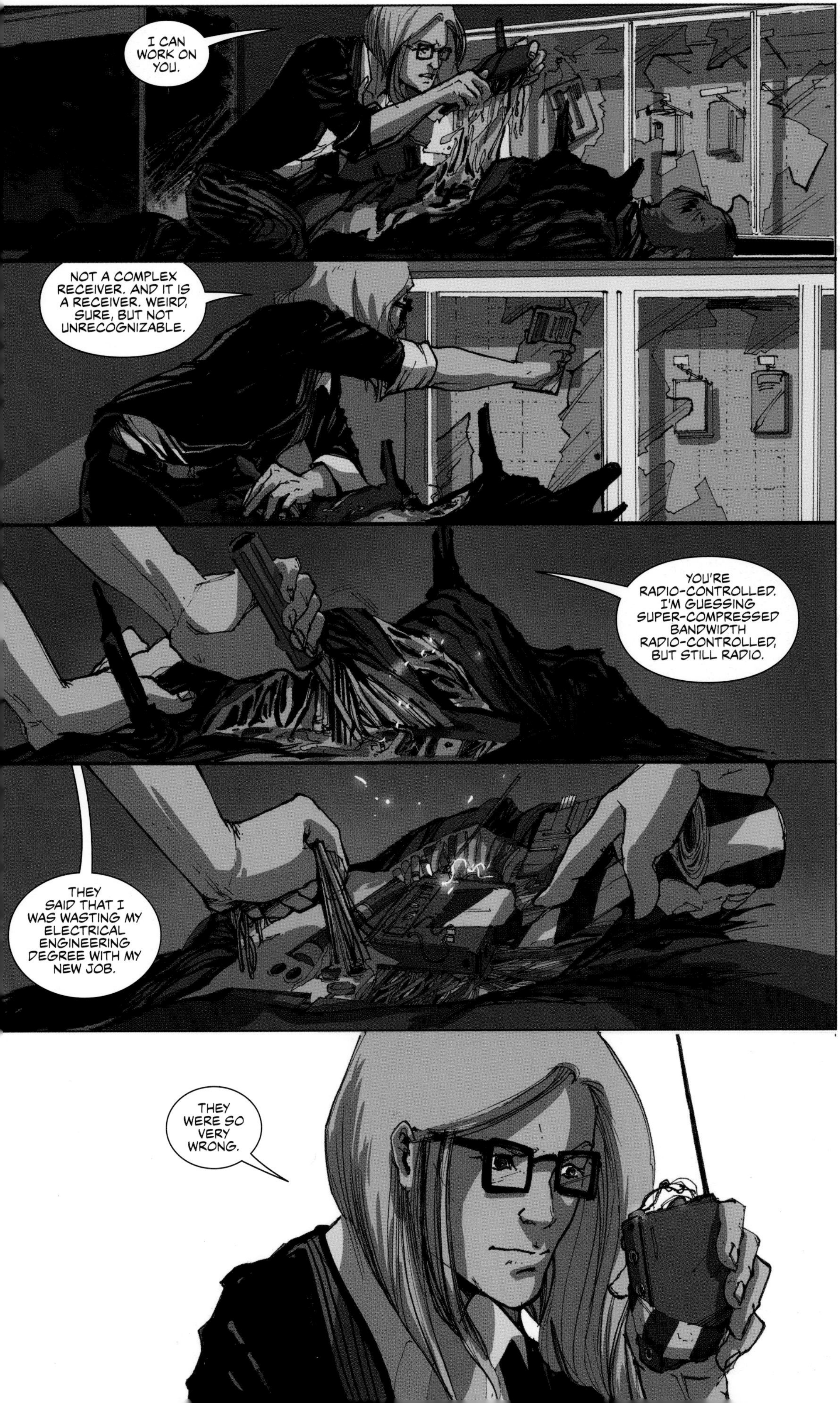
I CAN WORK ON YOU.
NOT A COMPLEX RECEIVER. AND IT IS A RECEIVER. WEIRD, SURE, BUT NOT UNRECOGNIZABLE.
YOU'RE RADIO-CONTROLLED. I'M GUESSING SUPER-COMPRESSED BANDWIDTH RADIO-CONTROLLED, BUT STILL RADIO.
THEY SAID THAT I WAS WASTING MY ELECTRICAL ENGINEERING DEGREE WITH MY NEW JOB.
THEY WERE SO VERY WRONG.

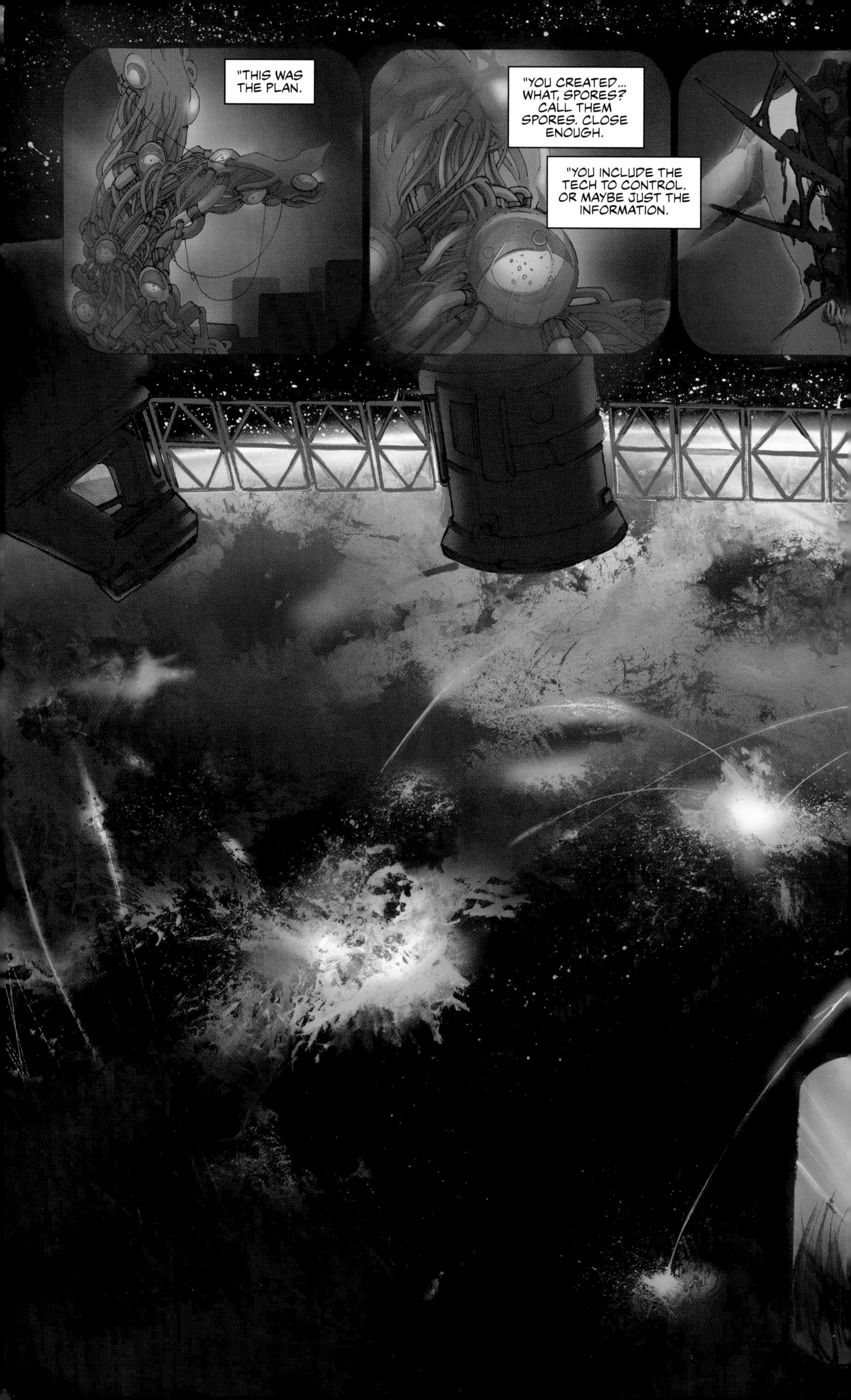
"THIS WAS THE PLAN.
"YOU CREATED... WHAT, SPORES? CALL THEM SPORES. CLOSE ENOUGH.
"YOU INCLUDE THE TECH TO CONTROL. OR MAYBE JUST THE INFORMATION.

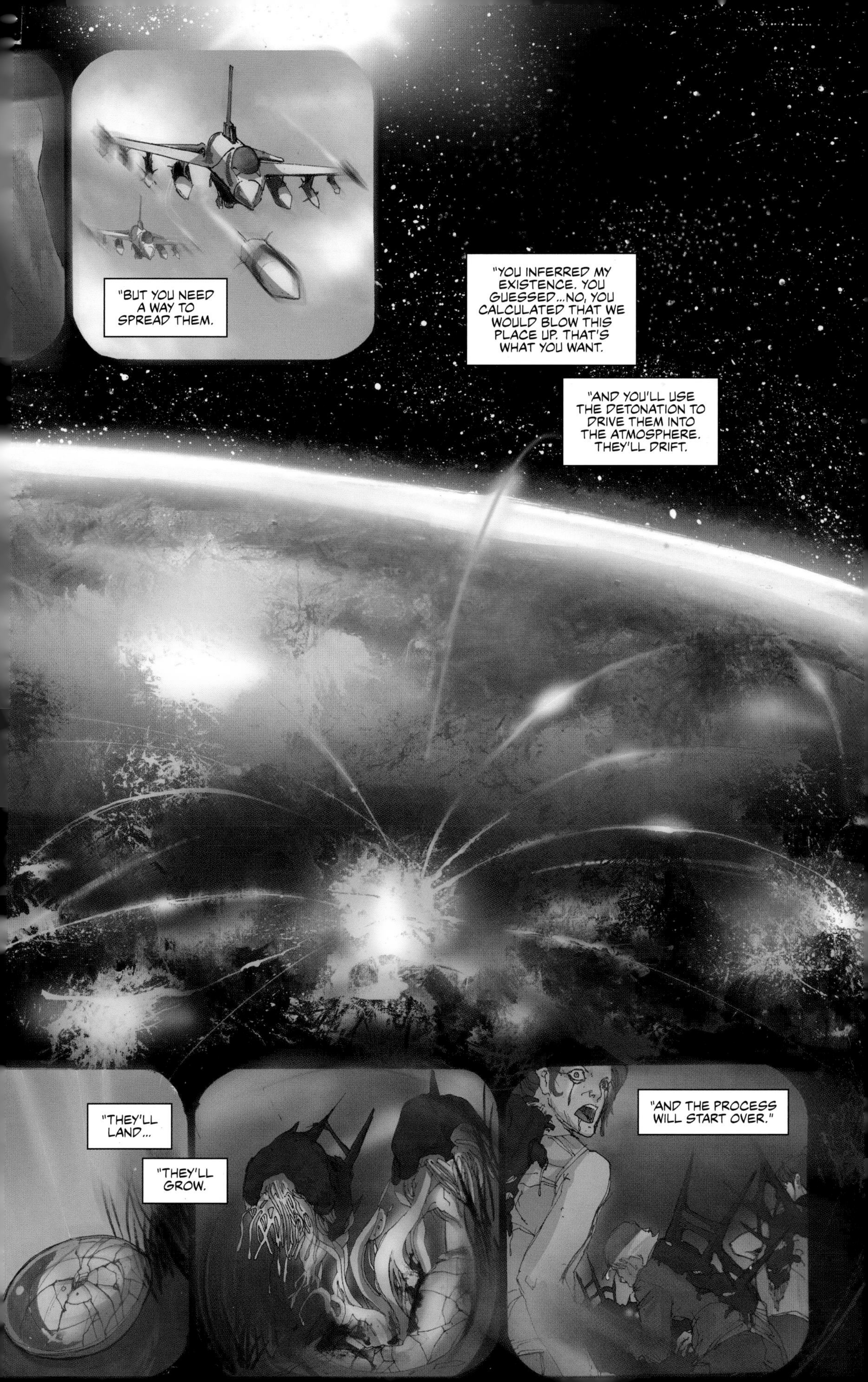
"BUT YOU NEED A WAY TO SPREAD THEM.
"YOU INFERRED MY EXISTENCE. YOU GUESSED...NO, YOU CALCULATED THAT WE WOULD BLOW THIS PLACE UP. THAT'S WHAT YOU WANT.
"AND YOU'LL USE THE DETONATION TO DRIVE THEM INTO THE ATMOSPHERE. THEY'LL DRIFT.
"THEY'LL LAND...
"THEY'LL GROW.
"AND THE PROCESS WILL START OVER."

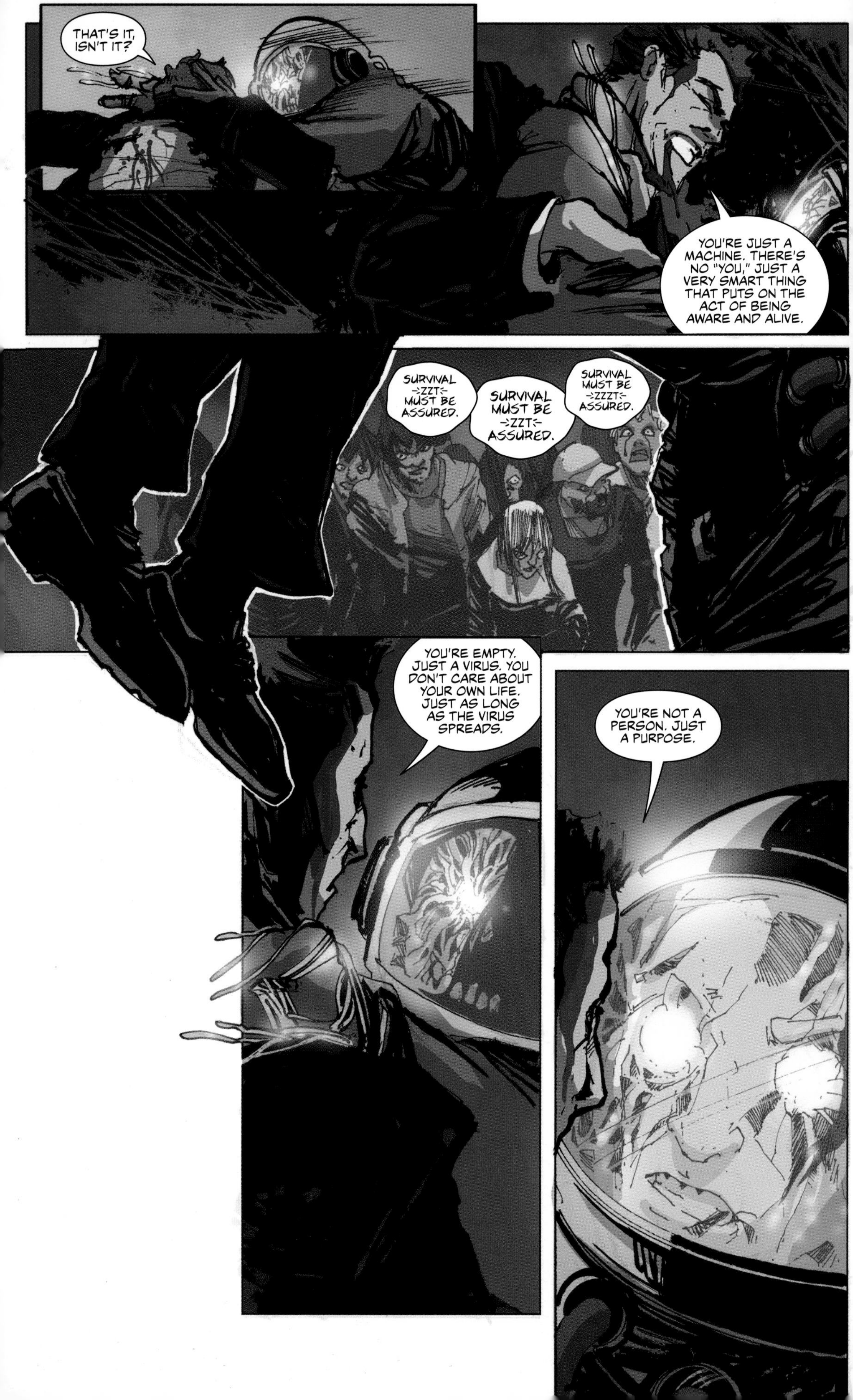
THAT'S IT, ISN'T IT?
YOU'RE JUST A MACHINE. THERE'S NO "YOU," JUST A VERY SMART THING THAT PUTS ON THE ACT OF BEING AWARE AND ALIVE.
SURVIVAL -ZZT- MUST BE ASSURED.
SURVIVAL MUST BE -ZZT- ASSURED.
SURVIVAL MUST BE -ZZZT- ASSURED.
YOU'RE EMPTY. JUST A VIRUS. YOU DON'T CARE ABOUT YOUR OWN LIFE. JUST AS LONG AS THE VIRUS SPREADS.
YOU'RE NOT A PERSON. JUST A PURPOSE.

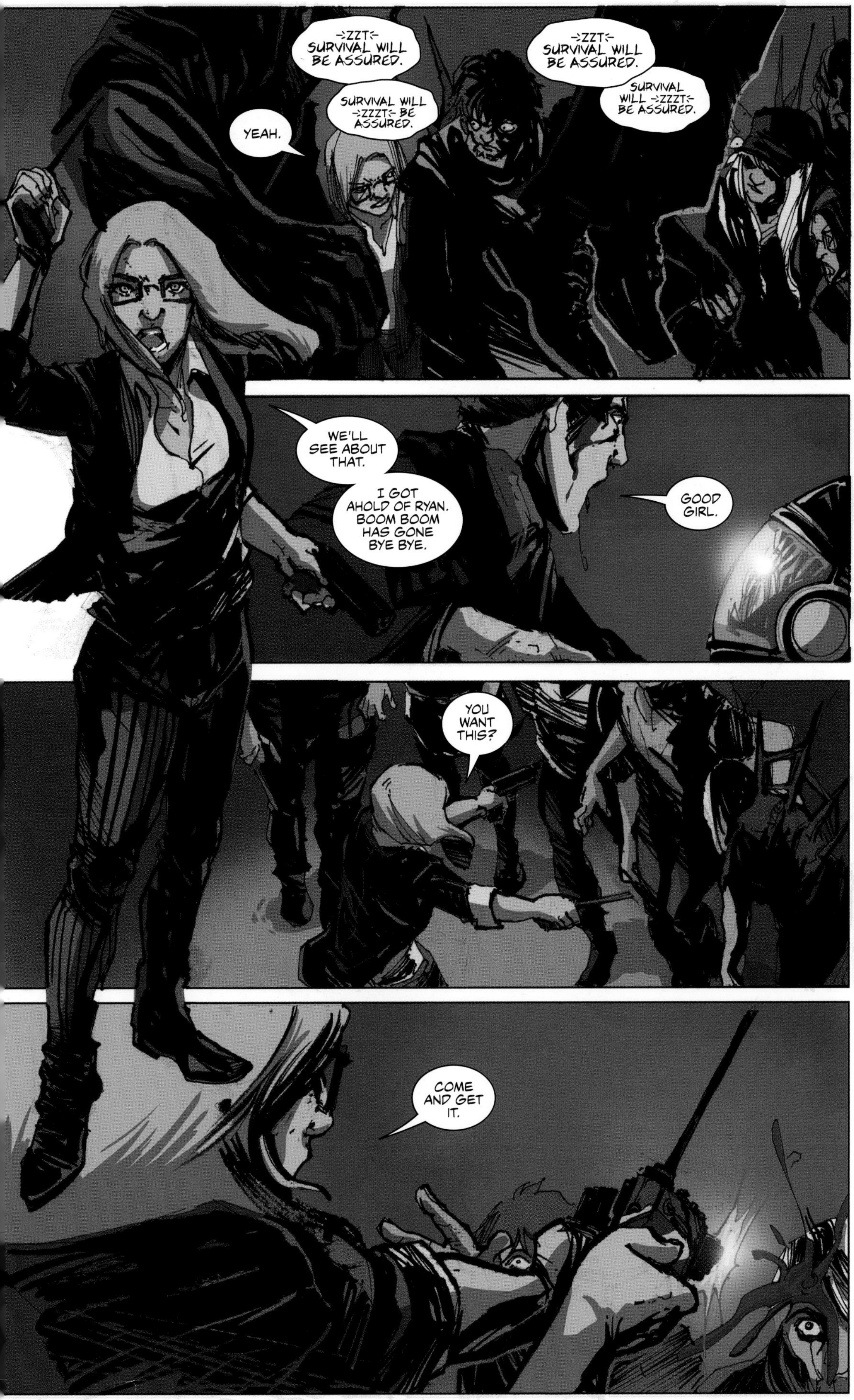
-ZZT- SURVIVAL WILL BE ASSURED.
-ZZT- SURVIVAL WILL BE ASSURED.
SURVIVAL WILL -ZZZT- BE ASSURED.
SURVIVAL WILL -ZZZT- BE ASSURED.
YEAH.
WE'LL SEE ABOUT THAT.
I GOT AHOLD OF RYAN. BOOM BOOM HAS GONE BYE BYE.
GOOD GIRL.
YOU WANT THIS?
COME AND GET IT.

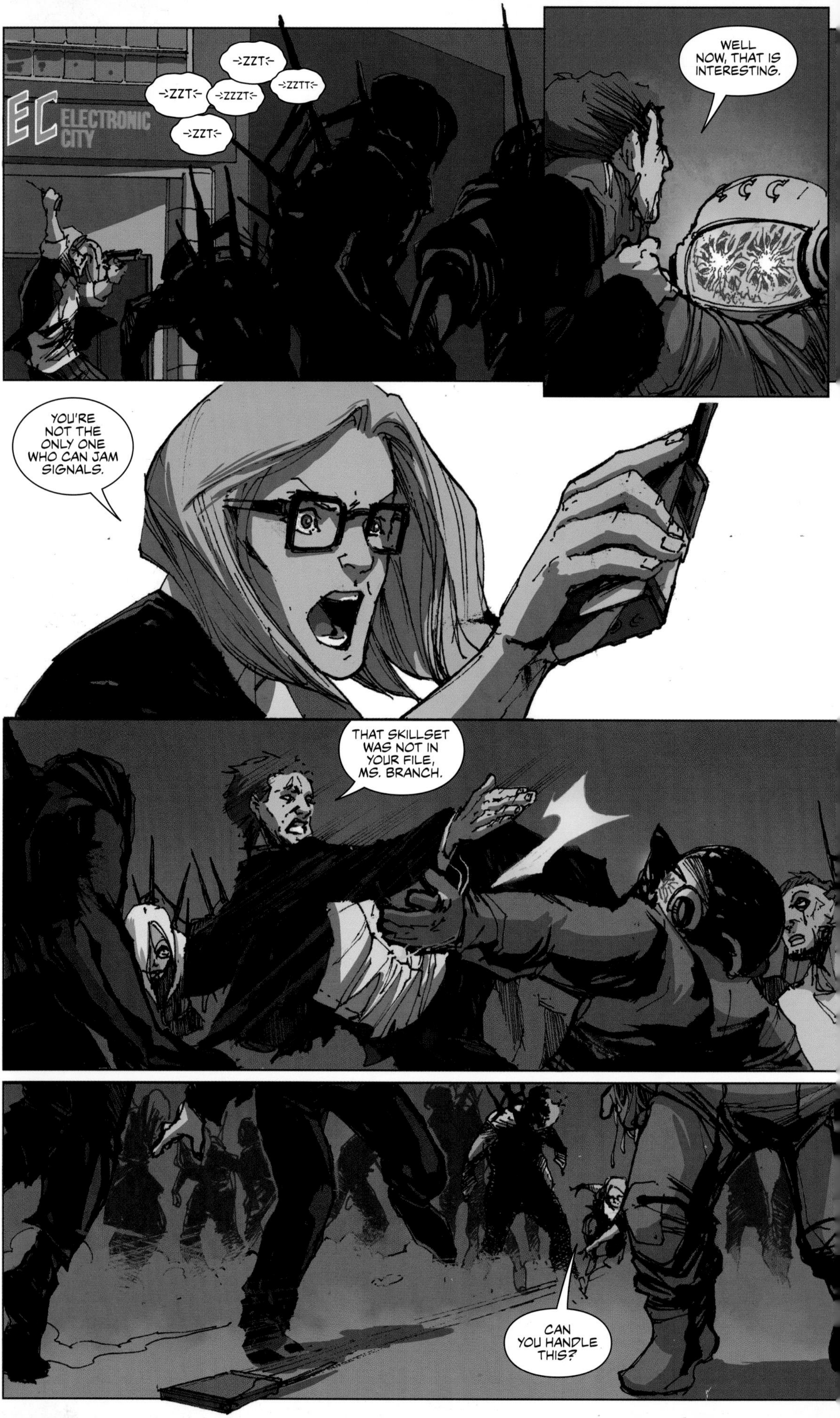
EC ELECTRONIC CITY
-ZZT-
-ZZT-
-ZZZT-
-ZZTT-
-ZZT-
WELL NOW, THAT IS INTERESTING.
YOU'RE NOT THE ONLY ONE WHO CAN JAM SIGNALS.
THAT SKILLSET WAS NOT IN YOUR FILE, MS. BRANCH.
CAN YOU HANDLE THIS?

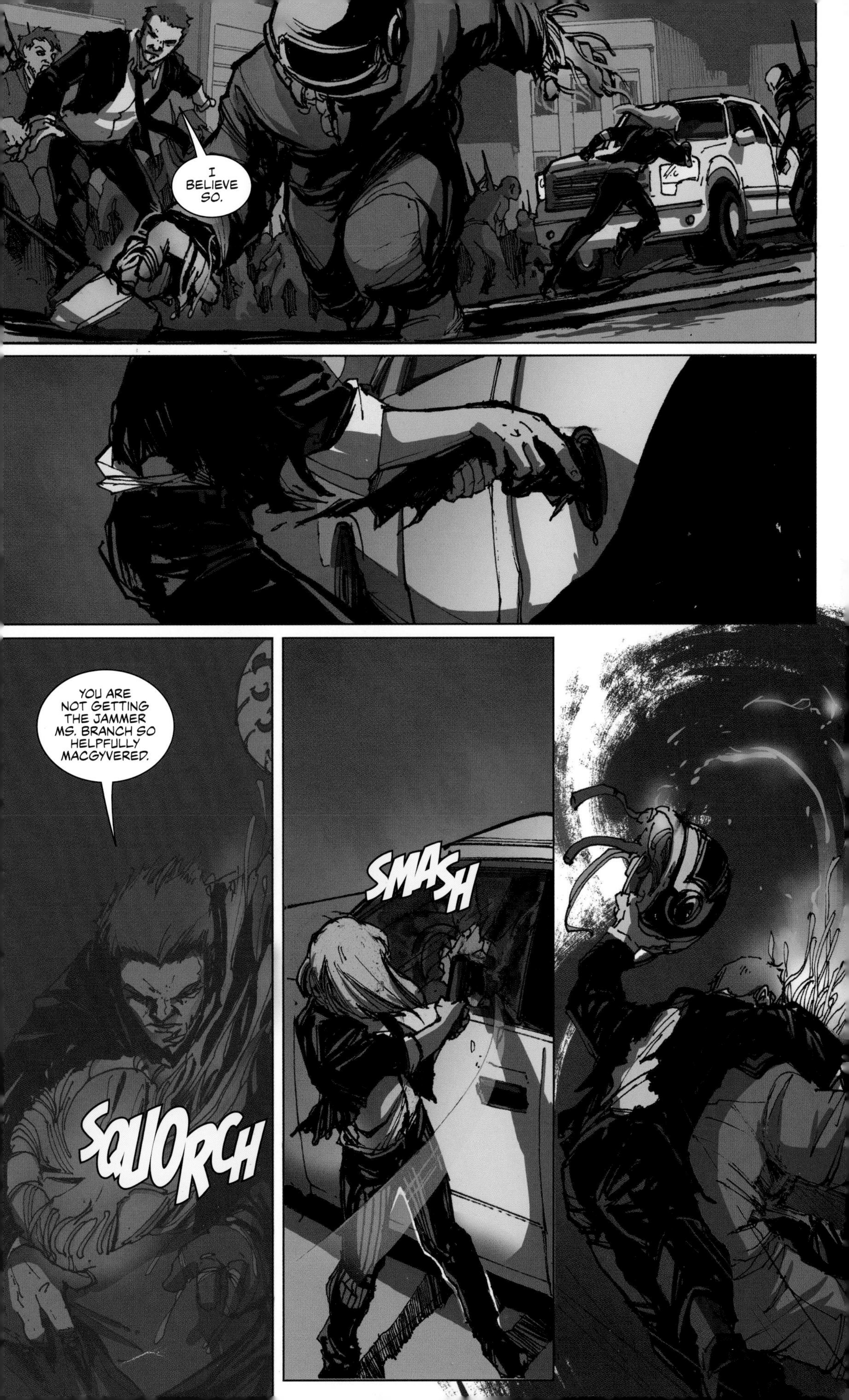
I BELIEVE SO.
YOU ARE NOT GETTING THE JAMMER MS. BRANCH SO HELPFULLY MACGYVERED.
SQUORCH
SMASH

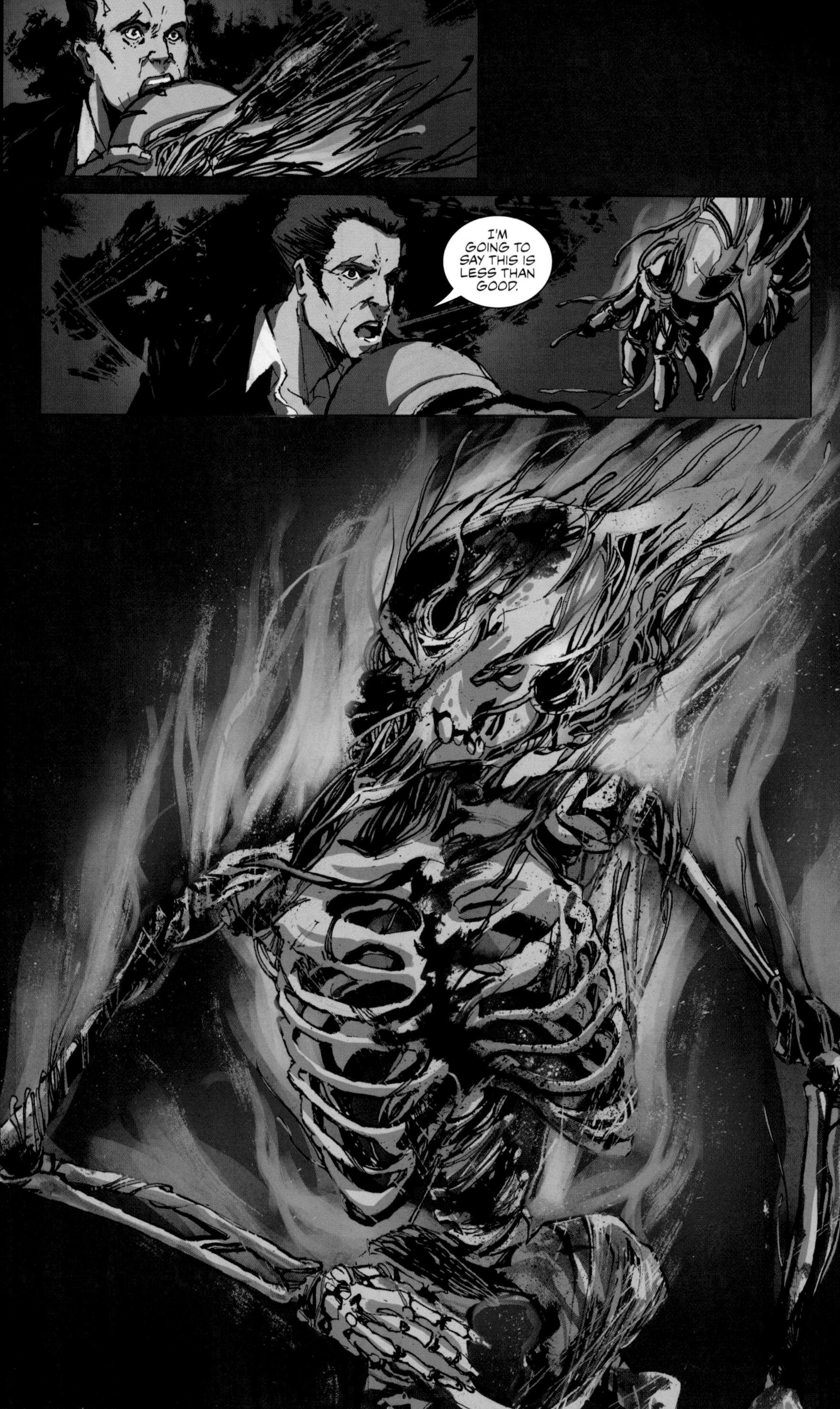
I'M GOING TO SAY THIS IS LESS THAN GOOD.

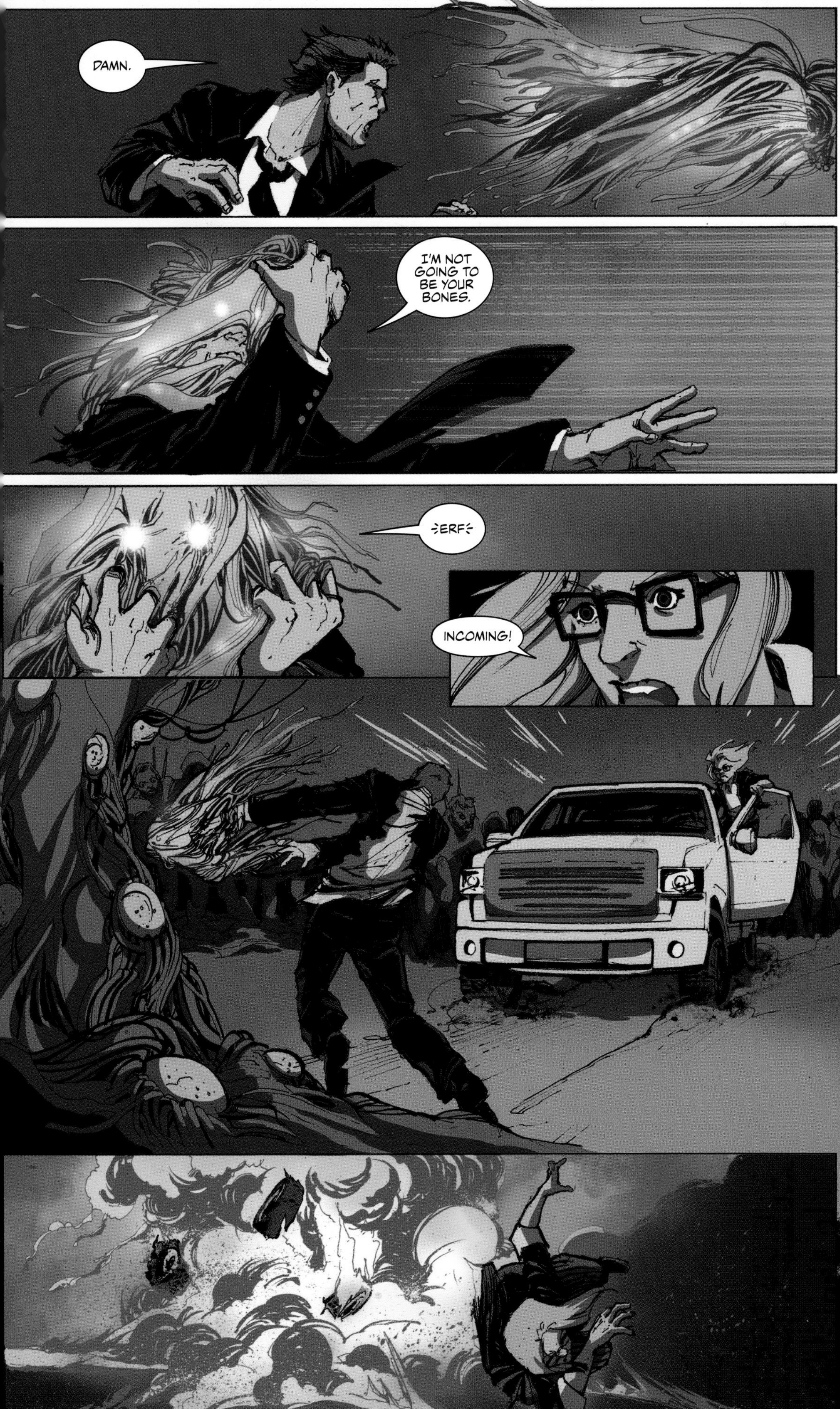
DAMN.
I'M NOT GOING TO BE YOUR BONES.
ERF
INCOMING!

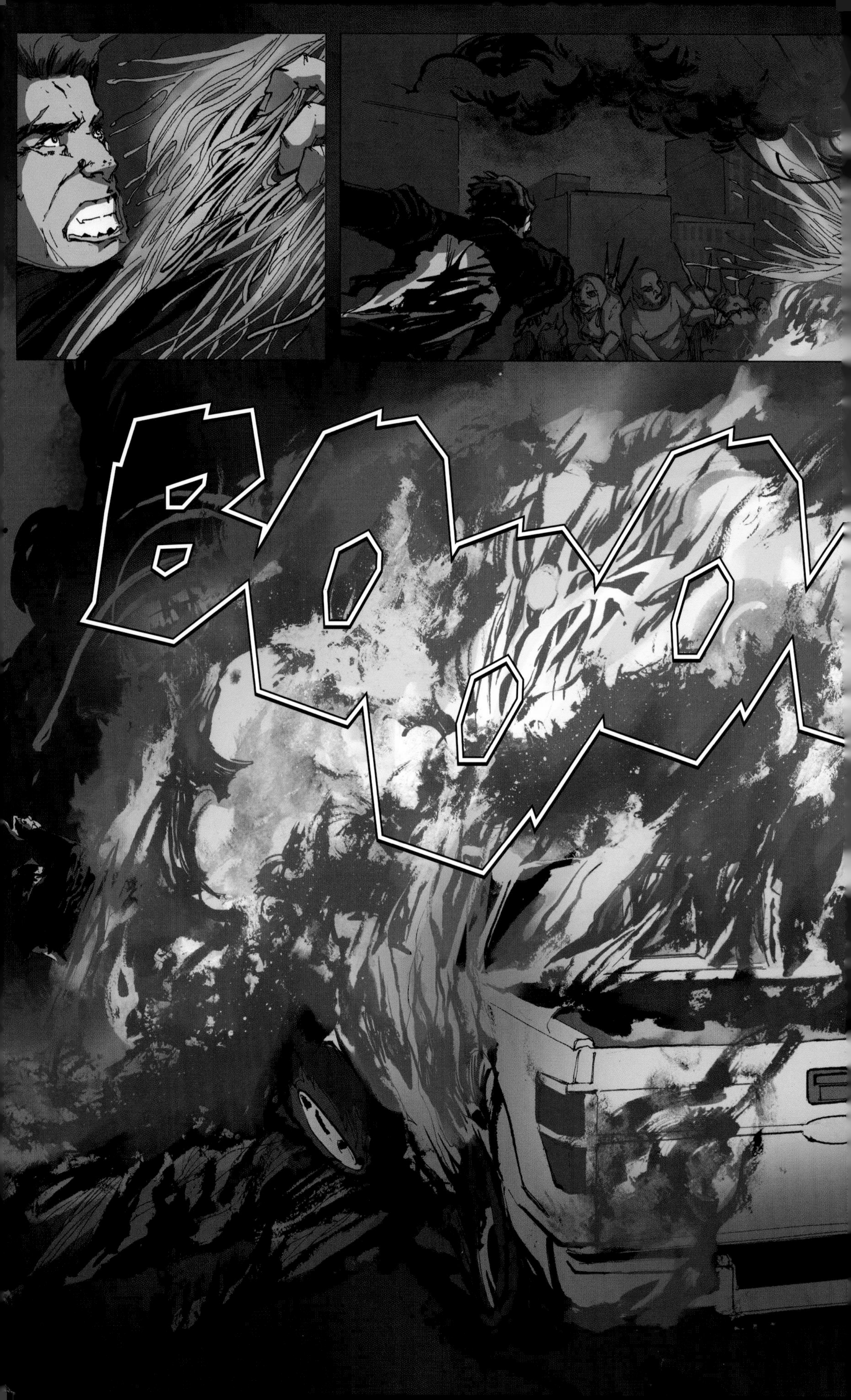
BOOOM

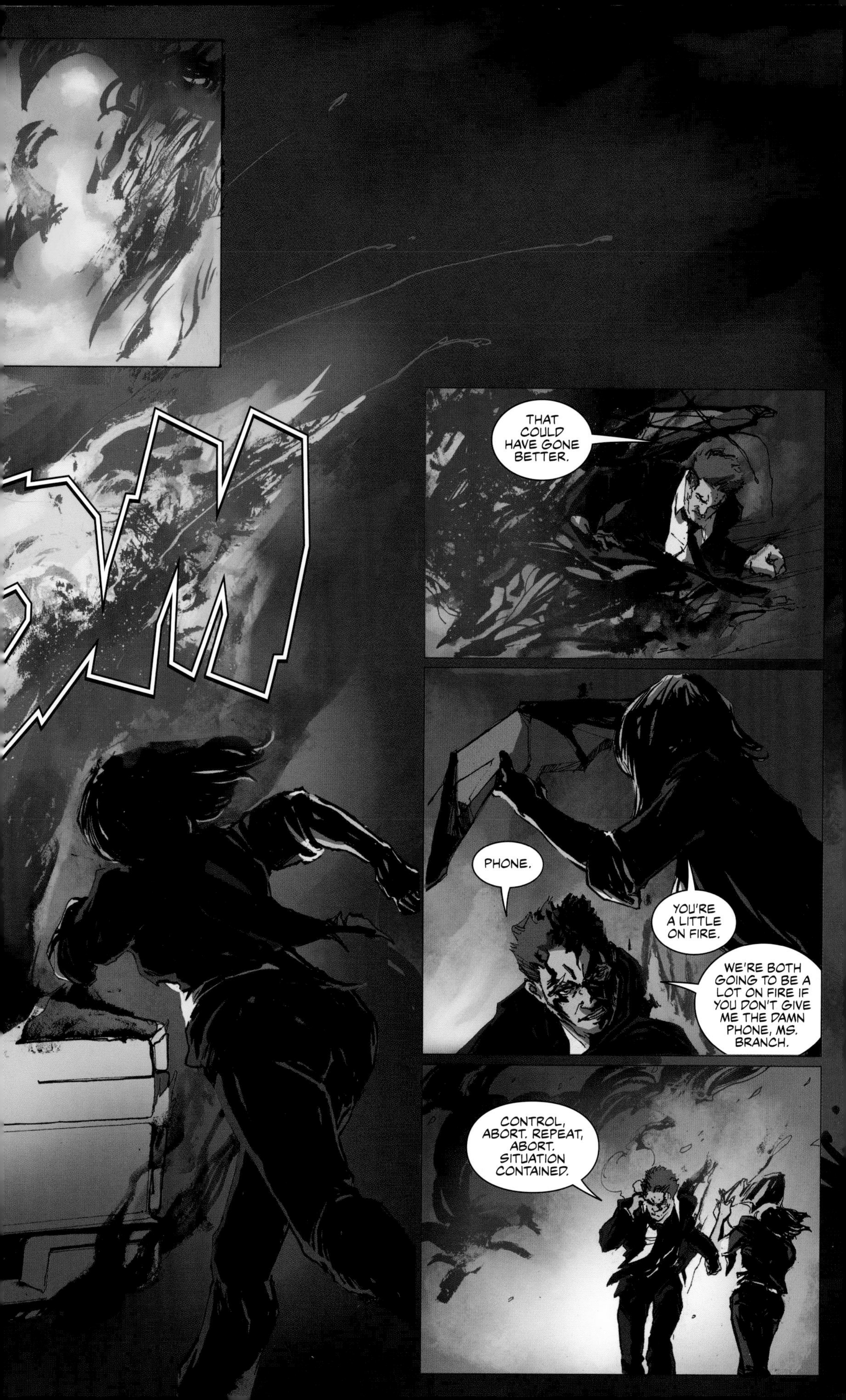
THAT COULD HAVE GONE BETTER.
PHONE.
YOU'RE A LITTLE ON FIRE.
WE'RE BOTH GOING TO BE A LOT ON FIRE IF YOU DON'T GIVE ME THE DAMN PHONE, MS. BRANCH.
CONTROL, ABORT. REPEAT, ABORT. SITUATION CONTAINED.

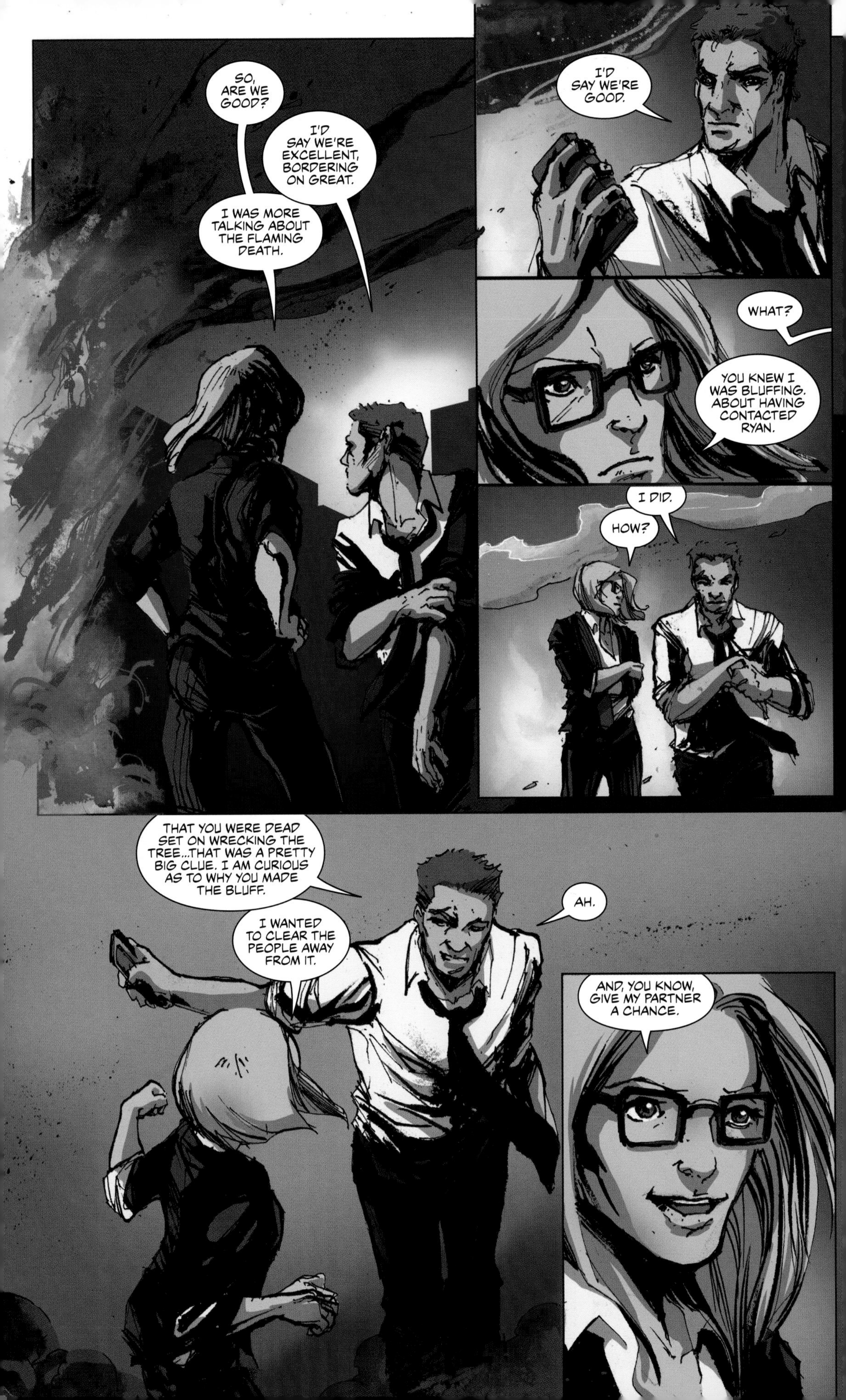

SO, ARE WE GOOD?
I'D SAY WE'RE EXCELLENT, BORDERING ON GREAT.
I WAS MORE TALKING ABOUT THE FLAMING DEATH.
I'D SAY WE'RE GOOD.
WHAT?
YOU KNEW I WAS BLUFFING. ABOUT HAVING CONTACTED RYAN.
I DID.
HOW?
THAT YOU WERE DEAD SET ON WRECKING THE TREE...THAT WAS A PRETTY BIG CLUE. I AM CURIOUS AS TO WHY YOU MADE THE BLUFF.
I WANTED TO CLEAR THE PEOPLE AWAY FROM IT.
AH.
AND, YOU KNOW, GIVE MY PARTNER A CHANCE.

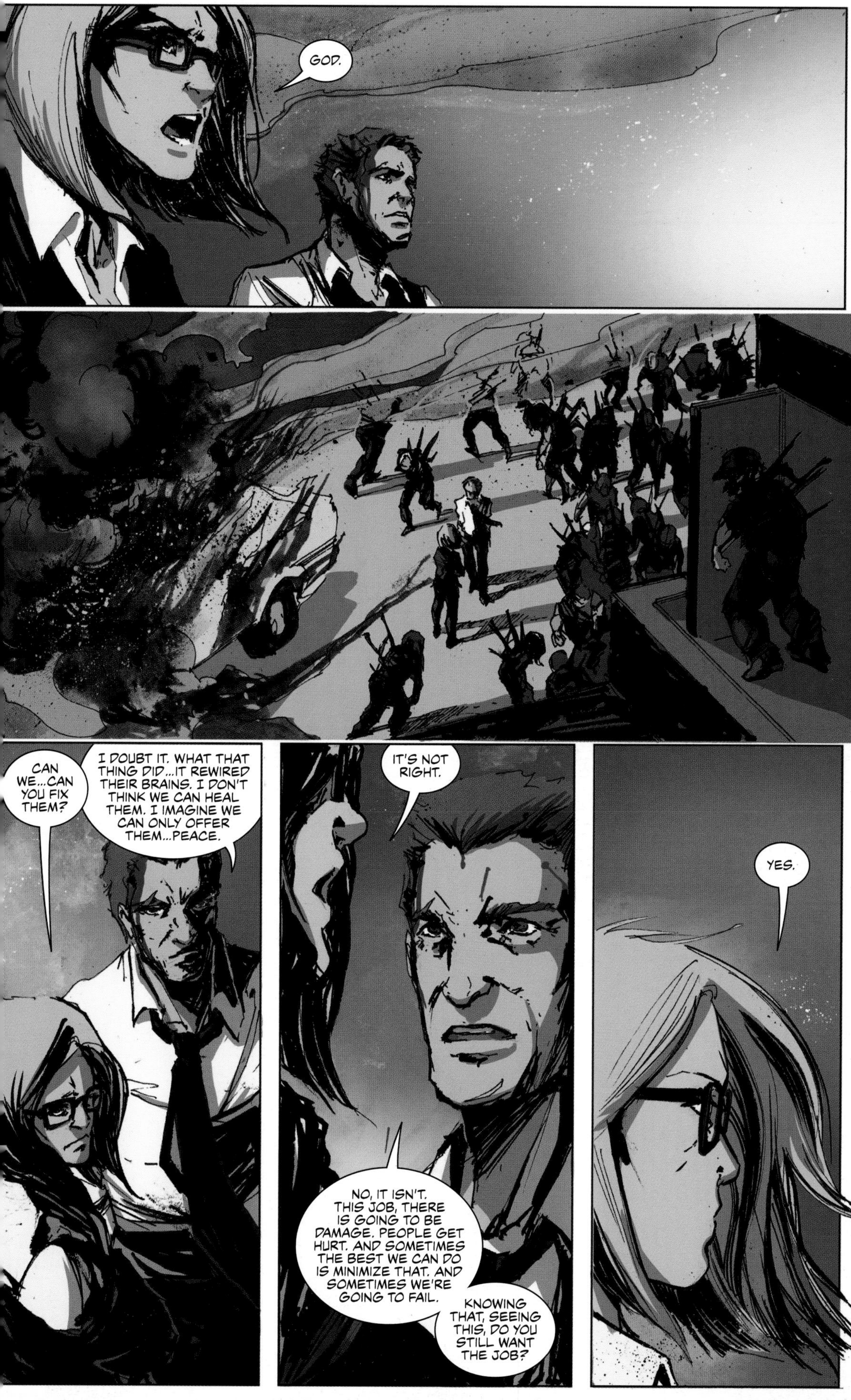
GOD.
CAN WE...CAN YOU FIX THEM?
I DOUBT IT. WHAT THAT THING DID...IT REWIRED THEIR BRAINS. I DON'T THINK WE CAN HEAL THEM. I IMAGINE WE CAN ONLY OFFER THEM...PEACE.
IT'S NOT RIGHT.
NO, IT ISN'T. THIS JOB, THERE IS GOING TO BE DAMAGE. PEOPLE GET HURT. AND SOMETIMES THE BEST WE CAN DO IS MINIMIZE THAT. AND SOMETIMES WE'RE GOING TO FAIL.
KNOWING THAT, SEEING THIS, DO YOU STILL WANT THE JOB?
YES.

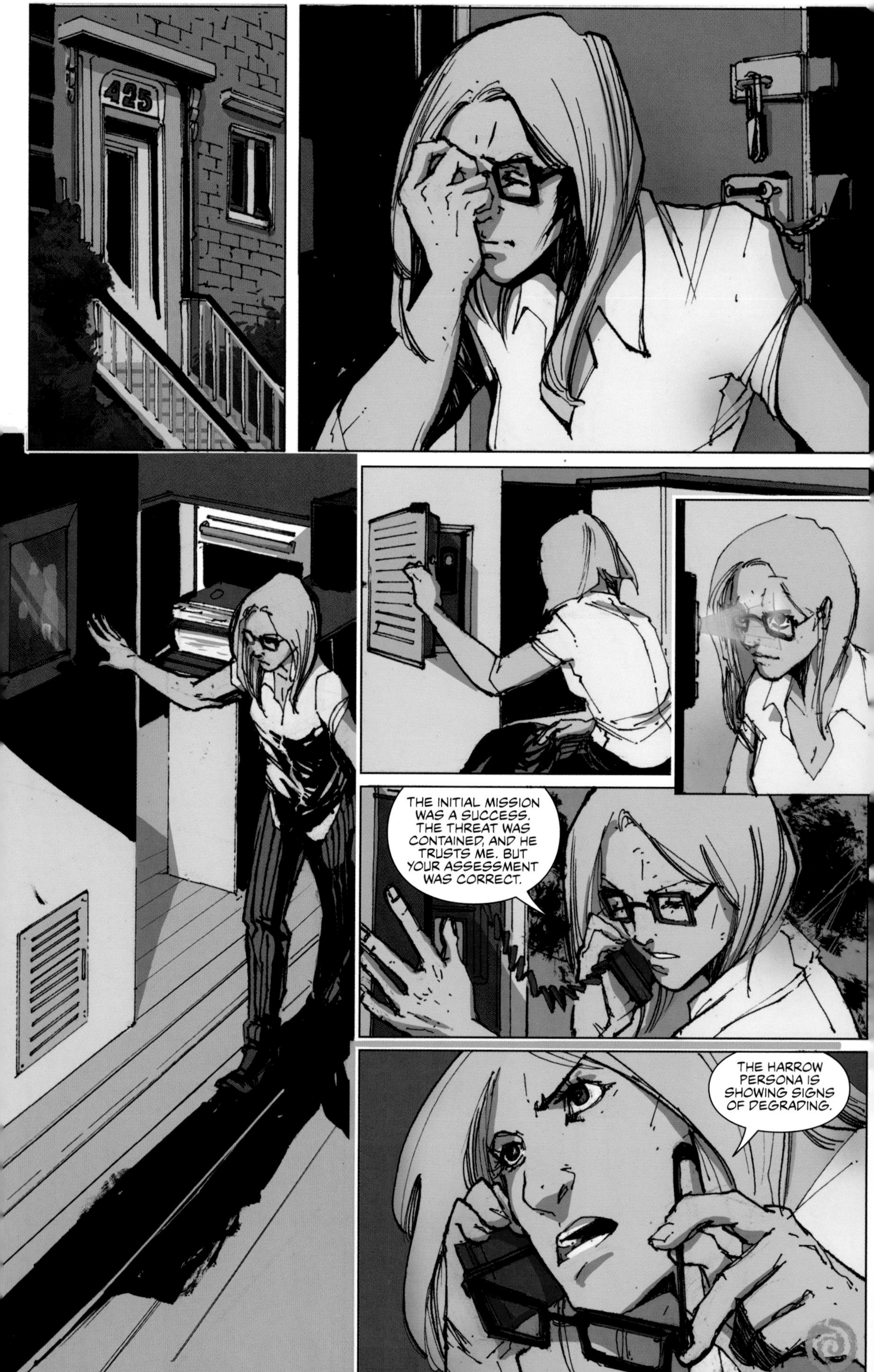
425
THE INITIAL MISSION WAS A SUCCESS. THE THREAT WAS CONTAINED, AND HE TRUSTS ME. BUT YOUR ASSESSMENT WAS CORRECT.
THE HARROW PERSONA IS SHOWING SIGNS OF DEGRADING.

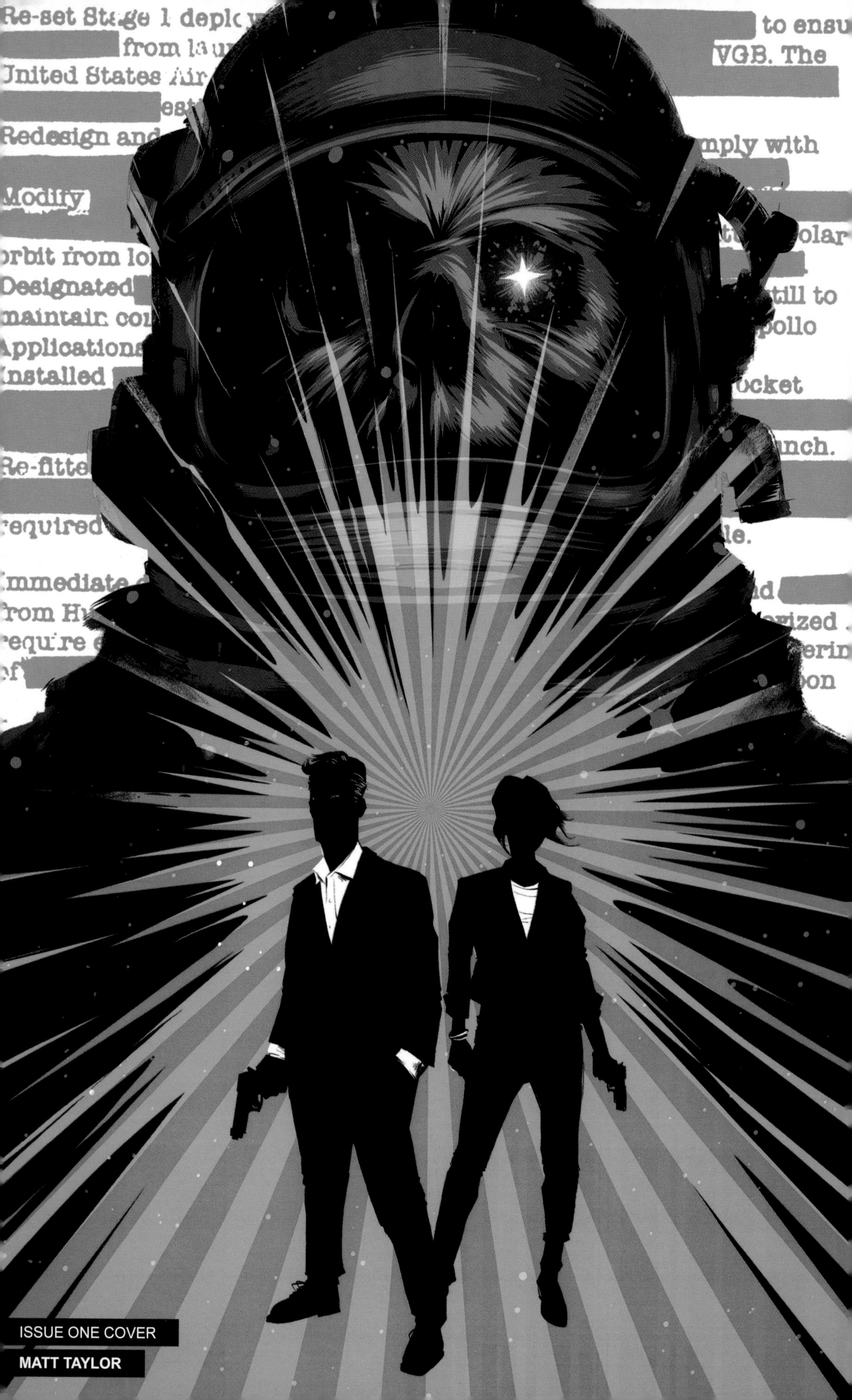
Re-set Stage 1 deplo
to ensu
from lau
VGB. The
United States Air
Redesign and
mply with
Modify
orbit from lo
Designated
maintain co
till to
Applications
pollo
Installed
ocket
unch.
Re-fitte
required
le.
Immediate
from Hu
ized
require
of
oon

ISSUE ONE COVER

MATT TAYLOR

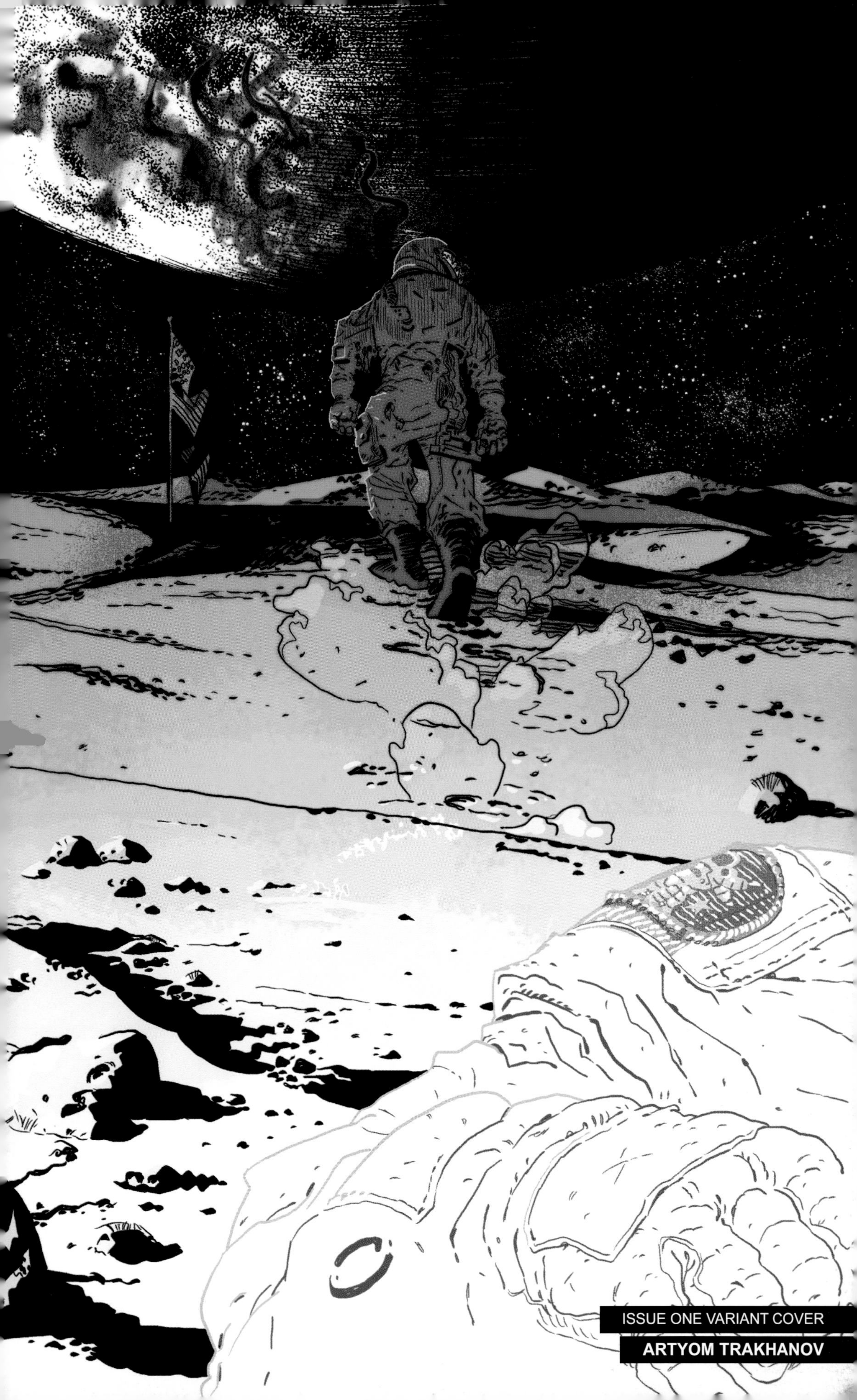

ISSUE ONE VARIANT COVER
ARTYOM TRAKHANOV

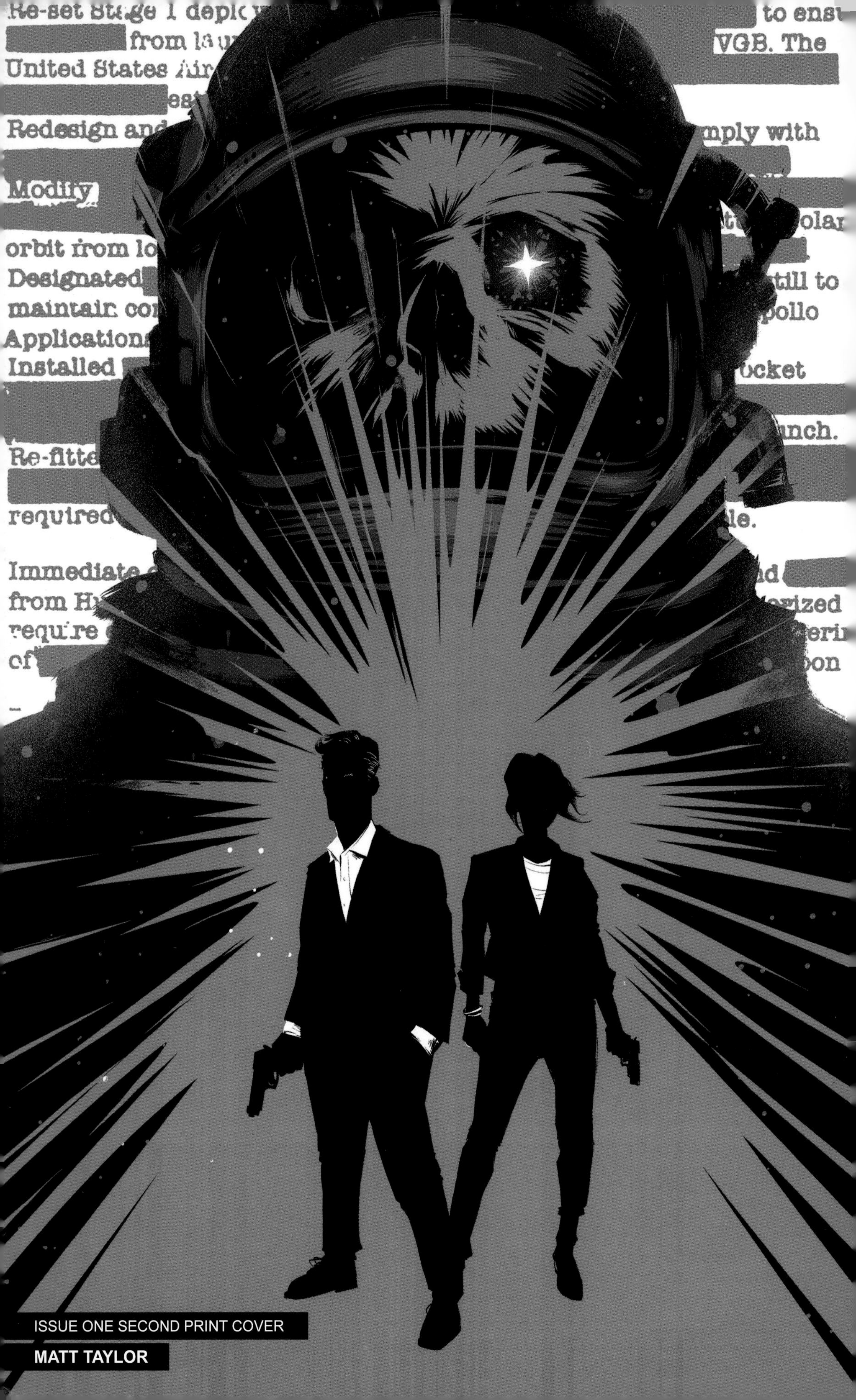

ISSUE ONE SECOND PRINT COVER

MATT TAYLOR

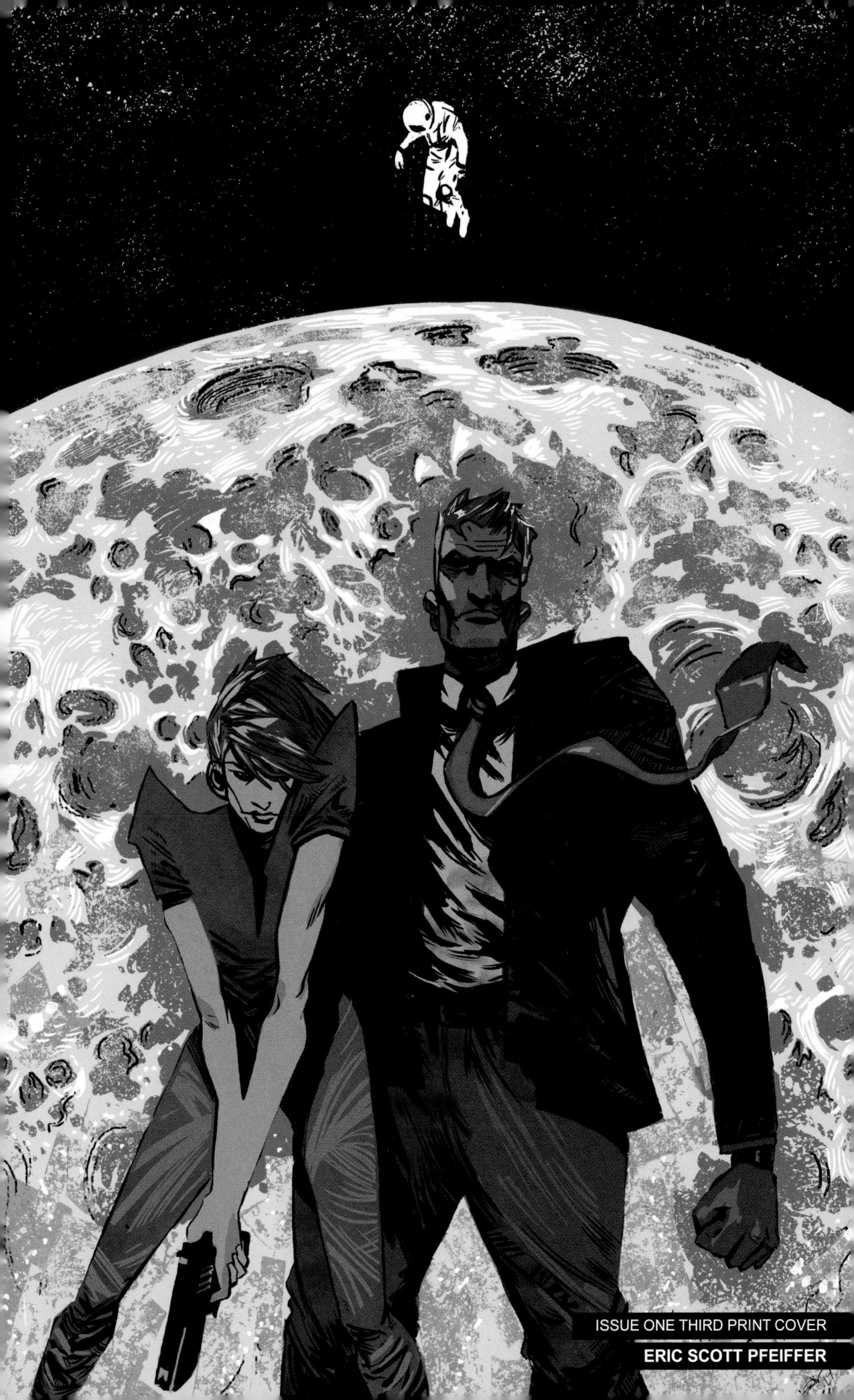

ISSUE ONE THIRD PRINT COVER

ERIC SCOTT PFEIFFER

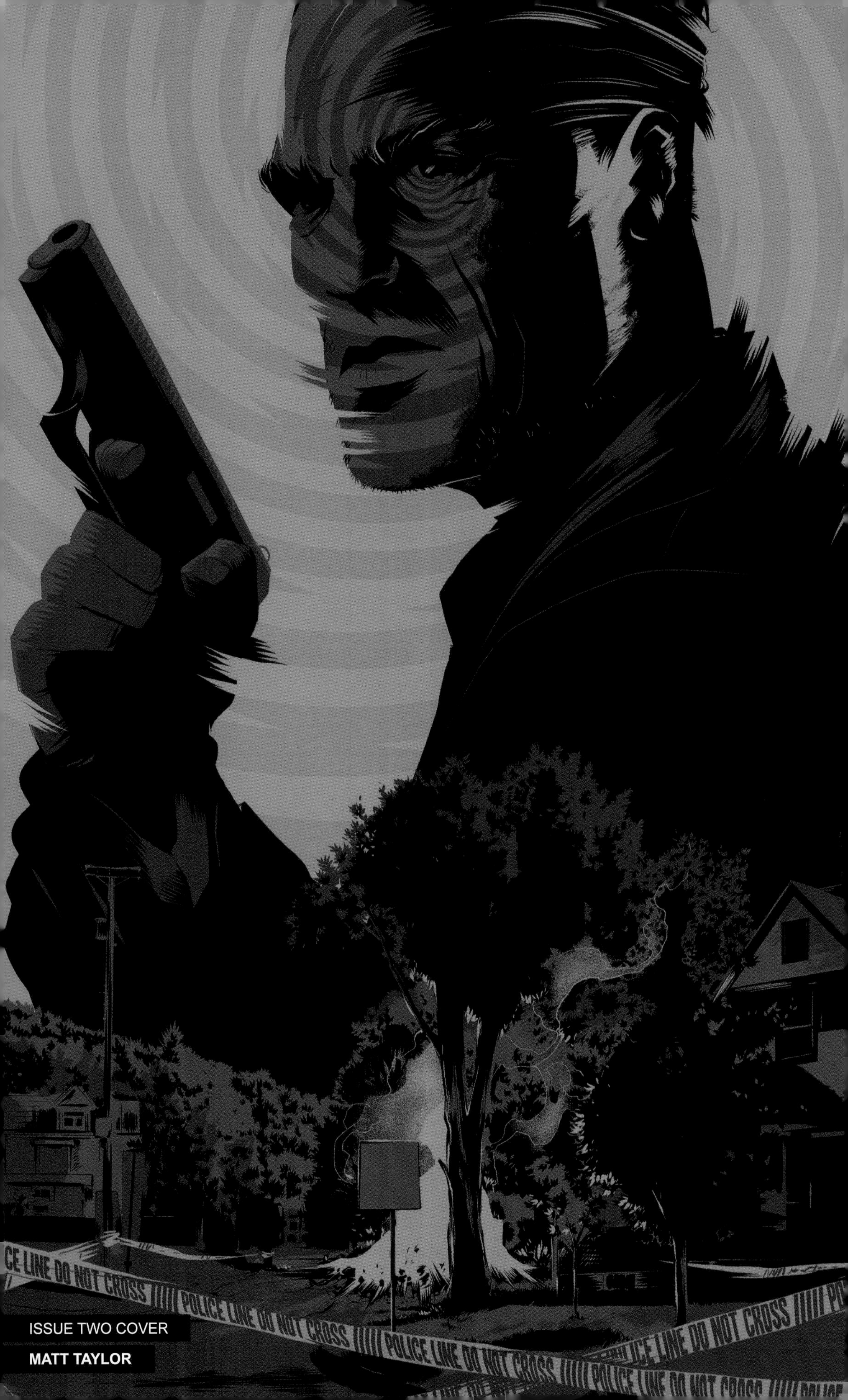
CE LINE DO NOT CROSS
POLICE LINE DO NOT CROSS
POLICE LINE DO NOT CROSS
POLICE LINE DO NOT CROSS

ISSUE TWO COVER

MATT TAYLOR

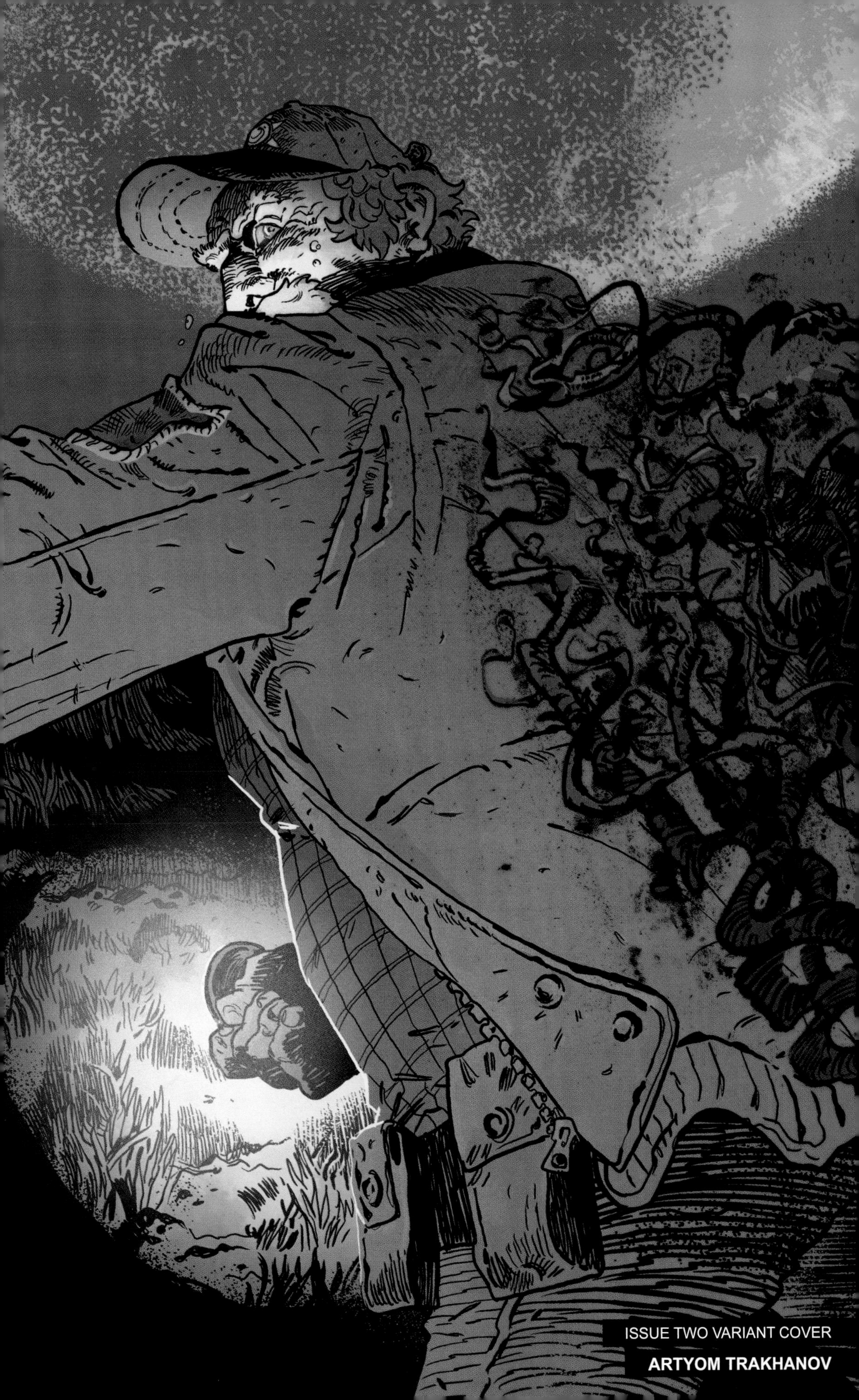

ISSUE TWO VARIANT COVER

ARTYOM TRAKHANOV

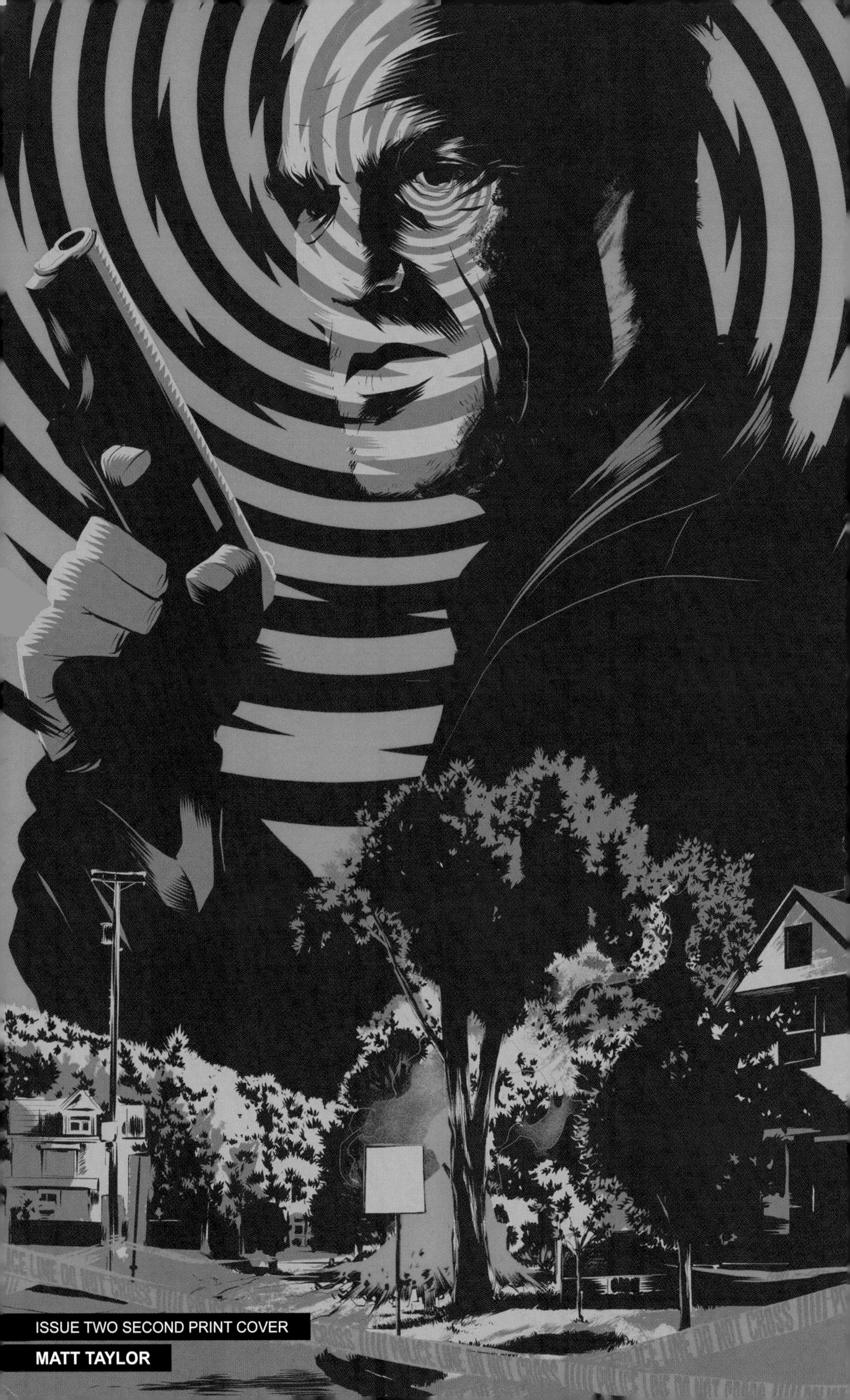

ISSUE TWO SECOND PRINT COVER

MATT TAYLOR

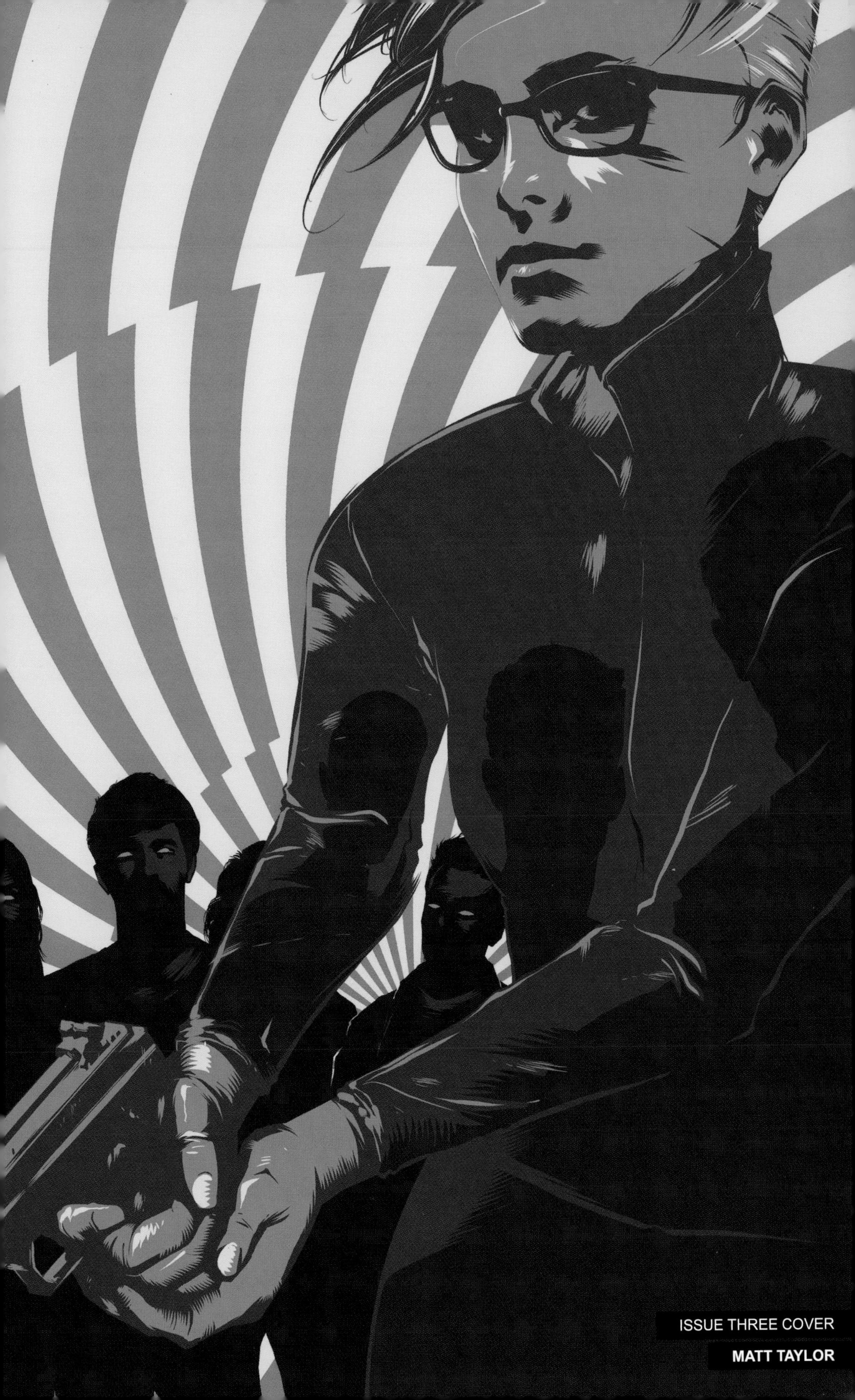

ISSUE THREE COVER
MATT TAYLOR

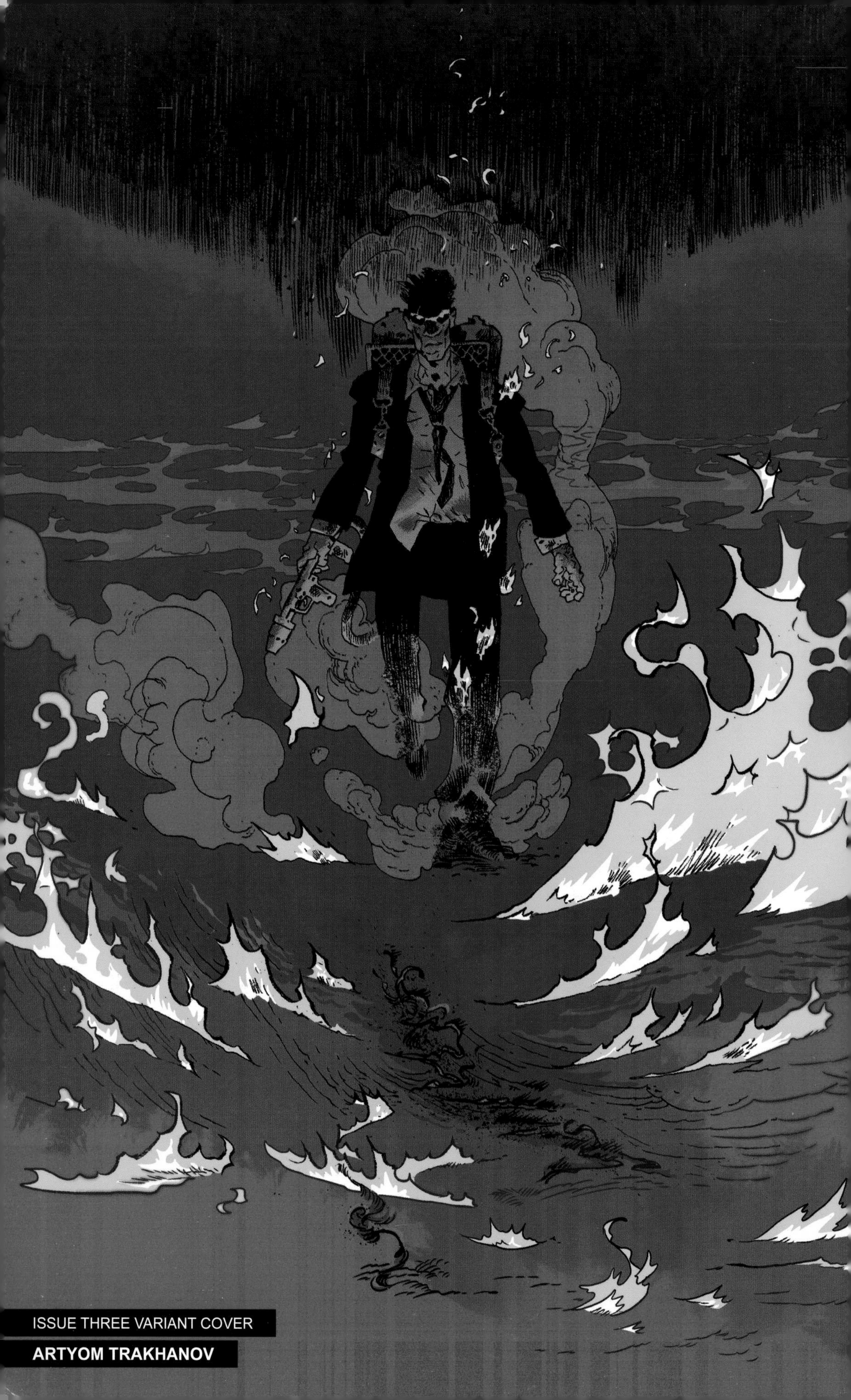

ISSUE THREE VARIANT COVER

ARTYOM TRAKHANOV